Edmund Wilson

EDMUND

A Study of Literary Vocation

WILSON

University of Illinois Press, Urbana, 1965

in Our Time / Sherman Paul

for Jared, Meredith, Erica, and Jeremy

Preface

Some explanations and acknowledgements are perhaps the only necessary preliminary to this study. Except for the dates of composition of two plays, which Edmund Wilson graciously supplied, I have relied entirely on public materials. The book represents my share of the work in a seminar on American Culture and Criticism, and to the students who participated in the spring terms of 1962 and 1963 I am especially indebted for stimulating and exacting discussion and for keeping me mindful of the different perspectives of the generations and the obligation that each generation has of providing the next, as Erik Erikson says, with "a safe treasure of basic trust." For intellectual hospitality and all the offices of friendship, I am grateful to William and Betty Rueckert, Robert and Jeanne Janes, Robert and Diane McColley, Jack Stillinger, and Milton R. Stern. My outstanding debt is to my wife.

I must also acknowledge the encouragement of Dean F. T. Wall of the Graduate College of the University of Illinois, the financial assistance of the Research Board of the University, and the year's leave made possible by the generosity of the Center for Advanced Study of the University and the John Simon Guggenheim Memorial Foundation. Alexander P. Clark, Curator of Manuscripts at the Princeton University Library, and Edmund Wilson willingly granted permission to quote from the letter to F. Scott Fitzgerald of July 31, 1922.

Urbana, Illinois   S.P.
May 1964

Contents

Contents

Prologue

      Edmund Wilson has maintained longer than anyone of his generation a distinguished position in American letters. Literary critic, social reporter, travel writer, poet, playwright, short story writer, novelist, chronicler, and historian — he is our pre-eminent man of letters, perhaps the last of the great professionals, the genuine *littérateurs*. Van Wyck Brooks, who did so much for the coming-of-age of American criticism, said in 1955 on presenting Wilson the rarely awarded gold medal for essays and criticism of the American Academy of Arts and Letters that he represented "a vanishing type, the free man of letters." He spoke of him as "one of the few critics who can also be called writers," meaning, undoubtedly, that he has the calling and has come into the creative life; that whatever its form his work is touched by imagination, comes from his being and reaches ours. In words so generous, just, and true, Brooks suggests what the survivors of his generation feel and our generation hardly recognizes — that here is a kind of man seldom present on our horizon.

      We think of Wilson, as he probably intended us to, when we read in *Patriotic Gore* of the old Romans of the old America. Justice Holmes, whose portrait closes the book, especially brings the author to mind, not simply because like Holmes he has acquired the "prestige of longevity," but because like Holmes, who was never corrupted or broken by the Civil War and its aftermath, he was never corrupted or broken by the wars and disasters of our time. Holmes's hard victory ends a long account of defeated and frustrated lives that in some respects might serve as a parable of recent history. And Holmes, who was close to the Calvinist soil of the old Republic, lives on, still vigorous in his work, into our time, gathering together the crucial American experience. In him, a father and a son meet; for in Holmes, Wilson's father is given the success his rectitude and ability deserved by a son whose own life was an attempt to forestall a similar defeat and to make good in his own achievement his father's failure. It is enough for Wilson that his father "got through with honor that period from 1880 to 1920!" It is enough for him that Holmes, who paid a different but still costly price, was able "to survive, to function as a first-rate intellect, to escape the democratic erosion." And it is enough for him that he has managed to survive by doing in his own way what Holmes had done — by striving for intellectual excellence, for greatness, for what Holmes called "the superlative."

Incorruptibility and professionalism — these requisites of intellectual endurance mark Holmes as they do every one of Wilson's heroes. We might call these qualities of character, as Wilson did in speaking of Pasternak, "the courage of genius." For him, one must have not only talent but the moral and intellectual courage that enables one to use his talents fully. He admires James and Yeats for their full careers; he defends those writers, like Elinor Wylie, who remain steadfast in their art. He respects and prizes Stravinsky even more highly now than he did thirty years ago because he now appreciates the fortifying example of "his persistence and craftsmanship" and the fact that "he has triumphed over exile and displacement, the disruptions of Russia and Europe, the temptations, on the one hand, of patronage and, on the other, of popular applause."

The qualities he honors are those qualities of character which in a long career he has earned for himself and without which he might have sunk in the currents of intellectual life. He can now write Waldo Frank that "I am astonished at your continued vitality and at your ability to produce something affirmative. . . ." And, in a postscript to the article on Stravinsky he had written in the twenties, he can say, distilling his experience as a writer: "In youth, we admire the heroes, the affirmers, the 'lords of life.' Later on, when we have had some experience of the difficulty of practicing an art, of surviving to grow old in its practice, when we have seen how many entrants drop out, we must honor any entrant who finishes."

one

The Landscape of Home

I

Within the large world of Wilson's work, we discover his world, its geography and history — and houses.

One point of the triangle that encloses his region is a cluster of once-fashionable or still-fashionable New Jersey towns, Red Bank, Lakewood, Princeton. The other points are Wellfleet on Cape Cod and in recent years Cambridge in Massachusetts, and Talcottville in Lewis County in upstate New York. Somewhat beyond lie Pittsburgh and Charlottesville. Toward the center are New York City and Stamford, Connecticut.

New Jersey, Massachusetts, and New York are the places in which his ancestors made and were overcome by history. One branch of the family had come from Ipswich, Massachusetts, and traced its lineage to the Mathers. In a recent genealogical poem, Wilson tells of "Priest" Kimball who had come West to Talcottville with his Mather bride and had been sacked because of his hell-fire Calvinism. In time, it seems, he had been recalled, and in a later generation two Kimballs married girls of the Talcott-Baker connection, thus forming the maternal family line. The Talcotts were Tories who had pioneered in the first westward migration after the Revolution, when a treaty with the Oneida Indians made settlement in western New York possible. They had driven their ox-teams into the wilderness bounded by Lake Ontario, the St. Lawrence River, and the Adirondack Mountains, and on the Sugar River had built Talcottville, a settlement which they ruled. From the river they had quarried the limestone with which to build a heavy-beamed house with walls a foot and a half thick — a fortress-like house graced without by a white-columned porch and a handsome fanlighted door and within by spacious well-proportioned rooms. In the time of the Talcotts, the house had many outbuildings, among them a dairy, quilting room, and ballroom, and it served the little community as town hall and post office, inn, social center, and store. The Talcotts supplied newcomers with grist from their mill and stone from their quarry; they speculated with their large land holdings but refused to sell lots to mechanics and water rights to manufacturers. When the railroad bypassed them, their speculations failed. The settlement never grew into the New England town they had hoped for.

Wilson's great-grandfather, Thomas Baker, who had married one of the remaining Talcott sisters, was a Jacksonian Democrat and a member of the New York State Assembly. He "bossed" the town and also "broke and sold the Talcott acres," creating a feud within the family that only later marriages ended. By that time, many members of the family had gone West or had been drawn to the city and much of the land had been sold. Eventually only the house remained, and Wilson's father bought it in his wife's name from her uncle.

Wilson now owns and sometimes lives in "the old stone house." It is, he says, a base of operations — one of the fixed points to which he traces his continuity and from which he surveys the world. The house belongs to the late eighteenth and early nineteenth centuries and represents for him an attempt to found a civilization more commodious than the narrow one of New England. It is a landmark of the time when there was limitless space, when men — he calls them a "sovereign race" — owned their land and governed their community. Though the westering they had pioneered had left Talcottville behind, in the timelessness of his recurrent dream, Talcottville is always on the road west, the place where a swift river runs, the place of the "wildness and freedom" for which, he says, he has always longed. Like so much of the past that stirs in his memory, it measures loss: it is the place to which the frayed Greenwich Village poetess of *I Thought of Daisy* returns to renew herself; the place in terms of which the Wilson of the thirties indicts a broken society and the Wilson of recent years feels his estrangement from the America of *Life* magazine and the tax collector; and the place which has enabled him to identify with as well as apologize to his dispossessed Iroquois neighbors.

Once the "new" America, Talcottville is now the "old" America. For Wilson, here begins the history of America — actually the story of those brought up in the old republican tradition — with which he has been most concerned personally. (On a large scale, *Patriotic Gore* is such a history, in some ways a *Magnalia Christi Americana* of the century in which his father's generation was broken.) His family, he tells us, never wholly abandoned the simpler habits and tastes of an earlier time nor never quite accepted the goals of post-Civil War America. They lived in modest prosperity on the margin of a rising plutocratic society and at a distance from the expanding industrial world. For generations, they followed the learned professions, had been doctors, lawyers, ministers, and professors; by training and tradition, they had been called to public service.

This is the tradition and the provincial world into which Wilson was born at Red Bank, New Jersey, on May 8, 1895. The landscape of this world is still spacious, children still romp in it. Four miles away is the seacoast with its summer hotels, race track, and garish estates. Yet Red Bank, the resort, he says, of the second-rate rich, is still an outpost of the older America, hardly a generation away from the North American Phalanx, the Fourierist community that had once flourished nearby. His grandfather, in the days of his country medical practice, had known the community well — he had brought Alexander Woollcott, one of its sons, into the world. His father, a lawyer in Red Bank, had supported a painter there; and as a child, he had himself been taken to the Phalanx for a visit.

For Wilson, Red Bank does not so much open vistas into the past as it establishes the point in recent history from which he himself begins. Where Talcottville is always of the early eighteen-hundreds, Red Bank is always of the eighteen-eighties: the "House of the Eighties," the house of his boyhood and youth, dominates the landscape. He seems never to have been happy in this house, and he never fully describes it or warmly evokes it in the way he does the house at Talcottville or his grandmother's house at Lakewood. He speaks of its bad architecture — it must have been one of "those monumental but clumsily-planned piles," as he says of the country house of *The Little Blue Light*; and, like the house in

"Ellen Terhune," it must have been in the shingle style and painted yellow. Nor was his mother happy with it. Even with its fine lawn and elms, the cow, chickens, and guinea fowl, and her resplendent flower garden, it seems to have been a gloomy place. It seems somehow to be abandoned by life, haunted in a peculiar Jamesian way. Perhaps a boy was abandoned in it, for the man he became is haunted by it. And for him, it is a fixation: there he finds the "one fixed point" his father kept "and left me for the day / In which this other world of theirs grows dank, decays, / And founders and goes down."

Edmund Wilson, Sr., who bought the house when he married, is in his son's account a representative man of the old tradition and of the generation that found itself incapable of adjusting to the sordid commercialism and politics of the Gilded Age. Like the poet George Cabot Lodge, whose *Life* by Henry Adams he includes in *The Shock of Recognition*, and like John Jay Chapman, whose reputation he re-established in the twenties and who merges with his father's portrait in *I Thought of Daisy*, the elder Wilson was "Bred to one world and wearied by this other"; like Hugo's father in *Daisy*, "the 1880's got him," and like Santayana's Last Puritan he was "visibly killed by the lack of air to breathe." He had been educated at Exeter and Princeton; at Princeton he was remembered for his oratory. Hoping for a political career, he had studied law. But the republican patriotism in terms of which he conceived his career was already becoming an anachronism. The patriotism that Wilson says both the North and the South had shared before the Civil War, the patriotism of a Justice Holmes who accepted responsibility for the success of our institutions and identified his interests with those of the Republic — such patriotism had been eroded by self-interest and money-making. (Wilson recalls that in his time at Princeton the children of "serious republicans" stood as a race apart among the future brokers and bond salesmen.)

From an office above a liquor dealer's in Red Bank, the elder Wilson practiced law in an independent way and followed politics from a distance. He advised the Republican Party and made campaign speeches, but he never ran for office; and though he might have been a corporation lawyer or a member of an eminent firm, he chose to take a variety of cases, and to take them when he needed to. An excellent trial lawyer, he often handled the difficult cases of other lawyers; for a time he was an attorney for the Pennsylvania Railroad and a member of the New Jersey Board of Railroad Commissioners. In 1908, the Republican governor appointed him Attorney General, an office he also held during the Democratic administration of Woodrow Wilson whom he foiled by successfully prosecuting the corrupt Republicans of the political machine in Atlantic City. As president, Wilson offered him appointments which he always refused. Only the possibility of becoming a justice of the Supreme Court would have aroused him and prompted an unwelcome move to Washington, but though he had had some assurance of filling the next vacancy, no vacancy occurred. Such success as he had, however, did not compensate for his thwarted political ambition. At the age of thirty-five he was already suffering from neurotic depressions and hypochondria. He spent much of his later life in sanitaria or shut up behind the felt-covered door of his room at home. Sometimes he went off to Talcottville, where he found the old village life, the wilderness and the solitude congenial.

An imperious, scornful, impatient man, he made everyone at home miserable with his suffering. Hugo Bamman of *Daisy* speaks for Wilson when he describes his father's behavior:

"He would suddenly appear in his dressing-gown, and freeze us with wild prophetic looks, and announce that the household was 'hurtling to ruin!' because he'd just got a caterer's bill or something. He finally had the whole household so that it was just like some kind of sanitarium . . . he couldn't stand to have a light burning or to hear a sound after he'd gone to bed himself . . . he used to nag us to go to bed in an insincerely amiable way that used to make me furious. Of course, he could be charming and sympathetic when any emergency or crisis arose, and he was able to embarrass us and disarm us so by having recourse to sympathy or charm just when we'd been resenting him at our bitterest, that when it actually came to a showdown, we were never able to stand up to him."

Like Hugo, Wilson admits that he never really liked or appreciated his father until after his death. Only then, it seems, did he begin to realize how much they had in common and how much he measured his own career by his father's standard.

He was an only child and in the trials of the household always sided with his mother, a lively dominating woman whose desire for a brighter home and social life had been frustrated by his father. Within the family she represented the forces of wealth and social prestige to which her husband refused to submit. She wished to move to a more attractive and expensive neighborhood, but he, having never invested his money, was unwilling to take on the burden of additional money-making and dismissed her carefully prepared plans. Though she respected her husband, she did not understand him; brilliant men such as he troubled her, and she hoped that her son would not be like him, would be an athlete. (How bitterly the boy resented what must have been a constant chiding on this score is apparent in Gandersheim's hatred of his mother in *The Little Blue Light* and in the depiction of the mother in *Cyprian's Prayer*.) Her response to her husband's neurosis had been a sudden deafness from which she never recovered. Once she had considered leaving him, but instead had had a collapse. When he died, she immediately set about building a new house.

The boy seems to have found little relief in this crippled household. Wilson remembers the "sensitive, intelligent, affectionate" Irish girl who managed the house and held things together. She taught him to walk. His fondest memories of this time are of other places: of Talcottville and the family reunions there (he kept a photograph of the falls of the Sugar River in his room), and of delightful visits to his Grandmother Kimball's house at Lakewood. The house at Lakewood is alive with maiden aunt and worldly uncle and companionable cousin. The smallest details are still vivid—the cookies studded with raisins, the sugar pills his grandfather gave the children, the horses' clatter on the wooden paving stones. Even to this day, he says, any odor like that of the mingled fragrance of fresh flowers and the smell of oriental rugs recalls the "singular amenity and brightness" of this house.

Life here had lost the Calvinist rigor he knew at home, where Grandfather Wilson, a Presbyterian minister, exerted an influence and Grandmother Wilson made Sunday mornings bleak by instructing him in the Bible. The Kimballs had rejected the severe faith of their fathers—Dr. Kimball took his ideas on religion and philosophy from Mill and Spencer—and they probably supported the "moral sabotage" of his mother who tacitly encouraged his antagonism to Calvinism. At the Kimballs', he botanized in grandmother's conservatory and went afield in search of wild flowers

in the pinewoods by the lake; or he found among the histories and
Bohn classics of Dr. Kimball's library other more attractive books
like Percy's *Reliques* and Burton's *Anatomy of Melancholy*. His
literary aunt copied into little books she sewed together for this
purpose the novels he dictated, and his uncle, when left in charge,
read to him as a matter of course from Bulfinch's *Age of Fable*. He
watched the splendid show of riders and equipages at the riding
academy across the way, and sometimes he was treated to polo
games or taken by his uncle in his runabout to a great estate to
play with the son of a millionaire.

The new house at Lakewood had been a concession to his grandmother's desire to keep up with the rich. Grandfather Kimball,
once a country doctor, now practiced among the wealthy, as did
his son who succumbed to their extravagant life. Yet, by comparison with the gilded establishments, the house was simple and the
life it consecrated old-fashioned. Like the house of the eighties,
where the boy felt the interior strain of the corrosive outside world,
so here, where all seemed bright and secure, he would be made
to feel the defencelessness of his world against the arrogant world
of money.

That world broke into his childhood on one of those days when
his uncle had taken him to play with the son of the railroad magnate, George Jay Gould. He had been impressed by the Goulds'
fenced-in domain; by the great country house, the lake, the sunken
garden, the private theater; by the rich boy's wardrobe of cos-
tumes, his expensive toys, and miniature automobile. Much that
he saw embarrassed or offended him, and something of the sinister
quality he attached to Gould troubled him there. But he was
shocked most by the rich boy's behavior, by his easy assumption
of the authority to command: driving in a pony-cart, he had or-
dered the footman to bring him some apples that had fallen to the
ground, and though his governess had remonstrated with him, he
had peremptorily insisted and, when the footman had done his
bidding, had told her, "These men must do their duty, Anna!" [1]

Even if this incident were made up in the light of later experience, it is still, as Wilson says of the stories people tell of their
childhood, profoundly symbolic. We need not accept the factu-

[1] Somewhat altered, this incident appears in chapter I of *I Thought of
Daisy*.

ality of the incident, but only the feeling he conveys by means of it: the feeling of insecurity. He tells us that he was impelled to return to this incident at the time of World War I and during the years of the Great Depression — times when, he says, he was "frightened about the things I have a stake in." Some incident as traumatic as this, or perhaps only the atmosphere the incident precipitates, shadows his childhood. There are signs of it throughout his work.

If we accept this fable of class displacement as evidence of his "wound" — it was written at the time he was working up *The Wound and the Bow* — then it might be said to be the determining force in his work. The threat to his world comes from the upper, not, as in the case of Dickens, the major example of his theory of the psychic wound, from the lower class. It explains his lifelong partisanship for the work of Edith Wharton, and, since, as he notes in speaking of her work, "the other side of this world of wealth, which annihilates every impulse toward excellence, is a poverty which also annihilates," it explains his sympathy for the lower class. He perseveres in the values of his fathers, values supplanted in the commercial world; he believes in the "superior virtue and value . . . of the spirit that studies and understands against the spirit that acquires and consumes; of the instinct to give light and life against the lethal concentration on power; of the impulse that acts to minimize the social differences between human beings, instead of trying to keep them up and make them wider; and of the kind of ambition that attempts to build on this thought and creative instinct instead of on the authority of the pony-cart." And his faith calls for the kind of public service that cannot be performed satisfactorily by repudiating commercialism in a withdrawal to art but only by using superior virtue to fight it head on.

One has his own memory of a house of the eighties. It is fashioned of interiors like those of Eastman Johnson's *Not at Home* and Stieglitz' *My Parents' Home*. But these recede, pushed back by the more insistent recollection of Hopper's *House by the Railroad*. And as one thinks of that stranded house he remembers what Wilson said of Dickens — that "behind the misfortune which had humiliated Charles was the misfortune which had humiliated his father."

II

Hill School at Pottstown, Pennsylvania, is not far from Red Bank. One takes the train to Philadelphia, transfers, goes northwest a short distance along the Schuylkill River, and then arrives in a dingy milltown, a place of slag pits and blast furnaces, a veritable nineteenth-century Coketown. Here one is in the world created by men like Henry C. Frick, Wilson's representative industrial pioneer. Here a man of the same stamp, John Meigs, the son of the Reverend Matthew Meigs of Connecticut, the founder of Hill, had made the school his enterprise and transformed it into a first class institution. Wilson, who entered Hill in 1909, remembers John Meigs's "iron regime," the paternalism and efficiency that made the school an oppressive bell-regulated mill, and the religious atmosphere, fostered by Mrs. Meigs, that something more than marriage had made a part of this world.

The religious side of prep school life was dismal enough, and though the three years he spent at Hill left ineffaceable memories of it, it did not break him as it had John Jay Chapman at St. Paul's. He attended chapel and Y.M.C.A. meetings, was exhorted to by a variety of evangelists – among them "reformed debauchees," and "Weeping Bob" who preached a "lachrymose and mealymouthed virility," and sophisticated liberal ministers who tried to awaken sympathy for the working classes – and by Mrs. Meigs who, in private interviews, did her best to save her boys for a life of "service." The extent to which he was troubled by this is more apparent in "Galahad," a story he published in 1927, than it is in "Mr. Rolfe," the memoir of 1942 in which he describes his life at Hill. The hero of "Galahad" is a boy with a severe and restrained temperament like his own, who, lacking faith, doubts his fitness for the presidency of the Y.M.C.A. He, too, hears the professional moralists – "Weeping Fred" is one of them here – and begins to question the Y.M.C.A. ethos, though for the moment he accepts what is said about the "clean" life and determines to live it. He is tried by a classmate's sister, a type of flaming youth and a symbol of life; she almost seduces him physically and does so spiritually, precipitating his rejection of the gospel of cleanliness and his flight from school. The boy, unlike the prototypal Y.M.C.A. boy of "The Death of an Efficiency Expert" (*The Undertaker's Gar-*

land), listens to his devil. It is evident that he will never lose his life in the routines of "service."[2] What Wilson says of his own experience might be said of him: "the code I was evolving for myself could never have much in common with the official morality of Hill."

Wilson remembers that under the constant religious pressure he had "tried hard to keep God in [his] cosmos," but that never having had any genuine religious experience, he could not accept religion as real for himself. The evangelists soon seemed humorous to him, and he came to feel that the religious activities of Hill were in bad taste. In his last year at school, two episodes marked the end of his religious preoccupations. The first took place on the train on which he was returning to Pottstown. He was reading *Major Barbara* and had reached the point in the preface where Shaw says that "at present there is not a single credible established religion in the world." This, and probably what Shaw had just said of the superiority of facing evil without illusions, shocked him into accepting a truth he had already entertained. Pondering this, he was interrupted by a boy from Hill, a simple muscular Christian devoted to sports and the Y.M.C.A.; and as he talked with his schoolmate, he reflected on the ignorance in which the boy was still enthralled. Such thoughts gave him an "ironic pleasure," and even in his recollections we feel the pride that went with it when he writes that "my faith had passed quietly out on the stretch between Norristown and Phoenixville, between two passages of banal conversation in which I had descended affably to the level of my companion." Nothing altered his views; reason stood firm against the assaults of faith. His last religious service at Hill, at which an eminent minister, himself a death's-head, spoke on immortality, only strengthened his conviction that to believe in doctrines for which there was no evidence was weak-minded and cowardly.

The way in which these episodes are placed in his recollections makes clear the negative part the religious activities of Hill had in his education. Fortunately, the countervailing influence of culture was strong, represented by Alfred Rolfe, one of the excellent teachers Meigs had taken the trouble to secure. Master of Greek,

[2] The efficiency expert dies by falling into a candymaking machine, and becomes a chocolate bar.

the "perfect Hellenist," Rolfe taught the language in the way that Wilson — like John Jay Chapman, a self-appointed mentor on such matters — feels it ought to be taught. He harnessed the student to the necessary discipline, but he made both the language and the civilization it expressed radiant for him, so radiant that even now, Wilson says, the human and heroic qualities that then glowed through Xenophon and Homer glow for him still. And Rolfe transmitted other things: a sense of the "high civilization" of the Concord of Emerson and Thoreau of which he was himself a product, and a sense of the exciting world of contemporary letters — it was in his rooms that Wilson discovered Chesterton and Shaw. He took pleasure in his favorite pupil's literary work for *The Hill School Record*, and his presence at Hill, the superiority that made him both out-of-place and commanding there, supported the boy who had so much to stand up to at home and at school.

Teachers who form us are rare. Seldom do we find the two or three Wilson found or keep in touch with them and acknowledge the debt we owe them. Wilson has done so out of deep affection, out of an awareness of spiritual paternity. Men like Rolfe are exemplars of the tradition that sustains him. The cultural authority Rolfe exerted was based on exacting discipline and conscious effort and on an appreciation of the qualities of the noble and the beautiful. It was humanistic. And it was Emersonian: individualistic and self-reliant, tough and resilient, without any dependence on religion — a precious fruit of New England to be prized and transplanted elsewhere. The narrowness that Wilson's forebears had escaped by migrating West, Rolfe escaped by taking the open road of the mind. Like others whom Wilson admires, he had migrated from the provinces and had come into the freedom of the "great social world" and the "great world of literature."

III

According to John Peale Bishop, Princeton is a place to loiter. It is a Sleepy Hollow removed from the urgencies of life. The climate there is soft and doesn't breed good Calvinists. And there, because the college affirms the "older aristocratic tradition" of the Middle States, the sense of the past, the Revolutionary era with its ideals of honor and physical courage, is still alive. This is the Princeton that Fitzgerald evokes in *This Side of Paradise*, the

Princeton where "Witherspoon brooded like a dark mother over Whig and Clio, her attic children, where the black Gothic snake of Little curled down to Cuyler and Patton . . . [and] topping all, climbing with clear blue aspiration, [were] the great dreaming spires of Holder and Cleveland towers." It is a sleeping college for Wilson, too, who did not wish to rest there but to awaken all about him from its winter sleep; it was, he wrote in *The Undertaker's Garland* (1922), the "most carefree of all colleges, where Apollo lies slumbrous and lazy. . . ."

When he matriculated in 1912, Princeton was still pretty much the college his father and uncles had known. Its campus life and customs, Christian Gauss says, had not changed greatly from those of the Golden Nineties. Horsing had replaced the more brutal hazing, but there were still the indignities of the class-and-club system and the violence of the freshman-sophomore rushes. These customs appealed to Fitzgerald but not to Wilson, who even then, writing in the *Lit.*, objected to them as examples of the "raw provincialism" of Princeton. He did not like the restrictions imposed on freshmen — that they keep off Prospect Street, the upperclass world of clubs ("those colossal monuments to the incurable mediocrity of Princeton taste and ideals"), and that they wear the prescribed costume of black shoes, black tie, hard collar, and cap. His feelings about college life were probably similar to those of Wilbur Flick, a fictional contemporary in *Memoirs of Hecate County*, who dodged the ordeal of the rush and lived in the manner of the aesthete at the local inn. "He was at least outside the college conventions — something for which I sneakingly envied him," the narrator writes, "and was not ashamed of his tastes, and my visits to his sybaritic suite relieved my freshman tension."

Wilson was something of a sybarite himself. He disliked athletics and preferred to read in bed, and he had already been admonished at Hill for losing himself in literary pursuits and neglecting his relations with his classmates. He had little in common with undergraduates who, as Bishop noted, placed athletic prowess first, the Triangle Club second, and admitted the *Lit.* into the curriculum. He had come to Princeton well-grounded in English literature and with a considerable knowledge of contemporary writing. After the elementary and miscellaneous courses of the first two years, he devoted himself to philosophy, Latin and Greek, and the modern languages — concentrated his studies, as he hoped the curriculum would someday make it easier for others to do, on what interested him, on what he needed. He soon established himself on the *Lit.*, T. K. Whipple, its editor, having put him, a freshman, on the board of the magazine; and for it he wrote one of his early poems, "Whistler at Battersea," extolling the isolated artist who was blessed by a "glimpse of art." Later he would write superb criticism of Henry James and Stendhal, and demonstrate in issue after issue, in story, dialogue, review, and editorial, how far he had advanced beyond the simple tastes of his classmates. They, like the undergraduates of Paul Rosenfeld's class at Yale, favored *Ivanhoe* and "Crossing the Bar," and had come abreast of a play called *Boomerang* and a writer named Tarkington. To them, Andrew Turnbull writes, Wilson seemed to be "a withdrawn, literary figure, a well-dressed 'poler' or grind, a smug, conceited little fellow who wouldn't talk to you because he considered himself the brightest person around. . . ." He wore orange ties and rode an English bike (a rarity then); he spoke in a high-pitched voice and, when excited, stammered and batted his eyes. Evidently, as he seems pitilessly aware, he was a Wilbur Flick. He was not the "duck" that Flick was, but he was called "Bunny"; he did not flunk out but was voted, with telling spite, the worst poet.

Christian Gauss, with whom he studied French and Italian literature, modifies this unpleasant portrait. He found Wilson neither rah-rah nor collegiate; he says that he was neither gloomy nor an aesthete. He like to joke and to make hoaxes, and in his group — the inner circle of the *Lit.* — he was eager and tireless, he "bubbled with ideas. . . ." Gauss remembers, as every teacher does, the brilliant student who made his preceptorials lively. And perhaps because it was a tribute to his teaching, he remembers that *The Evil Eye*, the Triangle Club production for which Wilson wrote the libretto, was set in *Niaiserie* in Normandy and the villain was called Count La Rochefoucauld-Boileau, and that in spite of its exotic and literary character — he found it reminiscent of Gautier's *Jettatura* — it was a howling success. Gauss, of course, was looking backward over a distance of nearly thirty years, years of friendship with the red-haired, stocky boy who had gone on to achieve so much; looking back — it is the most valuable part of his memoir — to the great period of the *Lit.*, the period spanned by the editorships of Whipple and Wilson, when, with the help of Bishop, Fitzgerald, Henry Chapin, and Stanley Dell, all favorite students of his, the *Lit.* had become a harbinger of new literary tidings and itself a part of the stream of modern literature.

But his memory of other things is dim, and he did not take the trouble to consult the college records. He attributed Wilson's failure to make Phi Beta Kappa to low grades in economics, when he had taken a course on the economic aspects of European history (he studied economics later at the Columbia University summer school) and had done badly in chemistry and coordinate geometry. He was right about Wilson's appreciation of Yeats, but wrong about his admiration for Amy Lowell and Frost — he did not admire them but some of the work of Masefield and Masters' *Spoon River Anthology*. And he did not dislike writers who tried to regenerate mankind: Shaw and Wells, he reminded Gauss, had been his gods at Hill and at Princeton; the *Fabian Essays* had set him up, and, as should have been clear to a reader of the *Lit.*, he had considered himself a social reformer.

The Nassau Literary Magazine, like *The Hill School Record* before it, provided Wilson the professional training that made possible for him the easy transition in the twenties to *Vanity Fair* and *The New Republic*. The magazine had the tasteful, sober format of the highbrow college periodicals of the time, but it also had a few touches of the bright sophistication that characterized *Vanity Fair* and some of the seriously critical and reforming tendency of *The New Republic*. In a heady way, it combined both art and politics — to be sure, a fledgling art and campus politics. Its art was politics, and in its sphere its intent was typical of the larger critical endeavor of the time: to raise by means of a serious concern with art and ideas the cultural quality of Princeton life. Its politics, as Wilson indicated in "The Fettered College," was directed toward the achievement of the complete freedom of the individual, specifically toward the elimination of socially discriminating customs and compulsory courses and religion. (He personally resented the time he spent on mathematics at the expense of English — he upheld the elective system which years later he repudiated — and he waged at Princeton a battle against the evangelical debauchery that had disturbed him at Hill.) And the "critical protestants" of the *Lit.* especially hoped to make good what the college lacked. They wished to furnish it with a rich tradition, to make it a place where great cultures would be studied, where students would turn out for a production of *Candida* rather than for the "dismal farces" of the Triangle Club and would some-day pass through the cloisters of Holder chanting *their* poems.

Wilson's own work for the *Lit.* is marked by the solemnity that he said in "The Fog Lifts" had made the *Lit.* a contributor to the "pervasive gravity" of the university. It is serious in the way that young men are serious; the situations in his stories are often those of the adult world, and they have about them the grimness that Gauss complained of in the stories Wilson sent him a few years later. When he attempts to be amusing, he is sophisticated: in "The Novel-Reader's Tragedy," a girl, bored by everything, reads Henry James, and then as the scene fades finds herself surrounded by people who speak as James's characters do and (he was a parodist early) like the characters of Shaw, Bennett, Wells, Mere-dith, and Chesterton. In "Human and Hamadryad," the situation is clever in the way his later dialogue between William Beebe and the iguana is, but the theme is serious. And his essay, "Ed-ward Moore Gresham: Poet and Prose-Master," is so perfect a hoax that it probably missed fire — he tried it again, with clues and in the form of a burlesque, in *Vanity Fair*.

Even then his mind searched out matters by means of the con-frontation of ideas or positions, by "encounters" and dialogue. His stories are dramatic but rigid, fixed by an intelligence too careful and analytical for fiction. His longest work, "The Thank-less Job," is Jamesian in the sense that it enacts the kind of situa-tion he appreciated in James: the conflict of the imagination with some moral duty that tests one's personal worth and ends, as in *What Maisie Knew*, with the moral triumph of choosing "the only decent person." Here, an orphaned boy is fought over by two women, a respectable schoolteacher and a woman of fash-ionable society. The latter wins him only to find that her world, represented by her vulgarly rich husband, corrupts him. For her the boy provides an opportunity to dedicate herself to decency, and in quest of this ideal, she leaves her husband and returns to her father, an old-fashioned American who possesses the rectitude she had tried to escape in her youth. The moral conflict in this story, as in the poorer story, "Below Stairs," is dramatized in terms of social classes and recalls the issues at stake in the episode of the pony-cart. It is interesting that by marrying into a grocer's family the boy finds a common America that is somewhere between the harsh respectability of the schoolmistress and the vulgarity of the newly rich.

One is impressed, here and elsewhere in his writing, not only by the fact that he seeks a middle ground, but by his feeling for human motivation and common good and by his moral touchstone of decency.[3] He defines himself best in an article on Henry James in which he objects to James's limited stage and suggests that some of the experience of Mark Twain would have given him an American inspiration and flavor; yet he sees what James accomplished on his restricted stage — the adventures of the imagination — and admires his "fine Puritanism." "He has given so convincing a picture," he writes, "of our single souls finding themselves thrust into a strange and interesting world, striving to understand everything about our relation to it and finally falling back on the only indubitable values upon which we may depend." These values, he says, rest on "the firmest ground in the world," on "the real excellence of the good and the real vileness of evil," and their imperative, in the words of Fleda Vetch, is that "You mustn't break faith. Anything is better than that."

Fine Puritanism is not the Puritanism that Mencken, whom he was reading, was attacking. It is moral precision, and it is connected with the artist's rather than the moralist's exploration of experience, with the adventure of imagination that, in James's case, led to an art whose impression was lifelike, one of real complex human relations. Wilson himself attacks those manifestations of the refined, the repressive, and the sentimental that Van Wyck Brooks, whom he was also reading at this time, called the malady of the ideal. In "Human and Hamadryad," the girl cannot renounce her soul in order to experience the pagan realization of being a tree, but she learns that souls need freedom and expression; and in "Into the Church," a wildly ironic story of a sick evangelist, genial commonsense materialism triumphs over senti-

[3] It may be significant for Wilson's generation that Fitzgerald in *The Great Gatsby* originally attributed decency rather than honesty to Nick Carraway.

mental Christianity. Yet he always tries to find the balance between extremes. His moral sense is sure, though perhaps some
would say priggish. He says of Stendhal that only his irony and
desire to analyze make his smoking room stories art, but his
deeper objection is to Stendhal's values: to the excess of irony
and the indiscriminate scorn that led him to simplify motives and
demean humanity — to think that the good are always stupid and
the intelligent always selfish.

Decency is an old-fashioned virtue; so one comes to consider it
in the work of Orwell and Wilson. Were it not for other connota-
tions, we might call it a bourgeois virtue. To be decent is not to
break faith; to stand by the values that in themselves affirm one's
humanity. The values here are those that were crystallized for
Wilson in the experience of the pony-cart, and they were probably strengthened for him at Princeton, where, Bishop said, an
attempt was made to create a respect for ideas and the suffering
men had undergone for beauty and wisdom. In his answer to
Gauss's memoir of those days, Wilson reported that his wife
(Mary McCarthy) had said of his group that "Princeton didn't
give them quite moral principle enough to be writers." It had
given them too great respect for money and social prestige —
both Bishop and Fitzgerald, he said, had fallen victim to this,
while he, having enough money at the time for travel and study,
had survived. He consoled himself, however, with the fact that
Princeton had given them other things that were good, among
them "a sort of eighteenth-century humanism. . . . " And he
added that "if we had gone to Yale, though we should probably
all have survived in the flesh, we might never have survived in
whatever it is that inspires people not to take too seriously the
ideal of the successful man."

IV

Bishop said that the really permanent feature of
Princeton was its best teachers. No doubt he referred to Christian
Gauss, the spiritual father of Wilson's generation there.

The enduring friendship of Gauss and Wilson, begun when
Wilson was a student and ending only with Gauss's death in
1951, was primarily the gift of the older man, a sign of the largesse
of his being. He had the teacher's need to bestow, but he did not

bestow, as older men often do, for his own advantage. Others partook of his generous spirit — Fitzgerald, Dell, and Bishop among Wilson's friends — but Wilson was the greater beneficiary because he needed more what Gauss offered him and because Gauss knew how to offer it to him. Gauss gave Wilson what his father had been unable to give him.

Wilson's need is felt throughout his work in the special attention he gives to filial relationships. One recalls his treatment of Marx's relationship with his father in *To the Finland Station* and that of Tom Sherman with his father, the general, in *Patriotic Gore*. And one notes in *I Thought of Daisy* the manipulation that makes it possible for the Wilson-hero to attribute to another his rebellious feelings against his father while he himself freely expresses his admiration. Where he identifies the course of his own career with that of his father, when the image of the old Roman is before him, he is warm and admiring; but even in *A Piece of My Mind*, his reflections at sixty, old hurts sharpen his words. He cannot, he will not let go, as Gauss once wisely suggested he do. Even his memorial tribute to Gauss, unlike memorials of other relationships in which he finds release, is tongue-tied. He has Judge Medina, another of Gauss's students, speak out directly what might seem the sentimental truth of his indebtedness, and he closes with some lines from Dante — untranslated, of course — which explicitly tell, as the rest of the memorial never does, that his relation with Gauss was deeply filial.[4]

He avoids in this way the kind of bondage that disturbed him in Paul Rosenfeld's relationship with Stieglitz. He wants a loving father and would be a loving son, but he does not wish to revere the father as a prophet nor accept obediently his spiritual guidance. He remembers his father's authoritative manner, his "dictatorial tone," the lectures at dinner — certainly it was this kind of intellectual bearing and style as much as the doctrine that later made him angry with Irving Babbitt. Gauss had a different intellectual and personal quality, and his relationship with Wilson endured, in spite of differences in age, temperament, and opinion, because he "never imposed, he suggested." From the start, he waived his professorial privileges; we are told that he lightly planted seeds of thought in the minds of his students, but more

[4] *The Inferno*, Canto XV, lines 82–85.

important, we notice that at the point where careers cross he was able to accommodate the more brilliant achievements of his friend.

The assurance that made possible this geniality was the result of his own modest success and of his habit of keeping open the windows of life. When Wilson first encountered him, Gauss was in his middle thirties and already chairman of the department of Romance languages at Princeton. This is the Gauss to whom his devoted students paid tribute in the *Vanity Fair* Hall of Fame — the Gauss who had strengthened the study of modern languages at Princeton and had stirred the younger generation of Princeton writers with his enthusiasm for French culture — and to whom they mischievously gave national prominence as the living repudiation of Mencken's idea of the professor. He became Dean in 1925, and his association with Princeton was permanently fixed. But Gauss was never parochial, neither bound by the affairs of college life that he enjoyed and managed so well nor by the village horizon. He began his autobiography by saying that in one lifetime he had lived through all the stages of civilization. He had known the primitive stage in Michigan where he was born and the advanced stages in the larger world in which he later always moved. Civilization was his passion, and what he did not know of it from experience he knew from his vast reading. He lived in the stream of history, fascinated by its movements and the personalities who had fronted it. He seemed himself to have about him the aura of history.

In early manhood, he had been a foreign correspondent in Paris and had known Oscar Wilde. Again in Europe in 1911, he had made a pilgrimage of the imagination, following closely the steps of Byron and Rousseau. This experience seems to have been a crucial one in his personal development, both altering and stabilizing his temperament. In a notebook he kept he recorded an episode of meditation in which what he had been seeking in Europe — and history — at last presented itself to him. Flora, whom he has secretly worshipped and whom he now finds in Italy "unrebuked" and one with Christ, tells him what the critics at home were already beginning to say: "You [the Americans] are adventurers, but you are running not toward but away from life. . . . You build empires, rush into the wilderness . . . be-

cause you cannot rest. . . . You are afflicted by your souls." Gauss
recognized his own malady of the ideal and tried to cure it. The
"fluid indeterminate element" in his teaching and conversation
that Wilson praises was the result of the yielding by which he
moved with the life he desired. Whatever Puritan iron had been
in his nature was annealed; even the determination for career,
the lack of which Wilson regrets, was relaxed. He did not relinquish certain traits of the older generation — the firmness, solidity,
and sense of responsibility that strengthened his fatherliness —
but put away dogmatism and was therefore at ease with and able
to oversee sympathetically the adventure of a younger generation. From the vantage of what he had learned from history and
literature and of what he had conquered in himself, he was able
to point out the inadequacies of the younger generation's estimate of life — to do so without rancor, never to the end of mere
denial, always in the interest of a larger and deeper life. That
"life allows every person at least one dream" was an article of the
generous faith that made it possible for him to take advantage
of the differences between the generations, to meet the younger
men as equals, and to share in their careers without too much
anxiety for them or any for himself.

Gauss gives the impression of liveliness of intellect and sympathy springing from serenity. He is engaged, yet detached;
serious, yet playful. This is the special quality of his letters to
Wilson and of many of the fragments and lectures collected in
his *Papers*, and it radiates from the various portraits of him that
Wilson drew. He is most fully presented in *I Thought of Daisy*,
where he figures as Professor Grosbeake, the "modern type of
sage, who taught wisdom in casual conversation and virtue only
by example." Some of his traits and views are those of Alfred
North Whitehead, whom both Gauss and Wilson admired, but
Gauss is always easily distinguished. The colonial house in which
Grosbeake lives in Cambridge is sketched from the memory of
frequent visits to the Gauss's house at Princeton where a room
was always ready for Wilson; Grosbeake's daughters are Gauss's,
his German wife probably Alice Gauss or at least a way of indi-
cating Gauss's German heritage. Though Grosbeake is depicted
as a mathematical philosopher, we are confronted with a philosopher of civilization who, in this episode, takes a more charitable

view than Sinclair Lewis' of the American businessman and the Middle West, and whose speculation, ranging over history, comes to rest on the need for moral leadership, for continuity of responsibility between the generations.

Grosbeake, at once modern and daring in his philosophical speculations and old-fashioned in character, is the only rock that appears in this novel of a generation at sea. He serves the hero as Gauss undoubtedly served Wilson: he steadies him, reminds him of the "human" in what Gauss, defining history, called the "changing field of human endeavor," and provides a broadly conceived humanistic tradition to which the modern prodigal can always return. To meet him is to be embraced by clarifying and enlarging and tonic thought, to be given again a universe to live in, and to be reminded, as the hero is, that "all that dignified mankind . . . had been built up through endurance and patience, through steadiness of purpose and good faith. . . ." He is an exemplar of decency.

Gauss's humanism was of a different kind than that of Babbitt and his own Princeton friend, Paul Elmer More, and in the battle over the "new" humanism he stood against them. Wilson depicted the differences in one of his best sketches, "Mr. More and the Mithraic Bull." Here the rigid and provincial More is granted his strength and achievement but contrasted with the flexible, humane, and worldly Gauss. We are told that Gauss had the freedom of knowing the literary life of Europe — a fact of great importance to Wilson and one that he notes also in the case of Paul Rosenfeld. Both had a large experience of art, and their work is diffused with an aesthetic responsiveness and warmth not to be found in More's work of disembodied learning and determined tradition-making. Yet in *Discordant Encounters*, Rosenfeld and Gauss represent traditional viewpoints against which the younger generation tests its aggressive modernism. They invoke a cultural tradition which Wilson shares and says is "easiest to call humanistic."

This humanism has a pagan element and may be defined by Gauss's preference for the French love of life rather than the English suspicion of life, and by what he said, when lecturing on Anatole France, of the characteristic of the French spirit.[5] He

---

[5] Irving Babbitt's remark that "the French language is only a cheap and nasty substitute for Latin" is in point here.

speaks of the *esprit gaulois* which loves even the coarser sides of life and is not afraid of passion or emotion; of the *esprit critique*, the dispassionate intelligence that will not be disarmed by sentiment or other considerations; and of the *esprit artiste*, the attitude in which one looks upon life as an art and views the world itself as a work of art. His humanism is neither Romantic nor Classic, but a compound of both. It respects the individual, his depth of participation in life — the need to be "deeply stirred with life"; and it respects self-discipline, not limitation for itself but the scrupulous intelligence that recognizes the limits and difficulties of moral experience, the necessity of achieving order and form, and the continuity of human effort that this requires. His Romanticism is not optimistic — he detested Browning — nor is his Classicism entailed, as was T. E. Hulme's and his disciples', by original sin. There is much in his thought that reminds one of the vital humanism of Ortega, for, like Ortega, whom he had read, he calls attention to those elements of culture and civilization without which both art and life become dehumanized. Even the religious solution he offers for the crisis of our time in *A Primer For Tomorrow* turns out to be salvation by human effort for human ends, a disinterestedness and a regard for those human sanctions that make civilization whole and worthwhile.

There are many touchstones of Gauss's humanism — for example, his extravagant defense of Byron and his appreciation of Flaubert's art. The best, however, are his letter to the younger generation and the dialogue of Gauss and Wilson in *Discordant Encounters*, for both show him on the defensive, forced to acknowledge that he is old and of the older generation and at the limits of his sympathy with the younger men. Gauss drafted the long letter in 1925, but apparently never sent it.[6] What it said was probably already familiar to Wilson, for within the year he enacted in "Mrs. Alving and Oedipus" the kind of "knock-down and drag-out" talk over it that Gauss had looked forward to. In this dialogue, the only one of the *Encounters* in which the participants are anonymous, Gauss is the professor of fifty, Wilson the journalist of twenty-five. Wilson increased the difference in age — Gauss was actually forty-eight and Wilson thirty-one — and set

[6] It is printed in *The Papers of Christian Gauss*, ed. by Katherine Gauss Jackson and Hiram Haydn, New York, Random House, 1957, pp. 71–94.

against the professor a brash young man whose narrow viewpoint is hardly that of the Wilson who wrote "A Preface to Persius." The issue between them is not a superficial matter of professional styles or momentary allegiances — not at all the kind of thing one finds in Ernest Boyd's "Aesthete: Model 1924." Gauss approved of the courage and sincerity of the younger generation and welcomed its attack on Puritanism and industrialism; he dismissed the inevitable difference in manners, even to some extent the difference in morals. What disturbed him was the younger generation's lack of historical and moral perspective and the boredom and nihilism from which its destructiveness sprang. He felt that it had no "attitude," only an "hostility," and that its conception of life was "void, sterile, false." The assumptions of the position he takes in the dialogue are clearly stated in the letter: the younger generation is "short on history, even recent history"; it has no conception of the heroic man nor of the tragic sense of life. For it life no longer holds the possibility of adventure or involves risks, and civilization itself is no longer cherished because no longer recognized for the precarious achievement it is. "Let us not fool with civilization," he advises its members, "unless we are sure we wish to be rid of it."

The journalist's view of tragedy might be called the liberal one. He believes that "impossible moralities" and "oppressive institutions" are always responsible for tragedy, that tragedy is the result of the conflict between conventional and enlightened ideas. Mrs. Alving, he claims, was brought to ruin by Puritanism and respectability; Oedipus was a victim of the taboo against incest, Antigone of official stupidity, Hamlet of the absurd authority of the past. Having progressed, the present generation is superior to the past; he is confident that his generation understands all those ills that were once ascribed to the Furies and that, no longer cowed by beliefs in fate and suffering, it is the master of the universe. He represents the contemporary attitude the professor traces to the early Shaw and to H. G. Wells: only destroy prejudice and convention, and all will be well.

For these simple views the professor is at first only a sounding board. He entertains them with the Socratic finesse that Gauss is said to have shown in preceptorials. He questions, adduces cases, and finally counters with views that are as profound and wise as their statement is eloquent. He reminds the journalist that conventions are actual facts of life, inevitable and necessary limiting conditions, and that tragedy deals with fatalities of moral character for which man himself is responsible. Tragedy, he believes, is the result of the universal condition of man, and the perfect society will not be without it. One must not seek to banish it, as he thinks the liberals of his time, much to their grief, tried to do; one must understand it and understand *with* it. He wants men of the world who know the worst of the world yet take it seriously, who can do without illusions yet maintain their dignity. He calls for mastery within the terms of life, not despair of or rebellion against them. The rebellion the journalist foresees will not, he feels, solve the problem of culture.

Gauss attacked liberalism, but was himself a liberal in the sense that he had what Wilson calls an "old-fashioned devotion to liberty." His father had come to America after the unsuccessful German revolution of 1848, and a hatred of Prussianism was a part of his heritage. Liberty, which he defined as "freedom for the inner spirit of man," was both a religious and cultural principle, a central tenet of his creed. He was a member of the National Committee of the American Civil Liberties Union, and when he spoke in the South he insisted, with a moral intransigence that suggests John Jay Chapman, another of his admirations, on addressing a mixed audience. That he had a tragic sense of life does not mean, as it did in the case of many in the twenties, that he looked backward or condemned modernism outright. For him history was a process to be directed by imagination and will; civilization need not decline if man remained creative. "If I started a philosophy of my own," he once wrote Wilson, ". . . I would call it *integralism*, which involves the fundamental concept that man and his historical and ethical environment are one and that to a certain degree he may make himself master of it." He was always forward-looking, insisting only that we proceed with the work of civilization better equipped, with something of his own moral awareness, devotion to liberty, and hatred of compulsion. The hostility of the journalist contrasts with the attitude of the professor. Because of the professor's quality of thought, moral depth, and humane manner, we feel that civilization would be safer in his hands than in the journalist's.

Wilson placed his memoir of Gauss at the beginning of *The Shores of Light* in order to indicate the critical point of view with which he began in the twenties. He dedicated *Axel's Castle*, his first major critical work, to Gauss, generously acknowledging his debt by giving his friend the book that had grown from his teaching. From Gauss, he says, he acquired the "idea of what literary criticism ought to be — a history of man's ideas and imaginings in the setting of the conditions which have shaped them." And he speaks not only of past teaching but of continuing kindness and instruction. To read their correspondence is to see the extent of that debt: to see Gauss assisting at every stage, offering critical aid and reading proof, counseling, suggesting, sustaining. One associates Gauss with Maxwell Perkins, the selfless editor who was more than editor, and following the long voyage of speculation that Wilson and Gauss shared, realizes how much Wilson relied on Gauss and how much he meant when he said in the dedication that Gauss "taught much in insisting little."

But the memoir testifies to something more: to the quality and strength of the allegiances by which both Gauss and Wilson judge men. The allegiances in this case are "old-fashioned." They constitute a tradition that includes the Emersonian individualism and self-dependence and the humanistic faith in the nobility of man and the beauty of his achievements so eloquently expressed in the memoir of Mr. Rolfe. Gauss, we are told, was a moral as well as literary teacher; he instilled "the determination to be a seeker after truth" and taught that salvation was to be achieved by the "vigilant cultivation of *'il ben del intelletto.'*" Like Alfred Rolfe, the old Concordian, Gauss's authority was moral and cultural. And as Rolfe had done in teaching Greek, so he had done in teaching French and Italian — brought a new dawn to the lecture room, a sense of something "human, heroic and shining."

two

Wanted: A City of the Spirit

I

In 1922, we find the serious young face of Edmund Wilson, Jr. in a *Vanity Fair* pictorial tribute to "The New Generation in Literature." The gallery includes among other photographs those of Stephen Vincent Benét, John Dos Passos, F. Scott Fitzgerald, and John Peale Bishop, and Wilson is singled out as a writer of brilliant and informed critical essays. His face, full front but half in shadow, is well-shaped and firm; the mouth is strong and drawn downward, the nose straight and fine, the forehead high, the eyebrow pulled toward the bridge with an intensity that determines the over-all impression. This is the picture that Zelda Fitzgerald said was "beautiful and bloodless." In another fully lit photograph probably taken at the same sitting, the sharp countenance melts into a boyish bland anonymity, and seems more in keeping with the open and unguarded yet intent young man we might have expected from the rendering of himself in an early play and novel.

But the resolute face is the one that as managing editor of *Vanity Fair* he had chosen to print, and it looks out at us in a way that confirms those aversions, recorded at this time in *Vanity Fair*, to everything, like tea, that messed up his day, or, like the stupid sea and indifferent countryside, that kept him from libraries, concerts, and the theatre, from politics and conversation — from the urban world of ideas. Cancel whatever is due to the sophisticated coloring of *Vanity Fair* or to the posturings of bright young men, here is a young man who has put away youth as much overrated.

He is glad to be free of its inadequacies, enslavements, and conformities, to be his own man in the large world of men. And in his work we come upon him with something of the shock that Fitzgerald had when, coming to New York City from arcadian Princeton, he caught sight of his friend "walking briskly through the crowd wearing a tan raincoat over his inevitable brown getup," cane in hand, confident, "wrapped in his own thoughts and looking straight ahead. . . ." The "shy little scholar of Holder Court" had been transformed into a man of the world; his new background, it appears, is sufficient to him and sustains him. In the retreating figure of his friend, whom he dare not interrupt, Fitzgerald has had his first glimpse of what for his generation was a compelling attraction, "the Metropolitan spirit." And even more explicit is the impression of another young man who a few years later observed Wilson during his evening hours at his desk in the Village apartment across the way. "He seemed in his own person, and young as he was," Lionel Trilling recalls, "to propose and to realize the idea of the literary life." The literary life — Van Wyck Brooks had by this time given currency to the phrase and body to the conception; and here was Wilson determined, perhaps by the closing words of Brooks's *The Ordeal of Mark Twain*, not to miss his vocation, "to put away childish things and walk the stage as poets do."

He had always been serious but the war had compounded his seriousness by initiating him into the world Eliot was soon to call the waste land. Only after he left Princeton, he explains in *The Undertaker's Garland* (1922), were his thoughts turned away from life by the overpowering presence of death. He had enlisted in the army because he wished to escape from bourgeois life — this is the reason he gives when reviewing his motives in the thirties. He had trained at Plattsburgh in the summer of 1916, had served in a hospital unit in the Vosges,[1] and toward the end of the war, with his father's help, had been transferred to an intelligence unit and promoted to the rank of sergeant. He had never been in much danger — no more than had the fledgling infantry-

---

[1] Like the Whitman he celebrates in *Patriotic Gore*, Wilson was a "wound dresser." One of his poems conveys this experience: "When all the young were dying, I dwelt among the dead — / Many I lifted from the homeless bed /And laid in that low chamber side by side. . . ."

man of his story, "The Death of a Soldier," who, journeying from
Le Hâvre in a 40-and-8 boxcar in the damp November weather,
had met his death, not by fire and not at the front, but by pneu-
monia at a field hospital. By helping the wounded to return to
battle, Wilson felt that he had contributed to the "business of
bringing death" and had been poisoned by the decay that was
poisoning the world. The epitaphs he wrote at this time speak
for an experience that in even more extreme forms has become a
major experience of our time: he learned how man is undone, his
humanity eroded, by a discipline that destroys the moral foundations of decency. He had had, as he wrote in "Reunion," one of
the bitterest reflections on his generation's experience of war, the
shock of realizing "one's capacity for becoming demoralized," of
having to admit to oneself "one's possibilities for cowardice, for
brutality, for bestiality"; and he tells in *I Thought of Daisy* how
within himself he had raged against "the violators of life."

Whether in France or the postwar America to which he returned, an America symbolized for him by the "black chimneys
of factories," he found that the "characteristic activity of our time"
was death-dealing. War, revolution, and industrialism had left
the earth "charred and sterile, littered with rubbish and bones."
For him, at least, the result was that it was impossible, as the
casualty of war says in "Reunion," to "ever live indifferently or
trivially again." The narrator of *I Thought of Daisy* explains that
because of his experience of war and of class domination he had
"acquired a scorn for the pursuit of money, position or rank: the
people who cared for such things seemed now to me sinister or
childish. It appeared impossible ever again to accept conventional
values complacently, to acquiesce in the prosperous inertia and
the provincial ignorance of America. One could never go back
again now to living indifferently or trivially; one was afraid of
lending oneself to some offense against that unhappy humanity
which one shared with other men." During the war, when Wilson
had been ill and had time to reflect upon his experience, he swore
that he would stand outside of society altogether and pledged
himself to devote his life to the "great human interests," to "Literature, History, the Creation of Beauty, the Discovery of Truth."

The impression we have of Wilson at this time hardly tallies
with the descriptions of the young intellectual in many of our

literary histories. One reads, of course, of "The Monkeyshines of Edmund Wilson" in Burton Rascoe's *A Bookman's Daybook*, that gossipy froth of the literary life — how he appeared one evening in a dressing gown and top hat, accompanied by Mary Blair [2] dressed in pajamas and Tallulah Bankhead dressed in a bathing suit and cutaway coat, and gave a vaudeville act. Many memoirs of the twenties, irremediably distorted by current interpretations and the colorful account of *Only Yesterday*, add their details. Matthew Josephson, for example, remembers that at a party in the Village Wilson fought with Burton Rascoe and bit him on the calf. Such incidents are recollected because we are expected to relish the good fun, to relive the heyday of youth, whether that of the twenties or of our own comparable college days. But even though in Wilson's case we may be grateful for the levity, we must admit that it is never central, at the most tangential.

The members of a generation have much in common, but Wilson experienced much of the life of his generation on principle rather than out of inclination. He was never quite one with his more boisterous contemporaries. The telling strokes of Ernest Boyd's "Aesthete: Model 1924" tell little about him. His thirtieth birthday may still be in the future; he may be an editor of a magazine; he may have gone to Princeton in the early years of "the Woodrovian epoch"; he may have answered the call to arms and returned to Greenwich Village enamored of French literature; and having written a competent book review, he may have awakened to find himself famous. But he did not feel these sharp words as Malcolm Cowley and Matthew Josephson did. He was not an expatriate nor an editor of *Broom*, and his literary baggage was already as heavy as his position was solid. He defended his generation, for he was with them in feeling, as Arthur Fiske says in *This Room and This Gin and These Sandwiches*, that the "respectable life was a living death." He, too, attacked Puritanism in *The Crime in the Whistler Room* and in the case of Dorothy Perkins who was tried for murder by respectable people, found a symbol of intense passionate life very much like his own heroines, Bill McGee, Sally Voight, Daisy, and Anna Lenihan. But he also admonished his generation, and because of his reservations or pronouncements seemed to some of his less well-established contem-

---

[2] An actress from Pittsburgh, whom he married in 1923.

poraries a stalwart of the older generation. Angered by Wilson's "The Muses Out of Work," Hart Crane wrote to Yvor Winters: "It is so damned easy for such as he, born into easy means, graduated from a fashionable university into a critical chair overlooking Washington Square, etc., to sit tight and hatch little squibs of advice to poets not to be so 'professional' as he claims they are, as though all the names he has just mentioned had been as suavely nourished as he. . . ." Maxwell Bodenheim spoke of him as "a fatuous policeman, menacingly swinging his club," and Josephson, apparently unable to revise an early opinion probably formed in response to Wilson's characterization of him in *Discordant Encounters,* still puts him in the "Uplift School."

There were critical schools aplenty in the twenties in which one might have put him, for the twenties were the coming-of-age of criticism, when the functions of criticism were needed, announced, and at last recognized, and critics began to take a conspicuous place in the intellectual life. Criticism, broadly conceived, oversaw the culture. A book like *Civilization in the United States* (1922), even more than anything by Brooks, Mencken, Babbitt, or Eliot, is the landmark of the period because it indicates in its very title that the time had come when Americans felt ready to undertake the inquiries once left to Matthew Arnold. And the title is significant in another way: it reminds us that civilization was the common object of criticism, and that for most critics, unable to shake the determining formulations of Brooks, it was profoundly a matter to be searched out in relation to the United States.[3]

Sitting in his critical chair overlooking Washington Square — by 1926 he was associate editor of *The New Republic* — Wilson had as good a position for viewing the intellectual scene as he would ever have. Herbert Croly, its editor, the architect of the new nationalism whose cultural program Brooks had articulated, undoubtedly influenced him, though it is clear in his early essays that he was already indebted to Brooks. Yet he never belonged to a school and never adopted an explicit program. The only thing

[3] In this connection, it is interesting to note Ezra Pound's *Patria Mia,* written prior to 1913, but published in 1950. In many ways, it anticipates Brooks's *America's Coming-of-Age* and the program of *The Seven Arts.* That the manuscript was mislaid may have been a misfortune for both Pound and Brooks.

that seems programmatic is his willingness to accommodate the various positions and attitudes of the time; and this, we feel, is not because he is confused or without resolution in his own thought, but rather because the competing schools of criticism canceled out in each other valuable elements of concern that he preferred to unite, and because at this moment in his adventure on reality more was to be gained by inclusion. One sees him attempting to define the great critic while at the same time he is trying himself as poet, playwright, social commentator, and reporter-at-large of the arts; hardly anything of creative or intellectual significance escapes him, and one is amazed, especially when looking back on so much that is brummagem in the writing of the twenties, by all that he managed to give the lasting impress of his intelligence.

Of all the schools of criticism, certainly the "Uplift School" is not the one in which to place him. The New Humanism of Babbitt and More always remained beyond the range of his sympathy, though, in scoring the fact that his generation of critics was badly educated and had never learned to write, he claimed that More was a master of ideas, the only critic of considerable learning and serious intent. None of the factions that formed around Mencken, Brooks, Babbitt, Eliot, and Mike Gold won his allegiance. Indeed he had the presumption to review the critical work of his contemporaries in a piece entitled "The All-Star Literary Vaudeville" (1926); and later, in "The Critic Who Does Not Exist" (1928), he charged that in spite of the existence of many schools of criticism, the literary atmosphere, unlike that of France, the cultural touchstone of his generation, was "a non-conductor of criticism." The schools, he said, did not consider it necessary to treat seriously each other's ideas nor to engage in a defense of their own — that would come later in the controversy over the New Humanism at the beginning of the thirties — although in *Discordant Encounters* (1926) he had staged the kind of give-and-take he had in mind. And there was no critic — he mentions only the second-rate Stuart Sherman whose new career at "the central desk of authority" was ended by death — who tried to make all of literature his province and to deal with it authoritatively. What he seeks is "a genuine literary criticism that should deal expertly with ideas and art"; he wants critics not of one or the other, not even first-rate writers who are nothing but literary critics, but men of letters who write poetry, plays, or fiction as well as criticism, men like Anatole France, Gourmont, Valéry, Proust, and Gide in the French tradition and Dryden, Coleridge, Poe, and Henry James in the Anglo-American, and historians like Renan, Taine, Leslie Stephen, and Georg Brandes for whom literary criticism is a part of their work. Of the French writers, then very much read by his contemporaries, he observes that they "came to intellectual maturity in [an] atmosphere of debate" in which the "language of criticism," common to all of them, awakened their intelligence to the responsibilities of art.

From this standpoint it is easier to look back on the career he was fashioning for himself in the twenties, to see why he had tasked publicly his friends Fitzgerald and Rosenfeld, the one for "lack of discipline and poverty of aesthetic ideas," the other for not being a critic of the "philosophic sort," and why he had upset Crane and others by suggesting that it did not "constitute a career for a man to do nothing but write lyric poetry." One sees better the direction in his own various endeavors [4] and realizes that the crucial critical issue for him was not the quarrel of the schools. He would contribute to the realistic scrutiny of American culture and the fostering of native expression, that preparation for the national culture Brooks had heralded; he would further the cosmopolitanism and aestheticism of which Eliot had become the representative; he would publish in *The Liberator* as well as *The Dial* and see his own experimental work performed by the Provincetown Players; and though he would join all the schools in a league against the New Humanists, he would try in his own work to emulate the learning and mastery of ideas for which he praised More. The essential issue for him was that of art and politics, of an art become increasingly private and privileged at the expense of its responsibility to the public and larger world of thought and action for which politics was the covering term. If any slogan spoke for him, it was the declaration of policy of the prewar *The Seven Arts*: "AN EXPRESSION OF ARTISTS FOR THE COM-

[4] In 1925, writing of Byron, he spoke of "the inexhaustible capacity for experience that is so satisfactory today in its contrast with the limitations of the typical literary man who agreeably diverts the hours of a safe and regular life by turning out novels or poems."

MUNITY." [5] Before the war, he had spent a summer studying sociology and labor problems at Columbia University; political journalism had been his goal. During the twenties, when a new kind of artist was replacing the old, he did not forget the generation before him, those men alive to both politics and art who for him had been the glory of the Village. Finally one sees that almost from the start the devotion to "ideas and art" (his own phrasing suggests a priority) had its not uncommon consequences: much of his art is criticism, a critic's art serving to provoke and to solve problems of ideas, while the best of his criticism is art. In his criticism one most often finds the "distinctive individual quality" which he says in *I Thought of Daisy* is the precious stuff of art — the honey, that "miraculous secretion of the mind which there was only one man to supply."

To enter the world of letters by way of *Vanity Fair* was not at all inauspicious. Assuredly, the magazine was just what Frederick Hoffman has called it, a "handbook for the sophisticate." It catered to the upper-class world or, perhaps like *The New Yorker*, to those who aspired to it. Along with the advertisements of automobiles and lingerie, so seductive to the Gatsbys of the time, it offered cultural amusement to those whose notion of sophistication was one of keeping up with fashionable and "modern" developments in art and thought. It did this very well: in its pages, one can learn of Einstein and Freud [6] and of the lively and the serious arts, and sample the work of writers like Masters and Anderson, Eliot, Pound, Huxley, and Lawrence. Its tone is frivolous; but one,

[5] In this, he stands closest to Brooks, but it must be pointed out that he did not contribute to *The Freeman*, under Brooks's literary editorship the most notable magazine of cultural criticism. He was not a disciple of Stieglitz, and, with the exception of Paul Rosenfeld, seems to have kept his distance from this group. Time, however, may reveal deeper allegiances: Brooks, in his memoirs, uses Wilson as his spokesman.

[6] Wilson wrote on psychoanalysis, but not in the parodistic manner of the time. He placed Freud with Copernicus and Darwin, and, though not accepting all of Freud's ideas, especially those on dreams, was truly excited by his discovery of the "abyss." Of significance to his later work is the fact that he saw in Freud the rare combination of artist and scientist, and that in placing him against the background of World War I made of him, as he would later of others against the background of World War II, a figure of light. (*Vanity Fair*, August 1920.)

searching our past, will find in it as wide a survey of the contemporary artistic scene as he would in the more serious *Dial*.

Perhaps the nature of the magazine explains why men as young as Wilson and John Peale Bishop were for a time its managing editors. It needed the daring and irreverence, the college-bred Menckenism they were able to bring to it, the kind of thing, at once the product of their temper at the time and of the tone they fostered in the magazine, that one finds in their joint publication, *The Undertaker's Garland*. But Wilson used *Vanity Fair*, as he would other magazines, for his own purposes. He did not limit his serious work by publishing it only in *The Dial* or *The New Republic*. Although nothing he wrote for *Vanity Fair* has the brilliance of the essay on *The Waste Land* in *The Dial*, several pieces define, as nothing else does, his point of departure, and they suggest why, in the absence of a serious and sustaining context for his work, he was glad to leave the "old mad-house" of *Vanity Fair* for a critical chair on *The New Republic*.

He took a stand at the start, and so was one to be counted. The first major article he wrote on his return from the war appeared in the September 1920 issue of *Vanity Fair*. It is called "The Gulf in American Literature," and is resonant of Brooks's *America's Coming-of-Age* as well as of the yet unpublished *The Pilgrimage of Henry James*.[7] For Wilson uses Henry James to explain the gulf in our culture between what Brooks had called the "highbrow" and the "lowbrow" and he calls the "refined" and the "vulgar." James is a "superior American of his generation" who represents the "tragedy of the artist in the America of the last half century," and he provides a focus for the literary-cultural issues of Wilson's time — the issues of a barren environment, of expatriation, of the Puritan conscience, of bridging the gulf.

That America did not feed James's soul is a condition with which Wilson sympathizes, for the "cheapness and oppressiveness of American life" are the result of the plutocracy that came to power in James's time and sits in judgment now. James belonged to a generation, like Wilson's father's, that had been broken, had

---

[7] Upon the publication of Henry James's letters, Brooks wrote "Our Illustrious Expatriate," *The Freeman*, I (April 28, 1920), 164–165, introducing critical themes Wilson takes up here.

been "born too old in a world too young." [8] Among the liabilities of his experience, the heaviest, as we now see from the vantage of *Patriotic Gore*, was the swallowing up in "the sordidness and stupidity of the industrial-commercial regime" of the eighteenth-century political philosophy of the Republic. The manufacturers and shopkeepers of this regime, not the contemporary artists, as the New Humanists believed, were "the anarchists of taste" — the phrase is the title of a companion article; they, not the artists, broke the rules, the old harmony of the preindustrial world. Like Rosenfeld, Wilson defends the necessity in art of beating out the rhythm of the age; he is an angry young man when this is the issue between the older and younger generations. And yet he looks back to other times and places, to the French landscape, to an earlier America. Listen to what he tells the French, in an article on the aesthetic upheaval there, about their Dadaist craze for the artifacts of American vitality — machinery, skyscrapers, jazz: "We, too, had an eighteenth century and we have forgotten it completely; it founded our literature, invented our social ideals, produced the political philosophers who gave strength and dignity to the Republic. . . . Be careful how you fling away the rope that unites you to the past from which you have fallen. . . ." Leave barbarism to the Americans who, he says, "would be better for living in a house that was even imitated from the eighteenth century." [9]

Wilson understands the personal necessity of James's exile. But expatriation, he believes, puts one in the unsatisfactory position of an onlooker. As his own manifesto, he cites the letter of Henry's — it was popular with other reviewers and critics also — in which he advises his brother William to keep his boys at home, to have them "contact local saturations and attachments in respect to their *own* great and glorious country, to learn and strike roots into its infinite beauty . . . and variety . . . [to] stick fast and sink up to their necks in everything their *own* countries and climates can give. . . ." James knew that "Its being that 'own,' will

[8] He says of his father: "Bred to one world and wearied by this other."
[9] This is basically Wilson's position in the dialogue between Paul Rosenfeld and Matthew Josephson in *Discordant Encounters*; the dialogue was not imaginary — Rosenfeld had been attacked in *Broom* — and Wilson clearly stood with Rosenfeld against Josephson, the apostle of Dadaism.

double the *use* of it." Yet what handicapped James in Europe, apart from the fact that Americans can never truly possess its culture, was the very thing that kept him from striking roots at home: the trouble with Henry James, as with the "educated American minority," was a Puritan conscience, a morbid fear of the "vulgar"; and nothing was more damaging because to fear the vulgar is to fear life itself.

The vulgar, as Wilson defines it here, is life, the vitality that he is one with the younger generation in demanding in "The Anarchists of Taste." [10] With Waldo Frank who wrote "In Defense of Our Vulgarity" for *The New Republic*, he believes that "our vulgarity is an ore which holds [new spiritual gold]. . . ." For the vulgar is also "the muddy and tumultuous encroachments of the democratic tide" whose literary spokesmen are Twain and Dreiser, men of the West. Now since this tide is strong, there will be no reconciliation in American culture; the "saving remnant," the "superficial literati," will be engulfed; and for the most part Wilson is happy with this prospect.

What disturbs him? For one thing, the vulgar is also just what James felt it to be — all the unendurable cheapness of an industrial and commercial and materialistic society. In this respect, the issue for Wilson is put by Rosenfeld in the encounter with Josephson: "whereas Seldes [he had just published *The Seven Lively Arts*] wants to call attention to the neglected virtues of the vulgar, you [a Dadaist] are attempting to discredit things that are fine." For another thing, artists like Twain and Dreiser have "no background save the soil," are philistine, illiterate, ill-equipped.

Wilson will do his best to make us see both faces of the vulgar. He will cover the seven lively arts. Yet the mood of the social documentary of the twenties in *The American Earthquake* is elegiac. The sense of loss, dominant throughout, is suggested by an early comment: "in general the respectable have disappeared and only the vulgar survive." And he will try to be for a generation of writers the literary conscience that Fitzgerald acknowledged he was for him. For a brief moment, he will find encouragement, as he does in his first article, in the fact of creative

[10] This issue is not a parochial one but perhaps the central issue of modern culture.

resurgence, seeing it as a reaction to all that is oppressive in society and believing that such forces of culture will somehow make a better world. But soon he will tell us that in much of this vitality, even that of his own generation, there is death at the root.

In the summer of 1925, Dorothy Perkins was sentenced to prison; in August 1927, Sacco and Vanzetti, Italian anarchists, were electrocuted; in the winter of 1928, Judd Gray and Ruth Snyder, "respectable" people who murdered her husband as "a step toward the larger freedom, the fuller enjoyment of life, which is so much in the air of our period," were executed. These landmarks of crime enclose the section of the twenties called "The Follies" in *The American Earthquake*, and they suggest something we have been reluctant to admit — that death was an overpowering presence of the decade.

There is nothing especially clever in two young men deciding, as they say in *The Undertaker's Garland*, that they can best interpret their country in a book devoted to death. Death and death-in-life are themes ready-to-hand — this is not the generation of Randolph Bourne whose banner was his *Youth and Life* (1913) but the generation of whom he had prophesied in 1917 when he warned that as a result of the war the only precious thing in a nation, "the hope and ardent idealism of its youth," will have been crushed out and "bitterness will spread out like a stain over the younger generation. . . ." The representative poem of this generation is *The Waste Land*, published in the same year as *The Undertaker's Garland*; and like Eliot's poem, the *jeu d'esprit* of Wilson and Bishop is an attempt to call the living back to life.

Its inspiration is not derived from Jessie Weston's book on the Grail legend but from Edgar Lee Masters' *Spoon River Anthology* — Masters is celebrated in "The Funeral of an Undertaker." But like Eliot's poem, this collection of stories and poems ranges over Western civilization: pagan Greek culture (the death of the last centaur who, in Greenwich Village, recalls the honor, the wise counsel of Cheiron, he had once forgotten), the Christian era (the funeral of Mary Magdalene), the nineteenth century (the death of a romantic poet who fights the battle of the generations over art and money; the death of a dandy — with echoes of Eliot's "Gerontion" and Stevens' "The Comedian as the Letter C"), the present era (the deaths of an efficiency expert, an undertaker, a soldier, a madman, and of Emily who seeks life in Hades). The solutions offered here are not religious ones as in Eliot's poem. In the preface, the young men deny immortality, and toward the end of the book they treat the death of God, who asks of man forgiveness for his botched creation. The solutions are pagan, naturalistic, social, and political, for the enemies of life are Christianity, bourgeois money-making, machine civilization and its ideology of service, holy war and its butchery — what might be called the Puritan complex. In spite of its theme, it is a book of considerable exuberance, and putting aside its lack of technical interest, this exuberance in behalf of life, accompanied as it is by political awareness, may account for its failure to capture much attention or to rally young men to its cause. Within a few years Wilson was to complain that the influence of Eliot had made the young men "prematurely senile."

The attack on Puritanism was also an attack on the older generation and the Anglo-Saxon leadership. Before the war, Mencken, Brooks, and Bourne had done much to rout them, but the generation that followed them carried on the battle for itself — for its own sake and pleasure — and in terms of its own experience. There is no question of which side Wilson took. And yet, whether in the meanings "vulgar" had for him, in the example of the centaur, or in those tournaments of ideas he called *Discordant Encounters*, one sees that the matter is never easily disposed of. His response is complicated primarily by his awareness of the fact that the past is not only the mortgagor of the present but a trustee of virtues. His own bourgeois background, for example, is not entirely worthless as some ideologists of the time supposed. The bourgeoisie, he believes, represents a stage in the history of the country and what it had achieved had been undone by the very forces the younger generation finds inimical. To one who had known the bourgeoisie as intimately as he had, it was not something to be expunged; it had genuine claims, and to forget them was to leave the younger generation empty and restless and destructive in its freedom.

This is the issue Wilson dramatized in his first play, *The Crime in the Whistler Room*. Produced by the Provincetown Players in October 1924, with his wife Mary Blair in the leading role, the play was his own contribution in behalf of the creative resurgence of his generation, a "fantasy," he has said, "of our first liberation from the culture and convention of the previous era." One of the several crimes in the play is the introduction of expressionistic dream sequences in what is otherwise an ordinary drawing room comedy; another, of a similar kind, is the use of colloquial speech. But these revolutionary literary gestures are not the ostensible crime of the title which is simply that the generations can no longer communicate with each other. Because of its inability to change, the older generation blocks the younger generation's quest for a larger life; but the younger generation, by repudiating rather than understanding the older generation, contributes to the crime.

Except for some of the dream sequences, the play takes place in the drawing room of the Streetfields' countryhouse on Long Island. This house was built at the beginning of the nineteenth century and has been "scrupulously weeded of the luxuriance of the Victorian era." The Streetfields are old Americans; in fact, Schuyler is editing the letters of his grandfather, once our minister to France, and has already written a biography of Gouverneur Morris, the Federalist statesman. The Streetfields are people of property, not Babbitts but an established upper class certain of its values such as one would not have found on Royal Ridge in Zenith nor even in East Egg; and they are people of manners, decorum, and taste who come to dinner in evening dress, follow a routine of bridge and reading aloud from Trollope, and confine their talk to family affairs which do not extend beyond Boston. Their taste is not advanced — *The Atlantic Monthly* adorns the coffee table, and Schuyler, who hasn't heard of Mencken, speaks up for the brilliant wit of Thomas Bailey Aldrich. What he says of financial matters applies as well to matters of spiritual economy: he has "made it a rigid rule never to invest in any new ventures."

The family's contact with the contemporary world is due to Miss Streetfield, a social worker at the Y.W.C.A. She is one more example of the evangelist of service Wilson despises, and her do-goodism, like her good manners, is a form of coercive righteousness. ("She wahnts to do good," Bill McGee, the girl she has rescued, explains; but Simon Delacy, up-to-the-minute in all of his attitudes, adds: "Something wrong with the old sex-life?") Miss Streetfield is an instrument of change in two respects, both of which are linked. She has brought Bill McGee to the house and is overseeing her education in respectability; and for convenience she has had a table moved in the Whistler room, a room whose harmony was established by the Whistler paintings and etchings hung there twenty-five years before (around 1895).[11]

Now the Whistler room is Schuyler's doing, and he is most upset by the action that takes place there. He is a genteel man, a Brooksian "highbrow," a Prufrock, the kind of patrician clubman one finds in Stuart Sherman's "Mr. Mencken, the Jeune Fille, and the New Spirit in Letters." In fixing his collection, he has fixed himself, has forgotten the rebelliousness of Whistler, his credo of art for art's sake, and his defiance of the philistines in his lawsuit with Ruskin. The taste that selected these paintings has not escaped gentility; what was once done as rebellion has become acceptable to taste, as if the people who had once shared in revolt had not maintained the attitude or could not relate it to the present — as Streetfield, for example, cannot see the relation between Whistler's painting of the little cockney girl and Bill McGee. In this respect he is one of those art lovers who, as Bourne said, has learned to appreciate a Japanese print, Dante, or Debussy, but has not learned nausea at Main Street. And yet, in spite of the fact that he fits these stereotypes, he is not a strawman. He is described as a man of some distinction; he represents the decline of a valuable type; he is the defeated writer of the post-Civil War period. And there is one speech in the play when, with Streetfield for his spokesman, Wilson achieves genuine eloquence.

If Schuyler Streetfield represents the defunct New England tradition, what is to be made of Bill McGee's father, the "lowbrow," the man of ventures from the West? McGee interrupts the action at a point of great boredom, when the deadly aspects of the Streetfields' life have told on the audience. But his "vitality" is undercut by obvious debility — and impecuniosity. He is charming and picturesque in a burlesque way which makes it impossible for us to take him seriously. We enjoy him but cannot place any hope in his hairbrain scheme, the Roosevelt Institute of Success,

[11] At Princeton, Wilson had written a poem on Whistler extolling the artist's heroism; the narrator of *I Thought of Daisy* has a copy of Whistler's "Battersea Bridge" in what he feels with shame is a bourgeois apartment. In connection with Bill McGee, it may be worth mentioning that Edna Millay went through college on money raised by a Y.W.C.A. worker.

which would perpetuate the evils of a vulgar business civilization. One thinks of him as a kind of W. C. Fields, and perhaps the name of his institute is intended to associate him with Theodore Roosevelt — with his brand of "practical idealism" and also with the failure of the progressive movement.[12] But finally one places him: he is another Col. Sellers, a folk character, a vulgar, boosting conman, the failure who worships success and who unthinkingly and idealistically allies himself with the most meretricious forces in our culture. The patterns of his speech are those of an age, having, we recognize, a western flamboyance; and, at times, he speaks, as he was probably intended to, in the manner of George F. Babbitt. He is, as Brooks says of Sellers in *The Ordeal of Mark Twain*, "the arch-typical American of the pioneering epoch," and it is apparent that he has "lost all sense of the distinction between reality and illusion. . . ." (The most painful scene in the play, that in which he clumsily performs as a magician, brings this home even to himself.) Nevertheless, where the Streetfields are barren, he has begotten Bill, all the vitality and passion for life that, respected and properly used, would provide the basis for a better life.

Bill is the first of several heroines in Wilson's work who represent the life for which others are responsible. The Streetfields repress her, but what of Simon Delacy who has given her the seed of another life? There is no question that this representative of the younger generation is modeled on F. Scott Fitzgerald. (It is interesting to note here the absence of the Wilson persona one almost always finds in his imaginative writing.) Delacy is described as "an attractive young man with a good profile, who wears a clean soft shirt . . . but looks haggard and dissipated. . . . His manner . . . alternates between too much and too little assurance, but there is something disarmingly childlike about his egoism." (In a critical article of 1922, Wilson wrote: "Fitzgerald is a rather childlike fellow, very much wrapped up in his dream of himself. . . . he is extraordinarily little occupied with the general affairs of the world. . . .") The brashiness of Delacy is also that of the Fitzgerald who, in one of the *Discordant Encounters*,

[12] In a *Vanity Fair* pole of critical values, with a scale of $+25$ to -25, Wilson rated Theodore Roosevelt -25. In recent years, he has considerably adjusted this rating.

tells Brooks, a man of dignity not unlike Streetfield, that he has made America "Younger-Generation-conscious."[13] In this encounter, one is made to feel the rather poor showing of the spokesman for the younger generation, not that what he says against Brooks isn't a fair statement of their complaint, but that in matters of character, especially of professional discipline, he is so obviously weak. What Wilson said of *This Side of Paradise* also represents his judgment of Delacy's action: "Its intellectual and moral content amounts to little more than a gesture — a gesture of indefinite revolt." When this was written in 1922, Wilson explained that revolt which could not fix on an object was typical of the war generation; but when he wrote this play, he was no longer willing to condone it.

Delacy's attitudes are primarily those of Mencken: democracy is a complete failure, God is dead, there are only slaves and masters, etc.[14] He mouths the cliches of fashionable cynicism as often as he hums a tune from *The Sheik* (jazz, which accompanies the dream sequence, is associated with Dada and death). Still he has a deep sense of the horror of his civilization. The macabre Horatio Alger story he concocts — it is called "The Skeleton in the Taxi" — might have been a part of *The Undertaker's Garland* or a companion piece to *Chronkhite's Clocks* (1926), an expressionistic pantomine in which Wilson ridicules the mechanization that dehumanizes man.[15] But Delacy's solution is the easy one of hedonism: "Oh, hell! Don't let them crab you! Remember you're alive and they're dead! Remember every moment of pleasure is a triumph against the forces of death!" He is careless in those relationships which, for Wilson, are always moral tests; one is not convinced at the end that he has truly accepted the choice set him

[13] Fitzgerald did, in the way of Simon Delacy but not in the way of Randolph Bourne, who was the spokesman of an earlier younger generation, a very serious one, with whom Wilson is spiritually affiliated.

[14] By 1924, Wilson had rejected Mencken's antidemocracy: "He extinguished the last spark of eighteenth-century political idealism. . . he excluded hope."

[15] Delacy says: "I have listened to their clocks and I thought: *That* destroys us all!" At this time Lewis Mumford was reminding us of the disasterous consequences of what he called "tick-tock." The title, of course, means "sickness's clocks." The work itself, written for a score by Leo Ornstein, is a good piece of its kind, fit for a Chaplin or, now, for an imaginative animated cartoonist.

by Bill's pregnancy. The choice is between death and life, and, as the dream sequences show, Delacy is sick unto death, worn out by the strain of his bravado in defying it, and full of fear. One feels the truth of his statement to Bill: "I can't lose my life for you!" He doesn't want the peace, security, and life her love promises. He lacks — as some are said to lack animal faith — her strength and decency.

By expressing the hidden motives of the younger generation, the dream sequences support its seriousness at the expense of the older generation. Except for Schuyler's great speech, the motives of the older generation are not revealed but taken for granted. To be dead-alive seems to be its fate. But an undertow of death also pulls at the life of the younger generation; indeed, a desire for death impels its libertarian excess. Only Bill, underprivileged even in this, has avoided it. In a dream sequence with her tutor, Bill fails to balance the equation of her frustration but does not accept the nihilistic solution of killing in order to live. Nor does she accept Menckenian values. Her dream of life suggests that what the younger generation is really seeking is not as destructive or harmful as the elders imagine — it hardly constitutes a "crime" — but that in a sense overlooked by both generations it is a crime because it shows a failure of social imagination. Bill dreams of an upper-class life similar to that of the Streetfields, even respectable, but happy and idyllic, somehow innocent and free of all anxiety, a life in which the goods of love and pleasure and spontaneity are purchased with a minimal outlay of responsibility and political effort.

The crime of the older generation is that, when the Whistler room is set aright at the end, all that has happened there will have been forgotten, the revolt of a generation, never understood, will have gone unnoticed. How spendthrift we have been in our neglect of these splendid energies! But were it not for Schuyler's speech, which also points up the transient nature of revolt, the younger generation might commit the crime of youth — the crime of which we hear in Eliot's "Portrait of a Lady": "'. . . youth is cruel . . . smiles at situations which it cannot see.'" For Schuyler explains his buried life, how in Paris in 1885 he had woven his life of Whistler's line, had driven in the Bois with the Prince ("my father's friend, the Prince!" — the accent of his speech is Eliotic), and had "relived the days when gentlemen served the State." He is, he says, a "priest of beauty"; and in his encounter with Delacy we are forced to place him with the conservators of value — with Rosenfeld and Brooks and Gauss of *Discordant Encounters,* who are superior in wisdom, dignity, and depth of passion for life to their younger assailants. Unlike these other representatives of the younger generation, Delacy begins to see beyond his own position: he sees in Schuyler an artist who has been betrayed by the same forces that are betraying him. While Bill turns back the Streetfields by naming them for what they are —"fakes" like her father, the other side of the Brooksian coin — Simon, in contrapuntal speeches, asks who has betrayed us — Carnegie or Bessemer, Hearst, Ford, or Wrigley, Jefferson or Rousseau, "a Nation of Pioneers?" And when Bill at last proclaims, "we're free!" Simon, at the end of his list, only repeats, "we've been betrayed!"

The Crime in the Whistler Room is the most thorough enactment we have of the Brooksian thesis. All the elements of the engagement with American culture, which was the ideological center of Wilson's coming-of-age, are here: East *vs.* West, rich *vs.* poor, old *vs.* young, Anglo-Saxon *vs.* immigrant, refinement *vs.* vulgarity, etc. And so is the weakness of Brooks's personal solution. For Brooks, a social visionary who believed in art as a social instrument superior to politics, liked to think after the war that Bourne would have withdrawn, as he had done, from matters of politics to matters more purely cultural. But if the betrayal, as Wilson's play indicates, is primarily a socio-economic one, the political field is not to be neglected. It may be true — as a statement of feeling about values, but not as a fact of action — that politics, as a character in another Wilson play about this period says, "is bankrupt since the War." But Wilson will not accept the notions that accompanied for many intellectuals the confession of political bankruptcy: that art itself, at some second remove, is in its way an instrument of political action, or that art is in itself a sufficient world. Nor will he accept Brooks's view, increasingly darkened by the postwar years, of the victimization of the artist. Wilson said in 1925 that Stravinsky "is the artist, not as victim, but as master," and he tried repeatedly to show that the cause of artistic failure is not so much environmental as it is personal —

due most often to a lack of discipline and sometimes to a mistaken conception of the responsibilities of art.

It is perhaps unfair to make this judgment in respect to the theatre, which in matters of discipline is seldom an exemplary art. But Wilson was intimately connected with the theatre and chose, in 1934–35, when he wrote *This Room and This Gin and These Sandwiches*, to use it as a sensitive guage of morale. He wrote the play with the intention of showing the consolidation of the creative movement in the twenties and its concentration in Greenwich Village. But the play, an accurate period piece (I present it here for this reason), shows instead the collapse and dispersal of the movement. And so it is full of nostalgia, a bittersweet farewell to *la vie de bohème*, at once lamenting and cherishing the carefree moment when this room and this gin and these sandwiches and a recital of Keats's "I Stood Tip-toe" [16] seemed a satisfactory way of life. (The mood is conveyed perfectly in a set piece in Wilson's report on Soviet Russia. He had gone with Russian companions to visit the Troítsko-Sergéevsky Monastery, and while eating a picnic lunch in a hotel room they had talked of the past and the future. "They had," he says, "cut themselves loose from the past and they didn't yet have the future, for which they had worked so hard. 'Come!' said G. 'We do have this little room, this vodka, this bread, this sausage, this view of the old monastery — these are *now!*'" Wilson is content; later G. sings a popular song.) [17]

Much of the political color of the play is due to Wilson's knowledge of Communism, even to his disillusionment, but the play itself is about the affairs of the Provincetown Players and its time span, from September 1924 to April 1925, is established by the fact of the LaFollette campaign. Within this brief period much of the history of the Village is compressed. Reference to *The Masses*, suppressed in 1918, is anachronistic, and so is reference to the "Payson" strike (the Paterson strike of 1912); but these are introduced to suggest the alliance of art and social reform in the prewar Village period. Similarly the case of Scarlatti's restaurant

[16] Lines 225–238.

[17] This incident may account for the fact that Wilson changed the original title, *A Winter in Beech Street*.

and the appearance of the landlady provide measures of what has happened to the Village, especially the destruction of the old life by commercialization. The moment of focus in the play is therefore that of the terminal crisis in a longer history of aesthetic and social idealism.

There is of course the threat of commercialism — the uptown theatre is to off-Broadway groups what established political parties often are to third parties, and this is a threat not only to the art theatre but to the artist who has, as Brooks maintains in the colloquy with Fitzgerald, allowed his art to become a business. Then there are the difficulties of personal relationships and the individual's abandonment of the cause, as if, in every case, it were only a stage to be outgrown. And finally, though Dan, the director, speaks of art as the true rebellion and as a political force (*Uncle Tom's Cabin* and *Lysistrata* are either produced or likely to be), and Bugs, the journalist,[18] writes a play about the strike, art and politics never really join. Both are aspects of rebellion, but they operate on parallel levels; and in the case of both, we are shown how easy it is for the idealist to give up, to be corrupted by the difficulties of his position, to sacrifice "spirit," "light," and "beauty" to the capitalist system. The cause of art is represented by the Beech Street Theatre group (the Provincetown Players) and the cause of reform by Bugs Brophy and assorted characters who represent almost every phase or shade of reform politics since the time of the Wobblies; whatever union there is is suggested by the proletarian background of Sally Voight, the leading actress, and by her illicit, unsatisfactory love affair with Bugs.

The hero of the play is not Bugs or Dan but an outsider, Arthur Fiske, the Wilson persona. Arthur is an architect: his allegiance presumably is to both art and society.[19] His background is upper class, and in the eyes of the bohemians and even in ours, he is standoffish, stiff, respectable, something of a prig. His clothes are those of the Eastern college man; and he is presented as a kind of chorus character looking through his rimless glasses on the antics of bohemian artists. He may be called bourgeois. Yet his concern for what he loves, his generosity, good manners, and de-

[18] Journalists, in Wilson's work, are writers closest to the political front.
[19] Randolph Bourne's fictive hero, Miro, is an architect, as is Trilling's hero in *The Middle of the Journey*.

cency distinguish him. In the end his steady sense of responsibility proves to be the needed virtue.

Arthur is not a Puritan. He would like to marry Sally, but he is not reluctant to live with her in the state of "free love." (The play opens with them in bed in a studio Village apartment, and may depict an episode of real life, when Mary Blair, Wilson's wife, was sick but insisted on getting up her lines.) Arthur is also something of a poet, an old-fashioned sort of one, whose limitations of aesthetic awareness — if they are not instead a criticism of those of others — are shown by his dislike of a modern painting over the bed ("erotic and fleshy female contours seem to be combined with machinery")[20] and of a play in which poetry has been made out of modern physics. In his way, Arthur has rejected the respectable life: he seeks in Sally the intensity of life Wilson had recognized in Dorothy Perkins, for he desperately needs to overcome the deathliness he has been left with by the war. His experience with Sally brings him back to life — or at least we are told that she had made a "genuine person out of a pair of spectacles and a pressed suit."

But Arthur is not at all happy with those excesses of art and morals that are excused in the name of experimentalism, and for his part he saves Sally from the destructive forces of others who feed on her creative life and subvert her idealism and from her own squandering of self. He may find a folksong about a New Orleans girl depraved, but he understands the heartbreak of the situation in "Careless Love" and is unwilling to see Sally, who literally enacts the song, be the modern girl who takes it in stride. His love is careless only because Sally won't let him be responsible. She believes (with Edna Millay) that "love ought to be all meetings and partings," that people should leave each other free and be different things to other people; yet she deeply feels the need to be cared for and suffers for her freedom. Sally decides to marry Arthur when she can no longer care for her own spirit— and the moral here is not what young readers still believe: that in marry-

[20] This suggests other details of real life. "Her apartment," Wilson wrote of Edna Millay, "was poorly heated, and I brought her an electric heater. I remember how miserable she seemed . . . wrapped up in an old flannel bathrobe and bundled in shabby covers. Above the bed was a modern painting, all fractured geometrical planes that vaguely delineated a female figure. . . ."

ing Arthur her free, hence genuine, creative life is over. No, the moral is that art cannot manage the long haul without discipline, that the virtues Arthur represents are also necessary to it. The "Omar Khayyam period" of which Arthur speaks cannot last. Death has also been sitting unnoticed beneath the favorite tree of youth, enjoying the verse and the wine. Sally's abortion, like the party of the dead in *The Crime in the Whistler Room*, is the price of careless spontaneity, the actual fact of a revolt gone aimless.

We are made to recognize in much that Wilson wrote about Greenwich Village the variety of personal motives that found in "art" the modus vivendi of liberation. The idealism of the true artist professed in the play is grand. It is nothing less than the program proposed by *The Seven Arts* before the war: "We don't want to cheapen anything! . . . we ought . . . to give people some image of the dignity and beauty of life . . . we've got to fight for life itself against all ugliness and deadness . . . we've got to fight for the intellectual life . . . etc." But this program is undone by personal messiness. (Signe says: "there ought to be a rule in little theaters that every member of the group has to sleep with the same person all season.") The capitulation to commercialism is also the result of failure of character, as is the dispersal of the group. Bugs, the self-dramatized victim of bourgeois matrimony, eventually ghost writes for a motor magnate (Ford); for convenience, Tracy will marry a Lesbian and will go to France and live in a chateau;[21] Fred, the D. H. Lawrence of the group, will preach his new religion. The postures of art are sickening. Even without Arthur as reflector, these people show themselves to be messy and contemptible. What Arthur cannot stomach is the underside of revolt that Wilson, writing of Byron in 1922, found so dismal. "One is chilled," he said, "to find the price these poets paid — and that other people paid — not only in pain and grief, but in sordidness and raw distress. How much good life was plowed under in the triumph of that noble defiance! And how messy the triumph itself appears when looked at in the process of its making."

[21] The general situation, not the particulars here, suggests John Peale Bishop and Wilson's anger over his defection. See the poem, "And You Who Faint at Either's Hard Expense." Wilson's memoir of Bishop is his coldest performance.

Joel Spingarn, who in 1910 had delivered a critical manifesto called "The New Criticism," published another manifesto, "The Younger Generation," in the June 1922 issue of *The Freeman*. Reading it now, one finds no reason to question Spingarn's good faith toward the younger men. He speaks of youth as Bourne had, as a spiritual condition, the "fresh vision of life" at the heart of all creativity; and he is as aware as anyone of the failure of civilization that so deeply disturbs the young. But any piece by an older man entitled "The Younger Generation" challenged the young; and the equanimity of this piece was enough to make them angry. Besides, Spingarn was speaking to them, telling them that their notion of "modernity" as the test of all value was merely a "fashionable theory," in fact, a disease resulting from a "constant and irritable sense of rebellion"; telling them point blank that the day for revolt was over and that the time for reconstruction had come.

"I myself," he says, "foresaw and approved of the revolt, even before my manifesto . . . in 1910." Yes, it *was* necessary to "destroy the academic dry rot that was undermining the creative and intellectual spirit of the nation . . . necessary to rid ourselves of the last remnant of the older American 'moralism' in thought and taste and action . . . necessary to destroy . . . the sterile forms which were made to serve instead of . . . realities. . . ." But destruction is no longer necessary; we need now to repossess much that is abandoned in a time of revolt — the realities of "discipline, character, morals, imagination, beauty, freedom, which are the groundworks of all that is noble in art as in life. . . ." It is time to build the "city of the spirit."

It is always time. But the young men were not ready to call a halt to revolt. A younger generation may be angrier with someone of the older generation who, in speaking for it rather than against it, puts the burden of rebuilding on its shoulders while the older generation is still in power. The younger generation in the twenties may have had a cultural but not an economic or political advantage over its elders; and probably because of this Wilson misunderstood Spingarn when in many ways Spingarn was voicing his own thoughts.

"Have you been reading the great controversy about the Younger Generation? — carried on by Spingarn, Nock, Seldes,

Rascoe, Rosenfeld, the New York Times and myself," Wilson asked Fitzgerald in a letter of July 31, 1922. The controversy, he explained, was a "great mess of misunderstandings" because everyone loaded his artillery "with nails, beer-tops, old pairs of scissors and fragments of broken glass" and fired broadcast. He was himself to do in *Discordant Encounters* what he proposes in this letter: to deal accurately with ideas and to pick out the opponent's vulnerable spots and take careful aim at them. In presenting both sides, he did this so well that Conrad Aiken, reviewing the book, complained about his negative virtue of "two-mindedness" and said that he felt defrauded at not finding Wilson's viewpoint. But the weight of a viewpoint is unmistakeably there: with Rosenfeld's serious devotion to art rather than Josephson's Dadaist game, with Brooks's sense of literary responsibility rather than Fitzgerald's frivolousness, with the professor's view of tragedy rather than the journalist's, and finally with Mr. Beebe's desire for rational mastery rather than the iguana's instinctual preference for drift. All but the last encounter are addressed to the specific issues of the battle of the generations and are weighted toward the position of the older men — men who had fought and were fighting Puritanism and materialism but who, because of what seemed, as in the case of Spingarn, cautionary counsel, were out of step with the brave new young. And they were first published in 1924, when Wilson challenged Spingarn in "Wanted: A City of the Spirit" and himself fired broadcast his nails and fragments of glass.

This is not his usual practice and suggests the demoralization his various balanced forms of problem solving were unable to prevent. He does not meet Spingarn's argument and even misses in the manifesto what is most valuable for him. The phrase, "a city of the spirit," has set him off; he disburdens himself of all the difficulties that he feels stand in the way of its achievement — of the realization of his own dream. Most of the difficulties are political. They go back to the fact that the United States, having become "the battleground of business," no longer offers a sustaining political ideal, to the failure of politics at Versailles and the decline of liberalism, and come forward to the Harding administration which, he says, has put political issues to sleep. The spokesmen of the time are cynics like Mencken and Lewis — in fact, as Brooks had already charged in *Letters and Leadership*, there were no critics or awakeners to whom to turn. Neither religion nor science provides the needed metaphysical stability. All is terribly hopeless. And for youth he sees only the alternatives of succumbing to the American city, of playing along and making money, or of remaining aloof and using the little margin of time and energy left one to do something valuable.

A major source of the strain this rejoinder exhibits is the paucity of alternatives and the fact that both of those offered are dismaying. He would like to do something valuable, but he does not want, as he says, to "hold myself separate." What appeals to him in the situation of the younger men of *Discordant Encounters* is the immersion in the vital present, an immersion, alas, achieved by an uncritical acceptance of the drift of things. Try as he will, he cannot quite give himself up to the vulgar vitality that he believes he must respond to in his role of American critic. America! America! how much he wishes to come to terms with her, to love what he feels responsible for! How he longs for a politics that would marry him to her and make him master in the house! And how much for his own assurance and ennoblement he feels the need of a metaphysics of mastery — of the "new idealism" of which Spingarn spoke but which he dismissed as Crocean; an idealism, as Spingarn explains, that banishes the old materialisms and dualisms because it assumes that "inner and outer reality are indissolubly intertwined"; an idealism such as Wilson shortly found in Whitehead, and found acceptable, and made the new foundation for his purchase on life.

II

In February 1928, Wilson wrote Gauss that he had finished a long article on Proust and was doing "a sort of novel." The sort of novel was *I Thought of Daisy*, and the article a portion of the material, much worked over during the twenties, that became *Axel's Castle* (1931), his first book of criticism. This book belongs with *I Thought of Daisy* (1929), another product of his life in the twenties, for it rehearses the crucial problem that the novel tries to solve — the problem of the writer's allegiance to society, a problem of the kind that was raised by such questions to authors as Eugene Jolas' in the Fall 1928 issue of *transition*:

"What particular vision do you have of yourself in relation to twentieth century reality?" Also published in 1929 was Wilson's first collection of poetry, *Poets, Farewell!*, which may be considered a signing off like Rimbaud's, a gesture in keeping with the resolution of both books. (The novel and the poems, rated lower than his criticism by reviewers, may have ended the literary experimentalism that had occupied him in the twenties and may have confirmed him in the direction he chose to take.) The difficulty of this resolution — and the price he paid for it — is indicated, I think, by the fact that toward the end of the decade he had reached a crisis in his personal affairs, had divorced Mary Blair and, as he wrote Gauss from the Clifton Springs Sanitarium and Clinic in February 1929, had "passed into a nervous decline. . . ." By this time the novel was finished and *Axel's Castle* was underway.

Gauss welcomed *I Thought of Daisy*. He said that it was the most penetrating analysis of the postwar intellectual that he had seen, and he told Wilson that "with more intelligence and with more penetration, you have done for Greenwich Village what Sinclair Lewis did for Main Street." Later in the year, on reading *Poets, Farewell!* he wrote Wilson that he should do "a modern *Confession d'un Enfant du Siècle*," an account of "a young man's life today at a crisis"; but Wilson, disgusted with the kind of subjective literature he had been treating in *Axel's Castle*, dismissed the project, saying that he intended to become more objective instead of personal. And yet, if not in the form Gauss suggested, his work in the twenties is such a *Confession* — the result of a profoundly personal involvement in the crisis of his time. As we look back on all of his work, the articles he has gathered together as "chronicles" and the plays that he feels should interest us as attempts to "dramatize the mentality, the characteristic types and the various milieux of the twenties and the early thirties," we see that his work, even the "objective" portions of it, is a confession of a child of the century. This, in fact, is what has made him one of those necessary writers in whom we can discover the consciousness of the time.

As a summary work of the decade, *I Thought of Daisy* employs in its fabric materials that Wilson had used in his previous writing. One may think of it as a more complex form of the encounter, dramatizing issues not in simple dialogue but in the denser, more concrete terms of fiction and in an intricate manner that Wilson calls "symphonic." The novel is not entirely successful; as Wilson himself is aware, it is too schematic, or rather, the scheme is too obvious and the author too concerned with making us aware of its thematic unfolding. Besides, the scheme itself is at odds with the story.

The narrator-hero — he is never named — is clearly the Wilson persona, an American intellectual of the twenties who is trying to "formulate an attitude toward life in the United States." "Formulate an attitude" — this is Wilson's phrase in the 1953 Foreword, one that hardly conveys the desperate attempt of the hero to seize and affirm "the American reality" and to find at last a working relationship and vital connection with contemporary, living culture. Having after the war put himself outside of society, he wishes now to establish contact, and one thinks of Hawthorne's predicament when the narrator says that "by way of literature itself, I should break through into the real world." Now the scheme deals with this problem and involves the creation of a different mood and point of view for each of the five sections of the book. But the point of view is never that of the character who is supposed to provide it; it is that of the narrator who assimilates all viewpoints to himself and tells the story throughout in the same prose rhythms and vocabulary. Events are remembered and described; they do not have independent dramatic existence. Because of the reminiscent quality, one feels that this fiction is a species of memoir and that the narrator is working out in several equations the calculus of his life. The novel is best compared with Trilling's *The Middle of the Journey*, another novel by a literary critic, in which intellectual preoccupations inhibit the full play of imagination. As one reviewer said: "The drive of Mr. Wilson's logic is not matched by a drive of the imagination."

What puts the scheme at odds with the story is the emotional undercurrent that pulls against the ostensible theme, the narrator's exploration of the reality of America represented by the protean Daisy. This powerful force has to do with Rita — with Edna St. Vincent Millay — for though the narrator *thinks* of Daisy, and sometimes resolutely, he loves Rita. The conviction in both cases is genuine. It is only that the feeling for Rita is stronger, and that in what for Wilson is both a confession, an attempt to bind his wounds and make reparation for his behavior (he sent the manuscript of the novel to Edna Millay), and a way of reorganizing his intellectual life, he is unable to keep the former from swamping the scheme of the latter.

That this is the case is significant. He was incapable of resolving his relationship with Edna Millay, the emotional commitment whose power to disturb him is still present in his work: in *Memoirs of Hecate County* and in the memoir of Edna Millay that closes *The Shores of Light*, the chronicle of the twenties and thirties whose very title is associated with her. In the memoir Wilson says that seeing Edna nearly twenty years after his last call in 1929 "exerted on me a painful pull, as if to drag me up by the roots, to gouge me out of my present personality and to annihilate all that had made it." His claim that Rita is only "partly derived" from Edna is not quite true: she is the only major character who is not an amalgam; she comes close to being the real person.

Daisy condenses into two years the history of the decade, and its documentation of life in the twenties is as good as Gauss said it was. But the narrator's personal history, involving an identity crisis, is even more interesting, a personal witness of the demoralization of the time and a fairly complete account of the intellectual issues involved in it. Like Arthur Fiske of *This Room and This Gin and These Sandwiches*, the narrator is a bourgeois, one, however, who has cast his moorings and is adrift, who gets caught in the maelstrom of Village life and saves himself only by grasping again the sure anchorage to be found in his past. His experience of demoralization is told in the first three sections; these are followed by the redintegration of the fourth section and the affirmation of the fifth. This curve of experience is complemented by the progressive development of two interdependent themes: one, the nature of art; the other, the nature of and the need for accepting "higher obligations." The general course of the experience is to and away from the Village — out of the Village into America; it commemorates a phase of Village history, but also, curiously, while moving into the present carries us backward in time to the America of the narrator's boyhood, to the bedrock beneath recent history, the psychological stratum, the deeper America that the writers of *The Seven Arts,* for example, hoped to bring to expression.

The first section of the novel is supposed to be dominated by the point of view of Hugo Bamman, who represents political or social obligation. He is a disaffected bourgeois, a composite character whose background and experiences are drawn from those of Dos Passos (Wilson admired his documentary novels), Cummings (he has had the experience of *The Enormous Room* and lives at Patchen Place), and Wilson himself (especially the family situation). Hugo is the narrator's boyhood friend, to some extent his double. His father is also a composite character, uniting Wilson's father and John Jay Chapman primarily, with something of Gauss and Alfred Rolfe: an old-fashioned American.

The narrator is sympathetic with Hugo's radical political position, but has not accepted it. Although he has been shocked out of his class by the war, has had an experience similar to that of the episode of the pony-cart, and longs for human solidarity, he does not find Hugo's revolutionary social idealism "real enough." Moreover, revolutionary intransigence has alienated Hugo, and alienation, above all, is the condition the narrator wishes to avoid. As Hugo's myopia suggests, he also has the partisan's nearsightedness and fails to see much that the narrator, for example, finds worthy in the bourgeois tradition and in modern literature. His radical position compels him to scorn such writers as Beerbohm and James and such contemporary literary movements as that connected with T. S. Eliot. His social view, accordingly, represents an alternative to rather than accommodation of contemporary art: the union of art and politics that he represents is of the prewar socio-political kind; but now (the time is around 1920) art and politics have been divorced. For the narrator, a minor poet, Hugo therefore represents a political rather than an aesthetic obligation, and stands in opposition to Rita, the priestess of art. At the start, the narrator finds himself in the situation of being forced to accept one or the other, and only by discounting these evaluations of art and politics is he able to reforge a literary faith that unites them.

Hugo is admirable in any case and not the least because he has managed to fashion, as the narrator would like to do, a career that honors the family tradition he has rejected. We are told that Hugo was "at the orders of a higher obligation"; and later, when the narrator compares his own feeble efforts with Hugo's success, we learn that in his way Hugo had "saved the honor of a family tradition which was otherwise largely moribund: he had truly assumed the responsibilities of leadership and shown the disinterestedness of public spirit, in the only fields where, in our generation, he had found it possible for him to work." By applying himself "to literature as to one of the old-fashioned professions," Hugo has made for himself a vocation comparable to his father's; by a rare "discipline of self" he has set himself off from the Village literati and has acquired the "solid and honorable character of a first-rate professional man."

The first section, however, is not dominated by Hugo but by Rita Cavanagh, whom the narrator meets at a cocktail party in the smart Village apartment of Ray Coleman, a newspaperman who is keeping Daisy. Here we are introduced to the old radicals, the theatre people, the minor writers, and the dissolute poets — to Village types who will figure elsewhere in the novel. And the talk is of experimentalism in art, which the narrator, with all the superiority of the good taste and knowledge of a classical education, at first disdains. The major episodes concern Rita, the recitation of her poems and her admiration for the daring scene designs of Bobby McIlvaine (a composite of Robert Edmond Jones and Lee Simonson). Rita's sensitive appreciation and her "passionate vehemence" in the presence of this work make the narrator feel "something of the awe of the infidel who overhears the prayer of the believer." He listens as she associates herself with the Pallas Athena of one of the drawings and, in discussing it, defines both her devotion to art and the terms of her relationship with men. Men, she says, "can't really believe in their hearts that her [the independent woman's] work is everything she lives for, that she puts above everything and everybody!" Such devotion — call it the absolute expenditure of self for the purposes of art, an expenditure that hallows even Rita's single standard of sexual relations, her *gamine* existence — such devotion is also a "higher obligation"; and later that night, during their long talk about poetry at his apartment, the narrator is drawn to it. As they talk the spring night through, the dark (which Edna Millay struggled against) is finally "washed with libations of light." The narrator wakens to a new world, has reached the shores of light; the life of the Village, he feels, is now his, and he has been set free at last "to follow poetry." He seizes the life of art in order to sustain his rejection of the "world of mediocre aims and prosaic compromises. . . ." He turns to literature because Rita has shown him that it "could be reality . . . as deep as life itself."

Against this version of art for art's sake, against this highbrow position — it is highbrow in the sense that it has been purchased by alienation and serves primarily the moral exaltation of the artist — there is a dissenting voice. It is the voice of Daisy's phonograph which interrupts Rita's recitation with the lowbrow jazz rhythms of *Mamie Rose*, the novel's theme song. This dissenting voice is linked with the narrator's interest in the literary use of common American speech, with Daisy's slang, and, by means of her background, with the "frank, vulgar, humorous, human" stuff of the American heartland and "the real, the live America" of motor traffic — with the America the Dadaists extol. Daisy, who changes throughout the novel, is the plastic stuff of America, its elusive, yet throbbing vital reality; and she represents the reality with which the art that the narrator really wants must come to terms. Daisy exists outside of the lonely castles of Rita and Hugo; their positions, however admirable, exclude her. But she admires both and perhaps can welcome them when the narrator has brought them together within himself.

Rita's devotion to art is at the expense of what Melville called the attainable felicities, and it is hard to believe that the narrator could have lived with her in the way he wished. His women must be homemakers. He might have provided for his poetess, but he would not, one feels, have sacrificed his own life for her (as Eugen Boissevain did for Edna Millay). Nor could he have faced competition with her: Rita, he says, demoralized his masculine self-assurance. One is aware in any case that Rita's devotion to art and her aesthetic beliefs — that imagination assigns value to things and that in intense subjective experience things have their being — make human relationships difficult. Rita uses others, absorbs them into her personality. Her independence and single standard are merely ways of asserting this right. They have not made her free, and must be seen, as the narrator finally sees them, as the inevitable weakness that underprops her strength. Indeed, it is because of some wound that she draws the bow of art and has its "compensation."

The second section of the novel begins several months later, in the winter, with Rita's departure from the Village. She has overextended herself, is weary of Village life, and ends her affairs, among them that with the narrator. He has not accepted her terms, is jealous and angry at the breaking-up, and, as a result, is poised on the slope of demoralization. Out of self-hatred, he rejects his love for Rita and his service to her aesthetic ideal. He turns — the very turning suggests the opposite — to Daisy.

Daisy is now living in the Forties, having resumed her work as a chorus girl. Exemplifying the popular culture that Wilson reported on in "The Follies" (*The American Earthquake*), she lives in an apartment, unlike Rita's spare waterfront flat, that is strewn with movie magazines, jazz records, tabloids, and women's garments. There, while awaiting her, the narrator plays a recording of *Mamie Rose*; but a bad needle distorts it and underscores what he feels are its mechanical and demonic aspects — a kind of nihilism which he connects with the blank wall to be seen from the window. Here, and throughout this section, he looks at Daisy's world through the severely discriminating eyes of Rita. The give-and-take of his meditations renders the difficulty of balancing their worlds, and also represents another stage of demoralization; for it is evident that he can accept Daisy's world only by thinking *resolutely* of her, only by taking all the vulgar trappings of her life as necessary complements of her vitality.

In some respects Daisy's situation duplicates Rita's. She is a free woman almost destroyed by her freedom. She has Rita's strength, and in addition a fine abandon and essential innocence; and though she too lives for the moment, she does not compel the moment, as Rita does, but gives herself to it. Rita is formed — no one will alter her — but Daisy is fluid, capable of identifying with the contemporary in all of its manifestations — with speed, jazz, movies, Broadway, sexual freedom. Where Rita represents the highest intensity, she represents exhilaration and excitement. But though her appeal is great (one feels Wilson's need to have it so), she is always presented as childlike. She belongs in fact with Bill McGee and Sally Voight who also come from Pittsburgh and have the same wonderful but indiscriminate vitality. Daisy's "romantic" honeymoon journey on the handlebars of Phil Meissner's motorcycle turns out to have been an attempt to induce an abortion, and in the course of the novel, she will even attempt suicide.

Daisy and Rita enact a discordant encounter similar to that between Josephson and Rosenfeld, and Daisy is not victorious. Only demoralization and drink make it possible for the narrator to think of a sixteen-year-old bathing beauty as "the real native American poetry!"; only the dream world of the movies permits him to say that he has found himself "almost safe again in that familiar American world, heterogeneous and absurd, which had ceased for so long to seem real to me, of which I had never for so long been aware save to repudiate it with scorn and impatience." He has of course forgotten that *this* familiar world is the world of men like Coleman, and he lapses into it only because he abdicates for the moment the critical rebelliousness that characterizes both Rita's and Hugo's positions. Rita, he feels, has rejected "all the natural bonds and understandings which make up the greater part of human life — comfort, security, children, the protection and devotion of a husband. . . ." And Hugo, too, seeing everything in terms of class war, has rejected "all the amenities of that civilized life of which he was himself the product. . . ." The narrator comes to popular culture because he has also abandoned *these* positions, for popular culture is not the middle ground he seeks. It is not a middle ground at all, but the opposite of that which both Rita and Hugo, the outlaws, represent. The middle ground is "that civilized life," that "greater part of human life," a reconstituted, responsible bourgeois life. To find it again, the narrator will have almost to begin from scratch, to retrace the course of American history and bring forward what has been lost.

It is clear in the next section, still in the winter of discontent, that the narrator has neither overcome his love for Rita nor found in Daisy a stay against demoralization, and that he must discover the underground, the demonic depths of misanthropy, before he can possess in clarity all that his previous experience has confused.[22] He tries to shore himself up by reading Sophocles — that is, by seeing what the New Humanist position offers him. But this

[22] This nightmare scene is comparable to that of the last story in *Memoirs of Hecate County.*

position is not strong enough to control or hold back the tides of real experience, and the demons of materialism and naturalism and cynical hedonism come forth to plague him. The scene of their emergence, appropriately, is Larry Mickler's apartment in an anonymous office building-rooming house located in the sordid petty manufacturing district around East 34th Street and Lexington Avenue. Mickler, the most odious character in the novel, is a would-be writer turned advertising man, the contemptuous maker of popular culture. His taste is "advanced": his shelves contain the works of a variety of modern writers, of whom the most important to him are Nietzsche and Dostoevsky. Modernism has disorganized him, and in terms of the critical debate of the time, it is evident that he represents the viewpoint of H. L. Mencken. He considers himself a superman and disdainfully criticizes democracy. He has read, not for wisdom or affirmation, but only to confirm his own feeling of human futility and his desire to enjoy the gratification of the moment. He speaks of human behavior metabolically, suggesting the reductive behavioristic and materialistic view of "human colloids" that serves as the philosophical counterpart of the action of this section. And he is a culturally destructive force: he shoots to smithereens a plaster cast of the Winged Victory — a symbol not only of the New Humanism, but, by association with Pallas Athena, of Rita's higher obligations.

When the party at Mickler's moves on to Sue Borglum's [23] house in the Village, we realize that the intellectual attitudes of men like Mickler and Coleman have done as much as the realtors to change the atmosphere there. Sue's fine eighteenth-century house, which sets the narrator dreaming of an idyllic life of love and poetry with Rita, is now the scene of a saturnalia. Studio parties seem to be a thing of the past; the anxious socialite has taken over.

At Sue's party, all of the major characters appear together for the last time, and each in his way measures the chaos by suggesting an outside referent. Rita, having returned from the country, brings upstate New York with her, and her renewed vigor and freshness contrast with Daisy's tousled and puffy appearance. Hugo, no longer wearing glasses, with his good manners, integrity, and cultivated intelligence, reminds the narrator of old-fashioned virtues and of the time when Hugo's father taught

[23] Louise Hellstrom?

him that men might belong to the world of history and literature. But these measures also remind the narrator of his failure. He has not been equal to any of the higher obligations, and although he had once refused to make love to Daisy in order to prove to himself his rejection of Rita's code of experience, he now uses Daisy in order to avoid her. He has not become a professional; he has not even become successful enough to shelter women, as Coleman has. Even when Daisy, herself demoralized, offers herself to him, he cannot, as Mickler would, go through with it. But the naturalistic considerations that impede him are in fact the testimony of his self-disgust; and it is contempt of his own contamination by Mickler's views that drives him finally to defend the Winged Victory, and, not finding Mickler, to vindicate his honor against the "horror" by assaulting Tony Scallopino, a Village restaurateur. The mounting chaos of Village life ends in drunkenness and violence, with everyone accusing someone of something, with everyone alone and in pain.

When the narrative resumes in the fourth section, months have passed and the major characters have escaped from the inferno of Village life. Daisy has gone off to Connecticut with Pete Bird, a deadbeat poet — they represent the exodus of intellectuals from city to country in the twenties; and the narrator has been to Europe, presumably to test the advantages of expatriation. It is now November, and he is at Professor Grosbeake's, where his redintegration begins — Grosbeake's letter that he had torn up in previous sections of the novel is now, as it were, put together again. Grosbeake, as we have seen, is a composite of Gauss and Whitehead, the spokesman of an acceptable humanism; and he provides the new metaphysics that replaces the mechanistic one of Mickler, the charitable view of America that may be said to repatriate the narrator, and the interpretation and example of higher obligations that reinforce both the bourgeois virtues the narrator prizes and those values of Rita's and Hugo's positions that still attract him.

Grosbeake's metaphysics is Whitehead's, a philosophy of "organism." For him the universe is not a machine, but an organism in the course of development. In his universe, there is no dualism: reality, as the narrator happily learns, is not outside one, but includes his moral and aesthetic values, and these are not reducible to animal processes. One is within the world, and his values are a creative force within it. God, in turn, is "the ultimate harmony implied by the aesthetic and moral values of which men were aware in the universe"; and revelation is simply the awareness of the necessity of this order and harmony — of the fact that to create order and harmony is the divine purpose that determines which possibilities in the flux of "events" are "actualized."

This philosophy restores the narrator's faith in creativity and order and is associated by him with the eighteenth century, with Watts's hymns, which recall the "grandeur of the universe [and] the moral principle it implied"; and in a variety of ways it is associated with the past and the creative idealism of Emerson. Grosbeake, the seeker for order and relationship, lives in Cambridge, in what is still a solidly eighteenth- or early nineteenth-century world, and he is connected in the thought of the narrator with Hugo's father who had awakened his "sense of the unity of life. . . ." The visit to Daisy and Pete pioneering in the country is a proper extension of this, for it reminds the narrator of Hugo's father's Adirondack camp (of the Talcottville of Wilson's own eighteenth-century origins). Both worlds come together in the common images of ice and snow that express the narrator's sense of purification and harmony, and in the fact, casually noted, that Pete is going to put in order a grandfather's clock.

Grosbeake also defines responsibility in a way that restores its civil meaning. Unknowingly he admonishes the narrator when he says that one must have enough character "not simply to drift about without preferring one idea to another"; but in speaking of Lewis' *Babbitt*, he develops the idea in its relation to the leadership of American business. Leadership, he says, requires men who are able "to experiment with ideas," that is, who have a wide range of experience, of "contact with realities," and a proper regard for power. When he notes that the American businessman leaves his son only an investment, that he inherits "no responsibility and no power," one thinks of Phil Meissner and the boy with the pony-cart, and realizes that what Grosbeake is asking us to be responsible for is the *continuity* of institutions. "The second generation," Grosbeake believes, "[should] take over some responsibility in connection with their fathers' work." The narrator says that he reflected on Grosbeake's words: the idea of continuity replaces that of the moment.

The Connecticut episode provides another school of responsibility. Daisy and Pete, whom the narrator visits on leaving Grosbeake, have taken an old house in the country and begun to restore it. Starting from scratch and drawing on forgotten skills, they have created from the litter of the abandoned past an "orderly and cheerful" living room. Pete is a gifted artisan who restores antiques, and Daisy is a model housewife. (She reminds the narrator of the girls of his boyhood; she is also a *jeune fille* whom he confuses with Grosbeake's daughters; and by means of her story of an aunt who married a nobleman, she is intended to remind us of a more self-reliant Daisy Miller. She is, of course, all our Daisys: the Daisy of the bicycle built for two, even Daisy Fay.) The narrator, suddenly a soft agrarian, considers their rural life an example of "pioneering heroism"; they have, he feels, established in a single room "amenities and decencies — this core of civilization!"

We are not expected to take this as a national solution, for even in the case of Daisy and Pete it is too marginal and precarious. It is, however, a temporary and personal solution that may serve as an example of the general need for simplification and reorganization. It represents a "usable past," a schooling in the national experience and a repossession of essential virtues. One might even say, because the narrator places the "wisdom of the country" against the "false values" of the city, that it represents a return to vernacular values, although these country values are not so much those values of spontaneity and freedom one finds in Twain as they are the "old-fashioned" values of Wilson's heritage. Now this example of pioneering, juxtaposed with what Grosbeake has just taught him, prompts the narrator's most significant realization: that "all that dignified mankind, all that kept them from the brawling and the squalor which, the night of Sue Borglum's party, had seemed to me the universal fate, had been built up through endurance and patience, through steadiness of purpose and good faith, through property well administered, through families standing together, through lovers true to their pledges!" And so he comes home — both episodes are homecomings — and his sense of well-being and the fact that he dismisses the demonism of satire signify his restoration to humanity.

Nevertheless, the narrator contemplates a satire which casts the previous events, especially those dealing with Mickler, into Wilson's terms of demonism. Wilson's demonism depends on his eighteenth-century beliefs in order, harmony, creative force, and decency — that is why it is fitting to introduce it here. His devils are those who have rejected his humanistic faith:[24] people of "anti-social views and habits," those who are neither romantic nor faithful in love, whose physical relationships are mechanical, transient, affectionless, irresponsible, sterile; those who have no idea of beauty, whose literature "consists chiefly of obscene anecdotes and stories of atrocious crime" (Mickler and Coleman) and whose poetry is imagistic, "devoid of . . . moral ideas and . . . ennobling emotions" (Pete Bird). The narrator who thus defines demonism is himself "addicted to sonnets."

Having purged his self-hatred in this way and having become aware of the complexity of human nature and moral problems that satire simplifies, the narrator contemplates the relationships that he has spared in his demonic musing. He thinks of Rita, of her lonely, desperate expatriation in Paris, and of the poem she has sent him; and searching deeply for motives, he finds the humanity of her art — "the sincerity of some personal sort" that had prompted the poem. And he remembers her description of the icy river (one more component of the winter landscape of this section) and how the image of the restricted but living stream was intended to establish personal contact, to recall the best moments of their love, that time when she, not he, had found in their relationship the value of "light" in a "world of darkness." These reflections are based on actual situations and letters, and Wilson makes magnificent amends to Edna: the narrator now places Rita within his preferred world and sees in her a defender of his own values of "light." In the same context, he also thinks of Hugo, of "what a great fellow he really was . . . how few there were like

[24] Larry Mickler's most brilliant advertising idea is a large electric sign of Mephistopheles jabbing a corn on a big toe. The narrator comments on the fact that here at least Mickler "had constrained his sadistic instincts to serve [a] beneficent end." By the time of *Memoirs of Hecate County*, the demonism of "advertising" men will be more subtle and more terrifying and impossible to condone.

him!" And the following day, when Daisy tells him of her attempted suicide, he realizes that she too had felt that "life without honor was horrible!" Instead of taking Daisy with him, as he momentarily wishes to do, he speaks to her of the need for responsibility, faith, and loyalty. On that already darkening winter day, as he prepares to leave, he wraps himself, like some character of Edwin Arlington Robinson's, in a mantel of "stoic fortitude" and is ready to endure "the closing down of night."

The final section of the novel, turning on several kinds of repatriation, is set against the August heat of the city and the leader present. The narrator, who meets Daisy for an excursion to Coney Island, is soon caught up in a reverie of his childhood and early manhood that is all the brighter to him because of the "faded and flimsy "façade of the pier and the Statute of Liberty which seems to him to be "a solid, dull slug of gray against a colorless burning sky. . . ."

The dismal port of New York! It reminds him of his repatriation after the war: "it seemed to me a long time ago." Then he had not been outward but inward bound; then he had seen Coney Island shining in the night, had entered the Narrows and had seen the trees and lawns and "large, white American houses" on the shore, had smelled the "luxuriance and rankness" of the land and then the "rotten" smell of the harbor where the chimneys of factories erupted into the night. He recaptures the expectancy of that time, his eagerness to enter again the life represented by those houses and his dismay at the heavy fumes of industrial life. And then America crystallizes for him in an image combining dismay and expectancy — and loneliness; a superb image, with the power of Rosenfeld's image of the Bayonne littoral and Fitzgerald's of the green breast of the new world: "Then suddenly I had almost caught my breath — I had been curiously moved by the sight of a single, solitary street lamp on the Staten Island shore. It had merely shed a loose and whitish radiance over a few feet of the baldish road of some dark, thinly settled suburb. Above it, there had loomed an abundant and disorderly tree. But there was America, I had felt with emotion — there under that lonely suburban street lamp, there in that raw and livid light!" A train adds to this scene its far-off shuffle and moan, and the imagination leaps with it "to the farthest reaches of a continent without frontiers!" The narrator remembers this homecoming as one that seemed to promise him "infinite freedom."

To approach Coney Island from the sea is to rediscover America, not so much the America of the discoverers, though that is suggested, as the America of the narrator's boyhood. Excursions to Coney Island, we are informed, once left from Christopher Street; and one is first greeted there by a Noah's Ark, which serves in this episode both to create and discount the nostalgia we have for our fabled Eden. The narrator postpones visiting the Ark until they are about to leave, and then, having done so, considers it a "sell" (Fitzgerald: "Its vanished trees . . . had once pandered in whispers. . . ."); here, in fact, he falls and breaks the roulette wheel he had won.

Within this context and of greater thematic importance is the discovery of the American past. Daisy, for example, more child-like than ever, is not conscious of and so does not possess a "usable past." As the moccasins she buys suggest, she is Pocahontas, the still redeemable American possibility. She had not been to the Eden Musée in her childhood, shows little interest now, and cannot remember the time when Teddy Roosevelt was a hero. The narrator, however, remembers when the Musée was located on 23rd Street and knows the waxworks well enough to notice the absence, among such figures as Grant and Brigham Young and Booker T. Washington, of the figure of the once-popular mimic, Marshall P. Wilder. For him the Musée recalls "that younger America which I had assumed we had forever left behind"; he feels close to that America again, and realizes that it had been not only the America of his boyhood, but a "boy's America." That the Eden Musée is at Coney Island may indicate what we make of our past, but at least for the narrator, finding the Musée in this place of recreation has been re-creative.

For Daisy the Coney Island excursion recalls her own more immediate past. The almost abandoned, old-fashioned summer hotel to which they go for dinner turns out to be the very one to which she and Phil had come on their motorcycle honeymoon. Here, an irate father had forced them to marry; here, under the aegis of Compton Mackenzie (Fitzgerald), began the career that ended with the Russian novelists (Dostoevsky-Mickler). And now, it is here that Daisy, who for others is every kind of American girl from pioneer housekeeper to Mack Sennet bathing beauty, tells us that she likes to think of herself as she appeared in the *Gambols*, as the "sweet and dewy" girl dressed in an old-fashioned white dress and pantalettes who became the college boys' pinup. She is indeed the child the narrator considers her. In her dream of life, she rather shamefully admits, she awaits a "great, big, strong, clean-limbed American," a Prince Charming who will take care of her.

Whether or not the narrator is Prince Charming is very much to the point as is the fact that he cannot even begin to assume this role until he places her. This he finally does during the last stage of repatriation, on the return trip by bus through sparsely settled Brooklyn to the city. On this journey of discovery, he sees again the side streets, the little suburban houses, and the "lonely and random street lamp . . . light[ing] untidy bushes and trees," and he feels that the America of which he had had a vision on his return from the war is still the essential America. The America in which Daisy and Rita and he had had their beginnings is still to be found in the present: there it is in the girls in their summer dresses strolling to the drugstore, wandering out into the evening, as they had done, vaguely expectant about the possibilities of life.

This suburban world is the common background of his generation, a fixed point, and a still vital source of renewal. To find it again is to find the American heartland, and to be reassured. It is against this background that Daisy tells her family history, compelling the narrator to recognize that it is *her* background too, that Daisy was "simply an American girl, who had grown up in an American town like other American towns. . . ." He learns that on one occasion in Pittsburgh even their childhoods had crossed, and he no longer thinks of her as an "alien." And in this setting, the moral he finds in the story of her family's financial decline is one of the democratic value of social mobility. "Americans," he realizes, "might turn into anything."

Daisy's plasticity symbolizes such possibilities. She is not so much a character as the stuff of character, someone to be told "what it's all about," to be shaped by a responsible intellectual. Of the men who had previously shaped her, "what hope," the narrator asks, "was there for Daisy with any of them?" Only Hugo, who pleases Daisy with his self-assurance and purpose, is worthy of her. But his professionalism, to which the narrator is now committed, is only one aspect of the ideal American Scholar: in his own experience, the narrator has found another — the acceptance of the common, the public, the "real" life. Neither Hugo, with his hatred of the bourgeois, nor Rita, with her contempt for the vulgar, accept the America that the narrator tells us he has "re-entered" and found himself at home in. They have taken account only of "American mediocrity and timidity"; he has taken account as well of saving virtues and strengths. These belong to the class from which he has come, and he will continue to exercise them in the interests of the common life. His repatriation is to the higher obligations of his class, to the stewardship of a "classless" bourgeois society.

At the close of the novel, Daisy restores the narrator's confidence. In his apartment, where once he had talked to Rita of poetry, he talks to Daisy of his recent meditations on popular art. Daisy takes this for what it is — a confession of love — and he possesses her. Of course he betrays his code of loyalty, but this is necessary to the logic of the scheme. When he speaks of the moment of love as "hot, moist, mucilaginous and melting," we are shocked perhaps by the crudity of expression, but we must remember that he also speaks of his thoughts as "unfolding like fresh new leaves" and must try to see here a mystical, Whitmanian communion with the body of America.

The Daisy he possesses, however, is the Daisy of the suburban America of his own past. The narrator does not affirm present reality, but rather an attitude toward it that has been strengthened by his homecoming. Accepting his past, he establishes the continuity of past and present, the lack of which had caused his demoralization.[25] He refuses to be alienated and hopes to find in art a way of serving the community. Daisy's response represents the approval of the older generation; and in so far as she also represents the younger generation, her admiration for Hugo, who is so much like the leaders of the past, confirms it for the present.

[25] It is in this sense that Norah Meade was right when she wrote in a review for *The Nation*: "If Mr. Wilson has freed his soul of a complex by

The novel concludes with the narrator's resolve to break through into the real world by way of literature itself. The difficulty of this resolution is made clear by the depiction in the novel of the literary situation — a situation thoroughly analyzed in terms of the literary movements of our time in *Axel's Castle*. We know from *Axel's Castle* that the narrator's resolve is not a simple one to be made at the expense of the genuine achievements of Symbolism, but that what he wants most, as Wilson declares for himself in *Axel's Castle*, is "the strength to be derived from a wide knowledge of human affairs, a sympathetic interest in human beings, direct contact with public opinion and participation in public life through literature."

The narrator determines to follow the vocation of chronicler. He will sketch Daisy, picturing her as he remembers her (for the sake of historical continuity) and as she is ("such pictures . . . would grow directly and freshly from life"). He gives up any pretension of literary elitism. He speaks modestly of his art as equivalent to carpentry, meaning, in one sense, that art is simply an honest craft like others and that the artist, as Mike Gold insisted, is a working man, and, in another sense, given in the passage on Yeats's prose in *Axel's Castle*, that art is individual handicraft and that his, like Yeats's, will be "the product of some dying loomcraft brought to perfection in the days before machinery."

The position at which the narrator arrives is one that Wilson had already been working from in the twenties. This may not have been evident until the week by week writing of that time was collected in *The Shores of Light* and *The American Earthquake. Daisy*, in fact, is a series of sketches such as the narrator has in mind, and it exemplifies Wilson's position, establishes it firmly, making it possible for him to move easily into the thirties. At the same time, this symphonic novel (by symphonic he means Joycean-Proustian, hence Symbolistic) exemplifies the conclusion of *Axel's Castle*: that it is possible to use the new literary techniques in a public way. In turning to politics, however, Wilson has not put by the claims of art. For him, politics is a proper stance toward the world, the commitment to turn outward to public things defined by his idea of "professional." It is not ideological.

this publication, then those who admire him in his more familiar literary roles will have reason to be thankful. . . . Not otherwise."

He does not reject modern art — American culture is in his debt for making its achievements known — but the stance of the contemporary artist.

Daisy reaffirms *The Seven Arts* program of art for the community. It belongs with Brooks's pleas in the twenties that the writer not secede from, but work for change within bourgeois society; with Pound's advice to American writers in 1928 that they get out of themselves and study society; with Santayana's belief that Americans should learn to accept what they have. It affirms the position of the generation immediately preceding that of the younger men with whom Wilson is associated, the generation to whom Wilson was apprenticed under Croly on *The New Republic*. That generation, Trilling reminds us, assumed "that politics and literature naturally live in a lively inter-connection"; they believed in a "national moral destiny," which "complemented and gave weight to the sense of a developing American culture." By working through the difficulties the twenties had put in the way of this faith, Wilson earned it anew, and demonstrated, as Trilling says so well, that his "literary feeling is directed toward . . . the general enterprise of literature."

Daisy not only works out the narrator's attitude toward America but a theory of art to complement it. Each of its sections offers a theory of art, and because each has a partial truth, it is not canceled out by but contained in the narrator's development. Even the pessimistic disquisition on literature in the third section, which Wilson told Gauss was not intended as his own serious opinion, contains too many of his working assumptions to be explained away.

The attitude toward art in the first section is apropos of Rita. On hearing her poems, the narrator feels that "literature could be reality" and recognizes in them the fact of "terror mastered by the mind . . . clutched and wrenched into beauty. . . ." In her poems and those of Catullus, Dante, and Verlaine that they discuss, he appreciates "that life of literature which rejects or suppresses nothing that goes to make our common life, but where all is passionate, noble and rich. . . ." There is nothing here to distress him as there is in the mode of life Rita has chosen to follow in her devotion to art. For Rita's mode is that of the *fin de siècle* writers (and by extension, Symbolists) Wilson mentions in *Axel's*

Castle who "want to stand apart from the common life and live only in the imagination" and who, as a consequence, are "thrown fatally out of key with reality." [26] Rita's private fairy story conversation with her friend, which the narrator doesn't understand but which obviously has meaning, is intended to recall Yeats's fairyland and the private meanings poets attach to images, images however still common enough to be eventually understood. Rita may be one of the "ice-eyed queens" of Yeats's fairyland, one, appropriately, who introduces the narrator to the service of art because Wilson himself had begun his own literary apprenticeship under the auspices of *fin de siècle* writers and, particularly, of Yeats.

In trying to reconcile what he admires in Rita's poetry with the subjectivity he disapproves of in her life, the narrator becomes aware of the inevitable conjunction of strength and weakness that is the essential idea of the wound and bow theory of the genesis of art. The narrator, it is well to remember, comes on this theory as a result of his own deepening psychological awareness; and the novel reminds us that it is a psychological theory which humanizes our appreciation of art by forcing us to consider the human triumph of mastery in art. The narrator may use the theory reductively, as when he traces Hugo's political art to his antagonism to his father; but even here psychological reductiveness is preferable to political reductiveness (one of the explicit points of instruction in *The Wound and the Bow*) because it reaches back to a deeper source and therefore to a deeper understanding of the human nature of art. In the narrator's case, as in Wilson's, to search out these origins does not lower his estimate of art but provides instead a schooling in "reality" that stirs his compassion for man and enlarges his appreciation of the humanity of art. This, in the end, helps him place both Rita and Hugo in his common America.

A theory of popular art is not discussed in the second section but withheld for the more significant context of the last. Instead we are given a taste of Dadism — "the joyous yell of the mechanical life," which, Josephson says in *Discordant Encounters*, we must "take . . . on its own terms." At the end of this section,

[26] This is not, of course, quite true of Edna Millay, who was politically active. Yet she did break down and retire to the country.

however, the narrator considers a sonnet the writing of which he had found unbearable because he had not been able to dramatize or impersonalize his feelings. Much of what he says about art has its origins in the idea that art is what it does. The germ of the long essay on literature in the next section is here, and in Pete Bird's remark that a cough drop "Eases irritation, just like a poem."

In the meditation on Dostoevsky the narrator is not angry, as it seems, over the fact that the artist restores in art the moral balance he lacks in life — he accepts the compensatory victory of art over personal deficiency and external chaos. Rather he is angry with the public for deriving solace from the artist's travail; angry that art can be used to cushion the moral shock of reality, that it is a "self-protective reflex," an instinct to justify ourselves. The artist at least braves reality, but not so the reader, for whom the artist provides a ready-made harmony.

This cynical interpretation of his own justification of art made Gauss unhappy. He believed that art attempts to re-establish the harmony broken by the space-time categories and the unwilled character of human life. For him the artist was someone like Grosbeake, not a fantast of harmony but an explorer of the hidden order; and, as we know, he did not consider art a sedative, a way of avoiding experience, but an initiator into the uncharted experiences of human life. Art orders, yet while doing so reveals the chaos of life, as the narrator explains by means of the Greek tragedies he reinterprets for the New Humanists. No, the narrator, himself an artist speaking for the artist, is angry with the misuse of art, with what Thoreau once called "easy-reading," with the "dons" who not only make it easy but, by altering texts, make it a retreat for the educated man.

The narrator goes too far when he speaks of the universal imposture of literature, and Gauss was right to reprove Wilson for his sentiments; but one imagines his pleasure when the instance cited turned out to be especially applicable to the New Humanists. The narrator's remarks on the English dons who made the Greeks serve their own view of life were taken from John Jay Chapman's *Greek Genius and Other Essays*, a brilliant attack on the school of "limp Grecism" in England, on such literary imperialists as Gilbert Murray and Jowett; and by way of Matthew Arnold and Sophocles, these remarks are intended for the New Humanists and especially to discredit their attempt to build "a fortress of absolute beauty and wisdom." The disquisition is intemperate, but this does not alter what the narrator maintains: that art originates in the "appetites and agonies of men," that it is always temporal and impure, always modified by differences in sex, race, and generation, and therefore never to be fixed in an ultimate tradition. If this view is "destructive," as the narrator claims, it nevertheless makes the adventure of art possible again for another generation.

Grosbeake's metaphysics, in the next section, simply puts the narrator's self-defensive and physically deterministic notions into an exploratory and creative context. For the artist has creative vitality — spirit — and his search for order is a cosmological necessity. He is a finite agent of the ultimate purpose of creation. His art is "readjustment," a coming to terms with a constantly changing universe, not "mere compensation" but "a necessity of universal development. . . ." In a world of darkness, as the narrator is reminded on reading Rita's poem to him, the artist embarks for the shores of light; and if his work eases irritation, it is because it provides human contact — communicates the moral and aesthetic values that enable and ennoble life.

This view encompasses the humanism of Gauss and Rosenfeld. It permits the acceptance of all art, especially contemporary art — unacceptable to some either because it is experimental or popular — which Rosenfeld said beat out the rhythms of the age. It is therefore fitting that when the narrator accepts America he should also accept jazz. When he hears *Mamie Rose* clearly at last, it is no longer a vulgar voice interrupting Rita nor a demonic scratching, but a work of art that he finds good and original in composition. Thinking about the Jewish composer (Irving Berlin or George Gershwin?) who had given the basic German melody of the song a "new accent, half agonized and half thrilling," he wonders — cataloging resources much discussed at the time — whether he had got it from Schoenberg or Stravinsky, from the traffic noises of the city, the life of the lower East Side, the chants of cantors in synagogues. But in themselves these resources are not enough to insure good music. The excellence, he finds, is the result of the "personal color or rhythm," of that precious personal element which he had once dismissed as of little importance. Now, reviewing the authors he had considered earlier, he concedes that the

personal element in their work had been the cause of their fame —
that their admirers had not been addicted to a sedative but rav-
ished by the taste of the miraculous honey of the mind. Art is no
longer tranquilizer, it is tonic food and drink, necessary nourish-
ment. To such an art he dedicates himself.

The literary faith arrived at in *Daisy* was already affirmed in
1927 in "A Preface to Persius." The idea that art is "provoked" by
discord, pain, and chaos and attempts to order, resolve, and ren-
der acceptable these "anomalies of reality" is clearly stated. What
is more, the critic, as well as the writer, is required to feel "the
shock of reality" and to stand firm against the "miseries and hor-
rors" of life. That Persius, a satirist in the time of Nero, and William Drummond, his eighteenth-century editor, had done so, and
that Wilson would do so now, account for the intensity of his
"sense of continuity with the past." But we must realize the situation in which these "maudlin meditations" take place in order to
understand why he also speaks appositionally of "this spirit of
stubborn endurance" — why, in fact, we are made to feel that the
position he takes, even though it belongs to a great tradition, is
a marginal and lonely one.

The meditations, published a month or so after the execution of
Sacco and Vanzetti, are set in an Italian restaurant in the Village.
The author is nourishing both body and soul: the dinner itself,
a product of a great human tradition, is splendid, and the book
he is reading, brought forward over centuries, is equally tonic.
The editor Drummond had been a member of Parliament, and so
reminds Wilson of other statesmen-writers, of those of the early
days of our Republic who represent his ideal. Those early days,
in turn, contrast with the present America where miners are
clubbed and children gassed — a present as tyrannical as the time
of Persius and whose Persius might well be E. E. Cummings,
who tells Wilson that the possibility of violence in New York had
made it unnecessary for him to go to Boston to see the machine
guns. Mediating on civilization and its breakdown in Persius'
time, Wilson is heartened by the subsequent extension and reorganization of civilization that made possible the continuity of
understanding between Persius and Drummond. But then he
remembers the new void that opened in Western civilization about

the time of Drummond — not a geographical void such as Rome
had been unable to fill, but a social void below the educated
classes. This "gulf of illiteracy and mean ambitions," he believes,
is America, and having pondered it, he declares that "there was
nothing to do save to work with the dead for allies, and at odds
with the ignorance of most of the living, that that edifice, so many
times begun, so discouragingly reduced to ruins, might yet stand
as the headquarters of humanity!" The necessity and difficulty
of this resolve are dramatically suggested when, on leaving, he is
jarred by a collision with a "couple of those bulky pink people who
. . . were dancing to the radio."

All of this may be considered a coda to the narrator's question
in *Daisy*: "where did you get that line about 'the downfall of
western civilization?'" To which Daisy replies: "Oh that was just
something I picked up at the Ritz Bar in Paris!"

III

Axel's Castle, the study of the Symbolists that established Wilson's reputation as a literary critic, is as profoundly
personal, as much an attempt to resolve tangled commitments, as
I Thought of Daisy. Having its origin in the malaise of the twenties, it is essentially a work of cultural diagnosis, a book of the
order of Brooks's *The Ordeal of Mark Twain* and *The Pilgrimage
of Henry James*. The "case" is Symbolism, and literary, historical,
and philosophical analysis discovers its meaning for the contemporary writer.

It is a major work, as important as Eliot's *The Sacred Wood*.
By showing the philosophical importance and methodological
seriousness of the Symbolist movement, it vindicated contemporary letters. More than any other book of criticism, it established
the writers of the *avant garde* in the consciousness of the general
reader: not only did it place them in a significant historical development, it taught the uninitiated how to read them. Superbly
written, clear, forceful, directed by a mind that tightly grasps
ideas and serves what it tries to understand, the book remains,
even after three decades of massive endeavor in the same terri-
tory, a brilliant landmark and stimulating point of departure.
That it probed the literary situation is evident in the response it
evoked.

For the most part the response was anticipated by Gauss who read the book in its various stages of preparation. When he finished reading the proofs, he wrote Wilson that the book would set him up as "the most intelligent and penetrating critic of our time"; for he had provided the most illuminating criticism of contemporary literature and of the present state of mind that he had read, and had written a book to be placed beside Ortega's *The Dehumanization of Art*. This praise spoke for the general consensus. Even the New Humanists admitted that the book was of the right tone — serious, moderate, and quiet — and that it was easy, natural, and lucid, a triumph of expository skill.

Gauss was pleased that Wilson had written of the modern movement in poetry in a way that would be "intelligible even to college professors." Indeed, Wilson had forced on the professors (the New Humanists) the fact that in the last fifty years there had been a literary movement that had behind it a new and at least disputable philosophy. The younger generation *had been* serious, and here was serious work to prove it, and to challenge the Mores and Babbitts. For himself, still debating the issue of "Mrs. Alving and Oedipus," he welcomed the treatment of the Symbolists. It seemed to him that the new literature represented the "soul" in its fight against "science" and upheld the tragic sense of life, and he did not agree with Wilson that "Symbolism is the last and ultimate stage in an evolution which is *now finished*. . . . " In any case, he felt that the New Humanists should appraise the Symbolists more highly because they were fighting their fight.

Yet Gauss knew that Wilson, in "Notes on Babbitt and More," had recently given the New Humanists "a solar plexus blow" and that they had their "clubs in soak for [him]"; and he feared that the dedication of the book, affirming historical criticism, would give them a chance to jump him. The New Humanists (if not the New Critics whom they had schooled) were too angry to find in the book the support for their position that Gauss had found; relativity of any kind was abhorrent to them. Their response to the book is best represented by Robert Shafer who considered it at length in *Paul Elmer More and American Criticism* (1935). Wilson, he concluded, had "written neither a historical work nor a genuinely critical one, but rather a piece of propagandism." [27]

[27] One should note as an example of the temper of the time the kind of Menckenian sally that even the New Humanists adopted. "When Mr. Ed-

Most troubling to Gauss was an argument of the book that made him feel, as he reported, "that I am following the hearse of poetry." This argument concerned the respective uses and vitality of verse and prose and answered in the positive the question which serves as the title of Wilson's final statement of the case — "Is Verse a Dying Technique?" He had himself published a book of poems by way of saying farewell to poetry, but the argument goes back to "The Muses Out of Work" (1927) and is not intended, as Gauss believed, to "lay a wreath on the grave of poesy," but rather to call the poets to the public world from which they, like the Symbolists before them, had withdrawn. Wilson wants the poets to follow the professions and to acquire a "real stake in society." For poetry is dying of the exclusiveness claimed for it by Valéry and Eliot; dying of the malnutrition of experience that comes from turning one's back to the world; dying, as in the extreme case of Axel, from the malady of the ideal. The argument is defensible on historical grounds, and Wilson advances it with sympathy because the withdrawal of the poets is related to the ascendancy of the bourgeoisie. But there is no question of the value of the techniques of Symbolism, the point of the argument being that these techniques are not limited to poetry but are available to prose, to novelists like Proust and Joyce who, in Wilson's view, are poets of full stature.

The cultural fact that Wilson addresses is the new conception of the vocation of poet that had its beginnings in Romanticism. He deplores the disengagement of the artist from the stakes of the world, especially the retreat that is made before engagement is even attempted, and he proposes another model for the writer, the exemplar of which is Anatole France. France, he had written in an essay of 1925, "had spoken, as few great writers do, for a whole civilization which he interpreted as well as led." Like his own M. Bergeret, he explains in *Axel's Castle*, France had at heart "the common interests of the community. . . ." Critical of much in society, he had nevertheless not dissociated himself from it, but had participated in the "public life through literature," had even occupied himself with politics and taken sides. And Wilson

mund Wilson mentions Ruskin," Shafer writes, "you might think that the poor old fellow had lived five hundred years ago. . . . when Mr. Wilson . . . set [s] the world of scholarship aright about Sophocles, he merely makes himself a laughing-stock."

has in mind critics like Ruskin, Renan, Taine, and Sainte-Beuve who used criticism as "the vehicle of all sorts of ideas about the purpose and destiny of human life in general"; whose criticism was not self-contained, neither "detached scientific interest" nor "detached aesthetic appreciation," and accordingly led to something beyond itself. If writers will no longer take up professions of public service, let them, he advises, make of letters itself a profession that gives them a place in society and unites them to the common enterprise. Wilson is speaking to the theme of Brooks's *Letters and Leadership* (1918). There Brooks had written of the poetically endowed members of the younger generation who "have lost themselves in a confused and feeble anarchism" and, like the run of Americans, were unable "even to imagine what it means to be employed by civilization."

Like so much of Wilson's work, *Axel's Castle* is dramatic. Several chapters contain discordant encounters, and the book as a whole is an encounter in which prose is the victor over poetry, and imagination in the service of social action is the only acceptable choice. The poets are treated first, the prose writers follow, and the concluding chapter, pitting the extreme forms of rejection against each other, closes out the story of Symbolism with an eloquent statement of the possibilities of the union of imagination (art) and science (society). Wilson explained an aspect of the organization of the book when he told Gauss that he treated Mallarmé with Yeats, considered Corbière and Laforgue with Eliot, and Ducasse with the Dadaists, and ended with Rimbaud because he wished to contrast him with Villiers de L'Isle Adam. There is some chronological order: the poets (Yeats, Valéry, Eliot) seem to have been placed according to age, and, with the exception of Gertrude Stein, this seems to have been the case with the novelists Proust and Joyce. To end with the oldest writers — with Adam and Rimbaud — seems an artful way of showing that the extreme positions had been taken as much as fifty years before *The Waste Land* and that by now the movement had run its course.

The book speaks for Wilson's own development and is directed toward what might be called the politics of art. In discursive form it works out the problem of the artist's relation to society that Wilson had tried to solve earlier in presentational forms. Looking ahead, one connects it with *To the Finland Station,* a study of the social revolutionary developments of the historical period treated in *Axel's Castle* — a study that might be called the art of politics.

The play of phrases is not idle. *Axel's Castle* ends with the hope that art and science [28] may someday constitute one system. For the Symbolists, who may have discouraged us about politics and action of any kind, have contributed to the disintegration of mechanistic and materialistic conceptions and, with modern science, have empowered the imagination for "the untried possibilities of human thought and art." These possibilities, however, are not to be looked for in literary art but in "social engineering." Even as late as *The Triple Thinkers* (1938), when Wilson was disillusioned with politics and intent on redefining his political role in such a way as to withdraw from direct action, he maintained that "society itself . . . is the work of art." And when he speaks of transcending literature, he does not mean to imply that he values it less — to love literature is always for him a saving virtue; rather he wishes to suggest an even greater challenge to the powers of imagination — "the possiblity of re-creating human society."

Axel's Castle begins where Wilson himself began, with the rebellious Romantics whom Gauss had taught him to admire and, in the first close study, with Yeats, one of his earliest favorites. As a youth he had felt the *fin de siècle* mood, had been enchanted with art and drawn to the fairyland of the imagination,[29] and he is therefore sympathetic with the poet who, harrassed by the bourgeois world, turns to it. Yet his own course had been otherwise, and he was aware, as he tried to show in the case of Rita, of the disastrous consequences of living in what he later depicts as a moonlight world. For Wilson, accordingly, the measure of Yeats's greatness is that he came to terms with reality — that in spite of the mask he felt he needed to adopt in order to preserve his poetic self and in spite of the substitute "science" of *A Vision,* his passion for reality was great enough to turn him increasingly toward the objective world. Yeats lived out the problems of the disorder of the age: the separation of art and science, contemplation and

[28] Providing methods and means of social reform, science serves politics. And politics for Wilson is an enterprise as much in need of rationality as of imagination.

[29] He is still concerned with it in *Cyprian's Prayer.*

action, Symbolism and Naturalism — dualisms which Wilson believes both the literary explorations of the Symbolists and the scientific explorations of Einstein and Whitehead have overcome. And Yeats is superior to all the other poets treated in *Axel's Castle* because he surmounted the disorder. Turning to the real, involving himself in political and social affairs, he lost none of his imaginative power, but acquired a deeper sense of reality and, to apply the phases of *A Vision*, passed from the all subjective to the more objective phase in which his soul became "the world's servant."

It is also a measure of Yeats's greatness that he loses nothing by the brief contrast with Shaw, one of Wilson's early idols. One would think that Shaw, so much like Wilson himself in shouldering "the whole unwieldly load of contemporary sociology, politics . . . journalism," would have forced Wilson to engage Yeats in a serious encounter. That he did not may be due to the fact that Wilson had perhaps already realized that Shaw's reputation was better upheld by considering him as an artist rather than as a social philosopher. But to consider him as an artist was no contest. Even in the matter of prose style, it is clear that Wilson prefers the old-fashioned garment of Yeats to the "impersonal instrument" of Shaw. Whatever makeweight Shaw may provide is quickly removed with the concluding section of the chapter. "Yet, in the meantime," it begins, "the poet Yeats has passed into a sort of third phase, in which he is closer to the common world than at any previous period." The poet of "Among School Children," passionate and wise, as profoundly critical of life in his poetry as in his prose, is left in our minds. The argument is behind him, and nothing is said to compromise his grandeur.

This is not the case with Paul Valéry. His concern with method apart from matter and with the algebra of language; his desire to penetrate himself by turning consciousness upon itself; his esoteric conception of poetry, his "aesthetic mysticism" — these Wilson finds repugnant. Justly appreciating his poetry, especially "Le Cimetière Marin," a supreme example of the Symbolist conquest of dualism, he is nevertheless repelled by the program for poetry that Valéry has made fashionable. In this chapter, therefore, Wilson vigorously attacks what has come to be called the "New Criticism." He questions the distinction between sense and suggestion by means of which Valéry maintains the exclusiveness and superiority of poetry, and launches the discussion of language as a technique of human communication that, whenever the occasion permits—in the study of Eliot, Joyce, and especially Gertrude Stein—he insistently pursues.

Wilson respects every activity of the mind, but he does not divorce such activity from the man. How a man lives and what he achieves as a human being are essential, moral inquiries of his criticism. He is a student of ideas and men. Thus, even when he acknowledges Valéry's "strength of solitary labor and of earnest introspection," he expresses his fear of the dehumanization that Valéry himself represented in the character of M. Teste (Mr. Head). It is also typical of his work that he reports Valéry's vicious attack on Anatole France on the occasion of his succession to France's chair in the French Academy. Lacking decency, snobbish and pretentious, destructive of valuable continuity, Valéry himself, according to Wilson's touchstones, exhibits the effects of dehumanization.

The attack on Anatole France sets the scene for the encounter between France and Valéry which Wilson himself stages. This encounter, he says, marks even more sharply than that of Yeats and Shaw the differences in method and attitude of the literature of the period before the war and the literature that followed; it establishes the poles of discourse for the entire book, and in it Valéry is roundly put down. Here the literary theories of both men are subsumed in their roles as men of letters. Anatole France, a popular writer, serves a "bourgeois clientèle" and supplies it with "a whole literature"; Valéry, an elitist, disdains the public, publishes little. One deals with "the events of life as it is lived in the world," and his extraliterary pursuits involve him in the world —in politics, where, significantly, he defends Dreyfus; the other deals with the "isolated or ideal human mind," concerns himself with politics only as a "detached intelligence," and prefers to pursue his scientific interests. These interests, impugned earlier when Wilson speaks of Valéry as a "super-dilettante" who acquired "a smattering of the new mathematical and physical theory," now add to his advantage because they represent Wilson's own excitement over the new universe of Whitehead. But in the absence of the kind of social commitment France has, these interests do not save him. When the representative characters created by these writers are contrasted, the social and agreeable M. Bergeret is easily the victor over M. Teste, the self-occupied and socially dissociated man whom, Wilson notes, would now be diagnosed as "introverted, narcissistic and manic depressive." Anatole France, deriving his strength from the public world with which the narrator of *Daisy* wishes so much to make contact, takes his place in Wilson's academy of letters and perhaps regains a place in the consciousness of the generation that had deposed him.

In turning to Eliot, Wilson confronts a contemporary, and rival. No other literary figure of his generation has preoccupied him in the way Eliot has. From the essay on *The Waste Land* in *The Dial* (1922) to "The Mass in the Parking Lot," a poem of the fifties introducing the "correctly garbed . . . T. S. Eliot, the Great Dictator," and "'Miss Buttle' and 'Mr. Eliot,'" a recent article in *The New Yorker* in which the Eliot cult and Eliot's own furthering of it are dissected, Wilson has felt the need to establish himself by taking Eliot's measure. In *Axel's Castle*, where he most fully considers Eliot's work, he encounters him in his own person, and his high praise — that Eliot "possesses a complete literary personality" — provides the opportunity of standing up to Eliot, the man of letters.

He does not face him as a poet, for he believes that Eliot's greatness as a poet is unassailable. Wilson acknowledges the "superior artist" whose taste is "absolutely sure," who, having brought a "new personal rhythm into the language" and left an unmistakable mark upon English poetry, deserves his prestige. Here he does much, as he had earlier in the pioneer essay in *The Dial*, to further that prestige, and considering his personal stake in Eliot's reputation, one can only admire his critical judgment and scrupulousness.

Wilson encounters the Eliot who, in *The Waste Land*, "enchanted and devastated a whole generation" and "made the young poets old before their time." When he first wrote about the poem he called his essay "The Poetry of Drouth," and he is still concerned with and set in opposition by the spiritual drouth that Eliot's "dry breath" represents in the intellectual world. As a clue to Eliot's position, he turns to his themes, and these, to the reader who has followed Wilson's work, are more readily connected with what he had said of Henry James than with what he says of Flaubert. Flaubert did affect modern literature by his profound distaste for contemporary civilization; he did teach many to believe that the present was inferior to the past. Yet Eliot's distaste for the present has a deeper source than Flaubert; its origin is psychological, cultural, American.

Wilson believes that Eliot is a "typical product of our New England civilization," that he belongs with the "highbrows" Brooks had criticized in *America's Coming-of-Age*. The moral idealism of New England, manifesting itself in Eliot as "excessive fastidiousness and scrupulousness," is the source of his distaste for the present. Eliot has the morbid fear of the vulgar that Wilson had noted in James, and his distaste for the present is in fact a distaste for life. Properly seen, it is really the result of "regret at situations unexplored, [of the] dark rankling of passions inhibited"; like Prufrock, Eliot has "dared too little. . . ." And *The Waste Land* is his personal confession of "emotional starvation," the sterility that desolates the land being due primarily, as Wilson detects in Eliot's recurrent garden scenes, to the "sterility of the Puritan temperament." However much one responds to the poem as a valuable assessment of contemporary civilization, as Wilson does, he is never permitted to forget that it presents "the peculiar conflicts of the Puritan turned artist." He is reminded of the poet's "horror of vulgarity," of his "ascetic shrinking from sexual experience," and — it will figure later in Wilson's disapproval — of his "straining after a religious emotion. . . ."

Wilson also recognizes Eliot's formidable distinction as a critic: he is the critic who has most profoundly affected literary opinion since the war. Yet, salutary as were the effects of his reaction to impressionistic criticism, his aesthetic ideas and the example of his critical practice have resulted in "pedantry"[30] and "futile aestheticism." Like Valéry, with whom he is associated, he believes that poetry is a "pure and rare aesthetic essence," that the aesthetic is independent of other values, and that poetry affords "superior amusement." Nothing, of course, could be more at odds with Wilson's aesthetic than these views, so that the objections to them, given in his discussion of the many impure uses of poetry in the past, point up the fundamental difference between Eliot's critical practice and his own. Eliot and Valéry, he says,

---

[30] Wilson includes a parody of Eliot's multiple and multiplying literary references.

talk "as if the whole of literature existed simultaneously in a vacuum"; they are, as he noted later in respect to Eliot in "The Historical Interpretation of Literature" (1940), nonhistorical in their approach, trying to see all of literature as God might see it and to call books to a "Day of Judgment." Such criticism, especially as it is practiced by the epigone, is too detached. It becomes a way of escaping from the broad human commitments of critics like Ruskin and Sainte-Beuve with whom Wilson here identifies himself.

As for Eliot's development beyond *The Waste Land*, it is praiseworthy because it shows that he is "too serious to continue with the same complacence as some of his contemporaries inhabiting that godforsaken desert," but it is not encouraging. Eliot now recognizes that poetry is related to morals, religion, and politics, but his positions on these matters uncomfortably suggest to Wilson the fashionable reactionary point of view of the neo-Thomists and the New Humanists. (In 1932, Wilson scored the "feeble fascism-classicism" of the New Humanists and found their viewpoint, among others, "queer" and of "no use in our present predicament.") Eliot's religious faith, he feels, is not genuine, is at best only the "low blue flame" of the convert who believes in the beneficence of belief; it is a faith "uninspired by hope, unequipped with zeal or force" and so thoroughly grounded in the conviction of original sin and the ultimate reality of evil that it precludes the possibilities of temporal salvation, those, for example, of political and economic reform, which Wilson believes to be within the power of man. Thus the leader in his generation of the party of the past is challenged by a presumptive leader of the party of hope. From Eliot, he expects no "guidance for the future. . . ." [31]

Proust and Joyce, who with Yeats are among Wilson's modern heroes, are not so much to be argued with as explained. They sup-

---

[31] Wilson never deposed Eliot; Eliot's power increased, with the help, ironically, of *Axel's Castle*. This accounts, in part, for the decline in Wilson's influence and for his embittered attacks on Eliot and the academics. Though one may agree with his views of Eliot, one must also acknowledge his rancor. "The Mass in the Parking Lot" and "Cardinal Merry Del Val" in *Three Reliques of Ancient Western Poetry Collected From The Ruins of the Twentieth Century* (the title itself suggests *The Waste Land*) are perhaps the best examples of his temper.

port Wilson's polemic by substantiating his theory of the applicability of verse techniques to works of prose; indeed the size and scope of their Symbolist novels suggest the richer possibilities of such appropriation. In giving the reader the hang (as he would say) of *A la Recherche du Temps Perdu* and of *Ulysses*, Wilson's accomplishment goes beyond that of "translation." [32] The form of these difficult works emerges in his study, and with it a sense of their imaginative and moral power. Proust's novel, moreover, provides the ground for significant psychological exploration; and both novels help him develop the connection between the "relativism" of their imaginative worlds and the "events" of the Whiteheadean universe. Having himself attempted a similar kind of fiction in *I Thought of Daisy*, his readings of these novels provide the best gloss that we have of his own intentions.

What makes Wilson's explanation of these novels so memorable is not the polemic thrust but the fact that they help him return to his own lost time, to the bourgeois world of father and son and of mother and son that he had left behind, that prewar world, as he says in connection with Proust, where everyone is "sick with some form of the ideal." Proust's hero is neurasthenic, like the author an only child still emotionally bound to his mother. His social world is morally corrupt, very much like the larger social world Wilson glimpsed in his childhood at Lakewood, a world, he writes, that "either ignores or seeks to kill those few impulses toward justice and beauty which make men admirable." Now Proust and his hero use their illness to escape contact with this world, and they permit their masochistic passivity to become sadistic — forms of behavior Wilson tries to avoid. One senses throughout the essay his refusal to be neurotic, and his pounding at the door of the world is exigent because of his knowledge of his father's and his own recent eclipse. Wilson prefers Proust-the-artist, for in his art, at least, he retrieved "the defeat of his will"; he prefers Proust-the-moralist with his Jewish "intensity of idealism and implacable moral severity. . . ." And even more than for the greatness of his art, he values Proust for affirming, as he himself does in *Daisy*, "the reality of those obligations, culminating

---

[32] The denigrating term of Stanley Edgar Hyman, whose treatment of Wilson in *The Armed Vision* (1948) accounts for Wilson's almost total neglect in the schools.

in the obligation of the writer to do his work as it ought to be done, which seem to be derived from some other world, 'based on goodness, scrupulousness, sacrifice. . . .' "

Wilson's analysis of Proust's illness, his recognition that "all of his thinking is sick" — that his notions of personal relationships and love are dismal and his belief in art as the only means of mastering reality is warped — undoubtedly supported the position Mike Gold had taken in 1930 in the controversy over Thornton Wilder. In 1928, in a review of *The Cabala*, Wilson had pointed out how deeply Wilder had been influenced by Proust, and later, by confirming Gold's opinion of Wilder's work as "a sedative for sick Americans," he had helped to precipitate a literary class war. But in the chapter on Proust, as in that on Eliot, he checks the vehemence one finds in the reviews he was writing concurrently. He ends the section on Proust's illness with a moving account of Proust's valorous struggle to complete his work before his death, and in the concluding part he interprets his achievement in such a way that the moral of his work — the fact that the artist has surmounted himself and become the historian of "the Heartbreak House of capitalist culture" — reproves those Marxists who summarily dismiss as decadent the work of bourgeois writers.

Nor is there anything decadent about Joyce in whose hands Symbolism is made to confront and master the modern world. Of the writers discussed in *Axel's Castle*, he is the greatest, "really the great poet of a new phase of the human consciousness," Wilson says, who not only reconciles Symbolism and Naturalism in a prose work but, without satirizing or sentimentalizing ordinary humanity, searches its heart and justifies its creative powers. In *Ulysses* he shows that "ordinary humanity . . . is . . . not so ordinary after all"; in Stephen and Molly and Bloom he represents the "body of humanity . . . laboring to throw up some knowledge and beauty by which it may transcend itself." And in the still deeper exploration of man in the dream of Here Comes Everybody, he gives us the very "psychological plasm," the source of human possibilities, from which all the forms of human experience have arisen. Wilson's only reservation is that *Ulysses* and *Finnegans Wake* (he considers a portion of the work-in-progress) are too systematic and synthetic — Joyce, like Proust, indulges himself and disregards the reader. But the works themselves, as his study shows, merit the challenge of their difficulty. From Joyce, for example, he draws refreshment of spirit and renews his delight in "the excellence and beauty of transcendent understanding itself." He finds the humanistic principle of salvation that, with Gauss's guidance, he had first appreciated in Dante: "the vigilant cultivation of *'il ben del intelletto.'* " [33]

Joyce's accomplishment, however, is not a resting place, a height to be scaled by other writers. There are other untried peaks in view, and we reach them by applying the philosophical lesson of his techniques to our way of being in the world: one must overcome not only the dualism of Symbolism and Naturalism but the dualism of the self and the world.

Now in the matter of technique, Gertrude Stein provides the example of Symbolist suggestiveness carried to the extreme of meaninglessness. Her experiments in dislocating words from their meanings are valuable for what they teach us of the mysterious logic of language, but they raise the central issue of Symbolist practice — that of suggestion *vs.* sense. Placed in opposition, suggestion and sense comprise another unnecessary dualism; for all language, as Wilson demonstrates, is suggestive. Language makes sense, however, only when it is not pushed too far beyond the boundaries of common understanding; its meaning depends upon the artist's willingness to acknowledge an audience, to endeavor to communicate. The lesson of communication applies to the Symbolists whose tendency to intimate Wilson traces to their preference for the solitudes of the imagination. But the lesson of suggestiveness applies to the New Humanists and the Marxists, both of whom, unwilling to accept its power and to fathom its depths, have too easily dismissed the Symbolists' achievement.

It is not the Symbolist technique but the Symbolists' way of being in the world that Wilson repudiates. He objects, as Gide had, to their "lack of curiosity about life," to their easy renunciation of the common experience. They have little of the Romantics' rebelliousness and eagerness to try the possibilities of life; and they impugn, as inferior, the reality of the social world, preferring

[33] The previous quotation may be taken as a translation of this phrase from the memoir of Gauss, which is also appropriate to this context because the issue of Joyce was one that they had recently discussed with Paul Elmer More. See "Mr. More and the Mithraic Bull," where Gauss, incidentally, is described as a "South German Dante."

instead the refuge they find in what they claim to be the superior reality of the imagination. Their malady is depicted in the story of Count Axel, who retires to his castle, resists the appeal of love and life represented by the romantic Sara ("Live? our servants will do that for us," he tells her), and persuades her to die with him. An equally extreme attitude, developing from within Symbolism, is the rejection of art — of the sickness of civilization of which Symbolism is a manifestation — for the life of pure action. This is the way of Rimbaud, a more attractive way for Wilson who himself feels the need to act,[34] yet as hopeless as the other.

The ordeal of Axel and the pilgrimage of Rimbaud — with these case histories Wilson points the moral of the contemporary cultural situation. Should the artist, as Valéry predicts, permit the popular media to take over the work of communication, we will have a mass culture and a minority culture, and the latter, according to Valéry, will be served by a literature "based on the *abuse of language*," a literature given over to the creation of illusions rather than to the transmission of realities. Literature will then become a game, the superior amusement by which we exercise our sensibilities. Such of course has been a direction in which literature (should we say the study of literature?) has been developing, but Wilson does not accept its inevitability. Symbolism dominates the literary world, but only, he explains, because of an extraliterary accident: as a result of the demoralization following the war, when the socially active writers lost credit and the writers whom he treats in his book, having maintained their integrity by pursuing their art, became the heroes of the younger generation. And since Symbolism offers only the alternatives of Axel and Rimbaud, the one leading to "some monstrosity or absurdity" and the other to a cult of the primitive that at best only postpones the artist's engagement with modern civilization, it has reached a dead end. Even the writers he has been considering, if they have not followed these extreme courses, still have not been able to muster hope or direct their imaginations to the "possibilities of human life." For the most part, they tend to look to the past and their social criticism is of little relevance to the present. Though they

---

[34] For example, consider Hugo, the political man of *I Thought of Daisy*, whose sudden trip to Afghanistan ("'it's one of the only places in the world that hasn't been Europeanized'") is obviously intended to call up Rimbaud.

are to be admired as literary masters, they cannot be accepted as social guides.

That the writer should be a social guide is, however, the momentous issue now. The time is 1930. Economic and social disasters raise a question of more importance to life than even that of the course of literature — "whether it is possible to make a practical success of human society, and whether, if we continue to fail, a few masterpieces, however profound or noble, will be able to make life worth living even for the few people in a position to enjoy them." For some minds, and often the most American, the foreboding is the ground of hope, and so for Wilson, whose dark question summons the bright promise of the socially directed imagination. Having begun with the Romantic rebellion, his book ends with the example of Russia, "where a central social-political idealism has been able to use and to inspire the artist as well as the engineer." It opens to new, untried worlds, beckoning the artist to resume in society the historical mission neglected by previous generations.

With *Axel's Castle*, Wilson concluded one phase of his career and moved forward into another, a phase well underway by the time the book reached the public. When it appeared in March 1931, he had already published the early installments of *The American Jitters*; and this book of social reporting, published in the following year, during which *Axel's Castle* went into its fourth printing, confirmed his own solution of the problem of the writer and for the Marxists, at least, made him a significant figure. Writing in *The New Masses*, Edwin Seaver said that one "could plot a graph of Mr. Wilson from Proust to Karl Marx" — from *I Thought of Daisy* and *Axel's Castle* to *The American Jitters* — and that this graph would show "a new and vital tendency on the part of American writers, a return to a sense of historic immediacy, to a new social awareness that has joined forces with the literary."

three

The First Truly Human Culture

I

"For me . . . the mark of the historic," Mary Mc-
Carthy explains in "My Confession," her account of moving left-
ward in the thirties, "is the nonchalance with which it picks up
an individual and deposits him in a trend. . . ." Besides raising
the question of individual responsibility, what she says tells us
something about the way in which we find ourselves in history —
find ourselves in those moments in history which are historical because their critical urgency awakens our sense of history. She is
describing the drift of history which carries one along and at some
point places him in the kind of situation we speak of as a confrontation with history; and it seems from the account of her experience that the drift is also preparing one, moving as it were in the
direction of one's choice, so that in choosing one feels that he is
consenting to history.

Her statement undoubtedly generalizes her experience of the
thirties. This is the way in which she found herself in history, a
fairly common experience of the time when Franklin Delano
Roosevelt said we had a "rendezvous with destiny";[1] and it may
explain the special character and momentous impact the decade
had for many who lived through it. And this is the way — for certainly her husband's experience[2] contributed to her sense of the

[1] The phrase is brilliant and ominous, for it makes acceptable the Marxian
conception of history, yet hints at the earlier rendezvous of Rupert Brooke's
generation — the rendezvous with death.
[2] At this time, Edmund Wilson.

historic — in which Wilson found himself in the history of that decade.

The drift that brought him to Communism is familiar because he has charted for us some of its major episodes. The trauma of class displacement is assuredly the most profound and crucial, then the disillusionment of the war and the discouragement and frustration of Normalcy — all so disturbing to the idealistic social faith which he has recently described in *The Cold War and the Income Tax* as "innocent" and full of "old-fashioned brotherly 'democracy.'" The basic terms of Van Wyck Brooks's diagnosis indicate the opposition Wilson felt between "the creative life" and "the acquisitive life"; and they suggest, as did Brooks's reminder that literary criticism in a country in need of reconstruction must become social criticism, the possibility of direct political action.

The antagonisms of the generations that had been so bitterly expressed in cultural terms had not however been made sufficiently political. That is why, on reviewing the critical positions of the twenties from the vantage of the crash, Wilson said that "we can see now . . . that they all involved compromises with the salesman and the broker." Not until August 1927, when Sacco and Vanzetti were executed, did it become stunningly clear, as Robert Morss Lovett testifies in his autobiography, that the doctrine of class war could no longer be discounted as merely a matter of partisan tactics. Like lightning on the horizon, the case of the Italian anarchists had crackled throughout the decade and with their execution finally but briefly broken into storm. Wilson, who spent the summer of 1927 on Cape Cod, wrote Gauss of the oppressiveness of Boston — "The Men from Rumpelmayer's," a narrative of that time and place, conveys very well the heavy atmosphere and the deadened feeling one has when he is unprepared to act in response to moral shock.[3] There is no evidence (beyond that provided by Matthew Josephson) that Wilson stood with Edna Millay and Dos Passos at the Charlestown prison. But the judicial lynching, as he called it, prompted his first piece of political writ-

[3] Here, as in "Reunion," Wilson brilliantly creates a sense of the off-stage horror. Daniel Aaron, *Writers on the Left*, New York, Harcourt, Brace and World, 1961, p. 419n, notes how "the agony of Sacco and Vanzetti forms a leitmotiv for a lobster dinner."

ing for *The New Republic*, the leader, "A Nation of Foreigners";
and it raised the question he put to Gauss and that led him in the
future to be a more attentive political witness — "What should be
done about America?" This was his Dreyfus case, for liberals like
himself the proper termination of the decade he characterized
in "The Age of Pericles," a short, crazy play approaching what we
now call the absurd, whose subtitle might have been "nihilism up
to no good." Although it antedates other installments of "The Follies" in *The American Earthquake*, its premonitory quality makes
it a fitting conclusion, a harbinger of what he called "The Earthquake" ("The stock market crash was to count for us almost like
a rending of the earth in preparation for the Day of Judgment").

The execution of Sacco and Vanzetti, Wilson wrote twenty-five
years later, "made liberals lose their bearings." This partly accounts
for the "nervous dissatisfaction and apprehension" that he says
had begun to manifest themselves in our intellectual life even
before the crash. Of this *I Thought of Daisy* and *Axel's Castle* are
sufficient testimony, as they are also of the determination to find
a new orientation for thought and action; and that he did not
know where to turn is evident in "A Preface to Persius" where
he can only counsel himself to stand firm and "work with the dead
for allies. . . ." As late as April 1929, the hope of social revolution, expressed for example by Dos Passos, seemed to him to be
a mirage.[4]

The crash caught him unawares, as it did many liberals, but
what is so remarkable is the quickness with which he found his
bearings and his function — that of teacher and admonisher of
hesitant liberals. Finding himself in history, he had also at last
found himself, and we can understand better why his major work
of this time should be *To the Finland Station*, a historical study
of man's relation to history; and having become a spokesman and
bellwether of leftward-tending liberals, and to that extent a leader,
we can understand his ready sympathy with the actors of history.
The jubilant feelings with which he responds to the crash do not
have the crash for their object so much as the opportunity for
action and leadership — for social engineering — that the crash

---

[4] In response to V. F. Calverton's plan for a symposium, Lewis Mumford
wrote in May 1929 that perhaps someone who verged "pretty far, by conviction or inertia, to the right" — someone, for example, like Edmund Wilson
— might be included. Cited in Daniel Aaron, *Writers on the Left*, p. 244.

created. He sees the occasion as another Civil War which will bring to an end the disastrous social consequences of the earlier one and replace them with something better. But let him describe that moment which, even in retrospect, is alive with the feelings of that time: "To the writers and artists of my generation who had grown up in the Big Business era and had always resented its barbarism, its crowding-out of everything they cared about, these years [the early ones of the slump when he was most active as a reporter and closest to events] were not depressing but stimulating. One couldn't help being exhilarated at the sudden unexpected collapse of that stupid gigantic fraud. It gave us a new sense of freedom; and it gave us a new sense of power to find ourselves still carrying on while the bankers, for a change, were taking a beating."

He carried on brilliantly, and the decade, which represents the watershed of his career — he was in his mid-thirties and early forties — was one of greater accomplishment and of more heated and extended engagement than we suspect from what he has chosen to reprint. When we review his career in the thirties, however, we do not find him (or for that matter many intellectuals) engaged in the tactical business of politics. He is not a political leader but an intellectual for whom the writing of current history — call it reportorial testifying — and a kind of policy-making at large have become the acting of history. He acts, but after the fashion of independent intellectuals: he signs various appeals and letters, among them the open letter in behalf of Foster and Ford, the presidential candidates of the Communist Party in the election of 1932; [5] he joins committees such as the National Committee for the Defense of Political Prisoners and the American Committee for the Defense of Leon Trotsky; he travels to Pineville, Kentucky, as one of Waldo Frank's delegation investigating the situation of the miners — only to witness the brutal beating of Frank and Allen Taub, which he writes up in militant prose as "Class War Exhibits" for *The New Masses.* But he does not join the Communist Party — submits to no discipline, does no party work — and the affiliations he has are with those independent Marxist periodicals, *The Modern Monthly* and *Partisan Review,* that oppose the official line. This may seem strange in view of his

[5] He voted for them, and thereafter for Norman Thomas.

admittedly welcome response to the Marxist faith, his admiration for Lenin, and the work he did in order to educate liberals in the fundamental reality of class war. Yet we must remember his intransigent individualism and his suspicion of Communist tactics (which was borne out at Pineville, where the delegation had been "used"); we must remember how easily the desire for action was satisfied by traveling about the country — Sherwood Anderson, for example, was politically fulfilled and happy visiting Southern mill towns [6] — and, most to the point, that Wilson had a program of his own.

His program is comprised in one statement of his first and perhaps most important policy-making paper, "An Appeal to Progressives," published in *The New Republic* on January 14, 1931: "if the American radicals and progressives who repudiate the Marxist dogma and the strategy of the Communist Party still hope to accomplish anything valuable, they must take Communism away from the Communists, and take it without ambiguities, asserting that their ultimate goal is the ownership by the government of the means of production." What he said to the dogmatists of art, whether Marxist or New Humanist — that art is "something that has to grow out of the actual present substance of life to meet life's immediate needs" — applied as well to the dogmatists of politics. He wants a Communism on native grounds; he is concerned primarily with America, not with the strategic necessities of the Soviet Union. And because of this, he remains, as he said of Dreiser, whose *Tragic America* he praised for beginning the work of selling Communism to America, an "unrussianizable American." His goal is the Americanization of Communism: on the one hand, he would bring Communism into line with the American democratic tradition; on the other hand, by way of Communism, which in "The Literary Class War, II," he says, "has for the first time brought humanity out into the great world of creative thought and work," he would vitalize American culture with "a new hope and purpose. . . ."

The second objective sets the task of *To the Finland Station*. Here Wilson labored to some purpose, funding the aspiration of a great tradition; and if he did not "Americanize Marx" as Dos

---

[6] During these years, Wilson was Anderson's political conscience.

Passos suggested, he at least, as Gauss recognized, humanized him. What is so curious is that he did not in a similar way seriously implement the first objective, but fell back on notions of the Americans that he had not critically examined.[7] For example, he writes that "we are the children of discovery and adventure and of resourceful improvisation to meet the necessities of new tasks." The pioneer, so often the villain in recent diagnoses of American culture, is now, we find in "Brokers and Pioneers," the hero he had always been in the popular imagination, recast however as a pathfinder to a frontier beyond bourgeois capitalism. This frontier is both the West, with which capitalism has by now caught up, and a state of mind, an independent psychology beyond the bourgeois psychology, which our frontier experience has bequeathed us and upon which, like the Populists, Single-Taxers, and Wobblies before us, we must now fall back. "What is best in our American tradition," he claims, "is our inheritance from this life of the frontier."

In this view, Whitman is one of our greatest writers because he succeeded in breaking away from bourgeois conventions, while most American writers, unable to escape their middle-class backgrounds, are seen to have suffered for it. The extent to which they did is shown by contrasting Henry George with Marx, Henry James with Flaubert, and Mencken with Shaw. Marx, Flaubert, and Shaw are the critics of the middle class he had recently written about in *The Herald Tribune Books*, men who were able, where the Americans were not, to get outside the framework of bourgeois thought; and they are very important to him, important, as we shall see, in the way the pioneer is, because they are examples of the strenuous endeavor he asks of all liberals — that they transcend their class and transform their psychology, that they become, in these essentials at least, "triple thinkers."

Communism was never for Wilson the parochial affair of Russia but rather the great enterprise of the human spirit set in motion by the Enlightenment. And so it kindled his idealism and evoked for him visions of the city of the spirit that man would build when he learned to rely on his ability to remake himself and his society. To put the pioneer against the broker, especially when the failure

[7] This is not to say that the notions are entirely without merit.

of the broker seemed to substantiate his belief that "capitalism
has run its course and we have got to imagine something better,"
was his way of recalling America to the enterprise she had in a
significant way once pioneered; and merely to mention pioneers
was a way of directing emotion to what for him was the truly
thrilling prospect revealed by the crisis — the fact that "the discovery of humanity and the earth has only been begun!"

Anything that darkened this prospect, any trangression of the
American boundaries of this vision angered him. He is most at
odds with the Communists when they exploit a situation for their
own purposes or adopt tactics that have no relevance to American
conditions. He is provoked, for example, by their interference in
the Scottsboro case, which he notes was due to the fact that "one
of their principle aims at the present time is to enlist the support
of Southern Negroes — to whom they have been preaching the
doctrine, arrived at from analogy with the Ukraine and completely
unrealistic in America, of 'self-determination for the Black Belt.'"
Invariably he supports indigenous radical elements — men like
Frank Keeney, whom he describes as "by birth and feeling . . . a
genuine leader of his people," and whose union of miners, he says,
represents "a spontaneous native labor movement." He admires
the well-behaved young organizers who have been trained at
Brookwood Labor College by A. J. Muste, and devoted intelligent social workers like his fictional Miss Dabney who admin-
isters relief in Kentucky. Though he leaves the impression in all
of his writing about the depression scene that hands such as these
are too few for the colossal task of social engineering, he makes
it clear that they are still the best hands for it. We simply need
more, and they will appear, it seems, when those artists and intellectuals who now indulge in "politicophobia" see in politics a creative challenge requiring imagination and intellect, and undertake
the work of selling the idea of Communism to the American
people.

And he believes that to do this one need not foster the proletarian art that Marxists like Mike Gold and Granville Hicks had
made the central concern of the literary left. If he lectured the
liberals on their solidarity with the middle class and on the fact
that as intellectuals they had no right to "succumb to the influence

of standards of living," he lectured the Communists on their mis-understanding of art. As early as 1927, he had said that the arts and sciences were classless; and as long as it remained an issue, he insisted that the artist belongs to two worlds, to a classless one and to the real one of which he is a part. In "Art, the Proletariat and Marx," one of many articles on this theme — "These are my opinions on this subject," he concluded, "and now let people leave me in peace!" — in this article he reminded the advocates of pro-letcult that such a culture was not the intention of Marx, Engels, Lenin, or Trotsky, that it was, as Trotsky maintained, not a culture at all, that it could be produced synthetically but for that reason wasn't art, and that, in any case, it had no relevance to America.[8] He was all for bringing the values of literature and art to the people, and he recognized that illiteracy in Russia made this a problem for which something as rudimentary as proletcult might be an expedient solution. But he did not think we needed it, for we had already a common language, easy communication, and — in books like *Huckleberry Finn* and *Leaves of Grass* — even a people's literature. Our cultural revolution, he said, need not be proletarian at all.

Perhaps the most striking thing about Wilson's appropriation of Communism is the fact that it did not lead him to identify his aims with those of the proletariat. It seems instead to have given substance to Brooks's rather vague notion of the creative life and to have led him to identify with the great Communist intellectuals who had made the salvation of man their mission. As early as 1928, in writing of Henry Clay Frick, he had impugned the heroism of our industrial giants — men, he said, without "dignified aims" or "honor," in no sense Nietzschean creators, scientists, artists, sports-men; and he could understand why the public, having no longer worthy heroes from the old West to acclaim, should turn in its de-sire for "a different sort of hero" than the businessman to Charles Lindberg and Commander Byrd. But they were not his sort of hero, the new kind of American he even then asked for and would soon recognize in Frank Keeney and Miss Dabney and in the kind of intellectual he himself aspired to be — one of those "men of

[8] A remark of William Carlos Williams is to the point: "There cannot be a proletarian art — even among savages. There is a proletarian taste."

superior brains who have triumphed over the ignorance, the stupidity and the shortsighted selfishness of the mass, who have imposed on them better methods and ideas than they could ever have arrived at by themselves." Much of the excitement of *To the Finland Station* is the result of the special interest he confessed to in "The Case of the Author": the special interest he had as a writer in "the success of the 'intellectual' kind of brains as opposed to the acquisitive kind." He will never let us forget that Marx, Engels, Lenin, and Trotsky were not politicians but "poets themselves in their political vision," men whose "genius . . . lay in the intensity of their imaginations and in the skill with which through the written and spoken word they were able to arouse others to see human life and history as they did." Nor will he let us forget that they were not proletarian, neither in their culture nor in their politics, although in the latter they identified their interests with the proletariat because they wished to guide it, to give it "intellectual backing." They came from the bourgeoisie, a bourgeoisie that had once been revolutionary, and they respected and valued its literature and wanted the people to have it; and yet – it is the mark of their moral superiority – they had made themselves classless. "They were aiming at a point of view and a culture beyond those of their bourgeois education," Wilson explains, defining his own aim; "but it was a point of view above classes, not a proletarian point of view – they were trying to develop an intellectual discipline which should lay the foundation for 'the first truly human culture.'"

This was the cause in which he enlisted and to which he wished to bring others. It was the cause of civilization itself, whose art and science, he believed, had since the beginning been "straining . . . to deal not with the individual or the class or the nation or the race but with the whole of human life. . . ." By joining with those who would "remodel society by the power of imagination and thought – by acting on life to make something new," the intellectual, he believed, would find true solidarity. To this end, he proposed that the bourgeois writer and the vanguard of the proletariat meet "on the basis of the classless Marxist culture, which is accessible to both – to say nothing of the general democratic culture which Americans have had in common since the days of the village store."

II

In point of time, *Beppo and Beth* comes first, for the time of this comedy is December 1929.[9] The play depicts, as Wilson says, "New York 'sophistication' reeling from the Stock Market crash," and expresses his satisfaction with the economic collapse. Yet, in the character of Beppo who is to some extent the author's persona, it presents the dilemma of an intellectual who is unprepared to see capitalism (his standard of living) go or Communism come. The Chinese servants who deliver the party line, or rather the Marxian analysis of the contradictions of capitalism, speak as Wilson himself did during the early years of the depression, but they are intended to be funny (that they are interchangeable unwearied spokesmen makes them so) and to represent only one point of view, and being Chinese, they are of course outsiders who do not offer an American solution. As for Beppo and Beth, they might stand in for the "Mr. and Mrs. X" of *The American Jitters* (1932), that couple of the salaried upper class who have no authority of their own and do the bidding of higher-ups. For Beppo has renounced political responsibility, is simply a Villager whose successful comic strip of cynical little tigers [10] has enabled him to move uptown. By the end of the play, he decides to refuse to work for Gibbs (Hearst?) and so not to support the tottering system, but his political awareness does not seem to have been widened. His decision represents a return to values he had abandoned in the twenties, not an advance to political action; and he and Beth will go off to Mexico, a primitive and wholesome culture where the artist is neither isolated nor forced to define his relations and responsibilities. In point of time, Beppo's predicament is first, his solution last; for the solution is of the sort that Wilson will himself arrive at in the course of the thirties.

The world of the middle-aged Beppo and Beth is a crazy, empty, neurotic one, a later development of the brave new world of *The Crime in the Whistler Room* and of the disintegrating Village world of *This Room and This Gin and These Sandwiches*. Beppo lives in a swank apartment-hotel that represents the capitalistic system — its speculation, manipulation, underworld connections, and superficial ends of conspicuous comfort and pleasure. He has,

[9] It was written in 1932, and published in 1937.
[10] His comic strip suggests George Herriman's *Krazy Kat*.

as Wilson was fond of saying, compromised with the broker. He was once married to Beth Badger (the pun is intentional), the smart new woman who for the first time replaces the Bills and Daisys of Wilson's previous work and who, significantly, follows the parasitical vocation of interior decorator. Beppo might be an older Simon Delacy who has not outgrown the Menckenian viewpoint. He maintains, for example, that there are only two classes, the "undistinguished mass and the civilized minority," that the mass is unfit to govern, and that politics is a dirty game in which he is not interested. He has even left the Village because he wishes to live a "real civilized existence"; he wants his daughter Mimi, the child of his *vie de bohème*, to be a lady. And now, two months after the crash, he is giving a party in his apartment in the Richelieu-Versailles Hotel. Here, in this shell of the capitalistic system in which he still thinks himself safe, we will see the civilized existence he has chosen to live.

The action of the play depends upon two developments. There are Beppo's personal problems — his new job, the marriage of his daughter to a racketeer, the general difficulty he has with the props of his life, his loneliness. And there is the intrusion and shooting of Luke Bostock, the owner of the Richelieu-Versailles. Though apparently unrelated, each development depends on the other: the collapse of the world that the Bostocks have made — and that the Beppos have allowed them to make — is the cause of Beppo's demoralization. Bostock, the stubborn capitalist who won't stay dead, is finished off in the last act; Beth attempts, and Beppo contemplates, suicide. And both outcomes are the result of the morality of the civilization Bostock has served in his aggressive, self-aggrandizing speculative way and Beppo in his willingness to take a job because it is a "good" job and only the pay matters. The touchstone of this morality is a brief dialogue between Chet, Charlotte, and Dr. Tinker (an amateur psychoanalyst):

Chet. W-what did your young man with the feelings of guilt think he was guilty of?
Dr. Tinker. Swindling people — selling them bad bonds.
Charlotte. How do you know he hadn't?
Dr. Tinker. He had, as a matter of fact.

Chet. Then h-how do you know it was a mother complex?

Dr. Tinker. If he hadn't been a neurotic, he wouldn't have worried about it.[11]

Bostock (Boss-talk) is the spokesman of the romance of American business, a capitalistic dreamer whose living counterpart might be Samuel L. Rothafel, the Roxy of the RKO Roxy Theater and the Radio City Music Hall, who Wilson said was one of those people "who have never recovered from the fantastic ambitions and imaginings engendered by the boom of the twenties." But Bostock, like McGee in *The Crime in the Whistler Room*, is also a folk character whose set speeches give him away. He comes from Connecticut and considers himself a Connecticut Yankee, and he talks in the manner of Lowell Schmaltz in Lewis' *The Man Who Knew Coolidge*. (He even recalls Colonel Sellers. He brags of how he built a million dollar hotel without investing a penny of his own. To which Charlotte replies: "You owe a million dollars, so that makes you a millionaire!") Now the romance of business of Schmaltz is the "triumph of American democracy of the real old-fashioned brand" of the Yankee — and as antidemocratic and socially destructive.

During the war, Bostock tells us, he had been turned away at the Ritz in Paris and had vowed to out-ritz the Ritz.[12] Having "vision" and "the readiness to take risks" — pioneer qualities upon which he says we will have to fall back[13] — he has seized the speculative paper of the twenties and on this foundation built ever larger and more sumptuous hotels. For him the hotel, upon which Henry James had delivered more accurate comments, symbolizes the American dream: "There's Life! Life as it ought to be lived! Glamor! Poetry! Passion! Excitement, Beauty, Success!" A great hotel, he says, was "the dream erection of my vision" and he "climaxed" in the Richelieu-Versailles.[14]

The capitalism of which Bostock speaks so extravagantly has

[11] In "The Case of the Author," Wilson said: "the bond salesman is the type of the whole office class in our society."

[12] So much for the American response to the condescension of foreigners!

[13] This comment is made when he is nearing death!

[14] See Wilson's remarks on the Empire State Building in *The American Jitters*, p. 163. In *The American Earthquake*, where this is reprinted, he has added: "One remembers that the Empire State Building is sometimes known as 'Al Smith's Last Erection.'"

another side. It is allied with the underworld, and we are expected to judge it as a racket. ("We cannot even complain," Wilson wrote in "An Appeal to Progressives," "that the racketeers are breaking the laws which are supposed to be guaranteed by the government, because the government differs little from the racketeers.") In fact, we are expected to find capitalism, that lawless, violent enterprise of robber barons, less worthy of respect than the efficient, crime-reducing racketeering of Jack Payne, the underworld knight-errant who is replacing Bostock. Payne comes out of the world of *The Great Gatsby*. He is a racketeer whom we are supposed to admire for his "frankness and boldness" and toughened awareness of life. But wised-up as he is, he is still a Gatsby who has beat his way in the world because all of his life he has been seeking "a real natural princess that burns with her own power!" This romantic readiness is intended to cast over him something of the purity of motive Fitzgerald tried so hard to attribute to his hero. But in Payne's case, it is borrowed, and even Mimi, to whom it is directed, says that he sounds like a musical comedy. The good life that Payne imagines is symbolized by the freedom (lawlessness) of his yacht, which is not only a symbol, like the hotel, of ultimate glamor but a pirate vessel, the plunderer's escape, much like Dan Cody's yacht in *The Great Gatsby*.

Neither Bostock nor Payne suggests a possible solution to the problem of the crash. They have, as Beppo recognizes, simply won out in the scramble for loot. Even he has scrambled for his share, and in his disillusionment, he finds America "goddam hopeless and stupid." His personal life, like the national life, has been without anything "to hang on to," and he realizes that he himself is responsible, that he is (as Harvey Stone said of Robert Cohn in *The Sun Also Rises*) "a case of arrested development." Driven by "the devils of the mind," he reaches for his gun.

Beppo sees nothing to choose between the "gangsters on one side and [the] Communists on the other." If Communism offers anything, it is the possibility of working for "something and somebody beyond yourself"; but this, apparently, is a possibility, outside any system, that one may choose for himself. It is the option of the artist. Yet as an artist who earns his living by drawing, Beppo has no sympathy with a retreat to "pure art" — all the more so when it is proposed by a kept artist. He does not believe, as

Chet does, that art, even though it "isn't used," is "the only thing left that can keep us from cracking up," or that the individual, eternal work of art justifies "a washed-up generation" on which "the sun may be rising and setting. . . ." Beppo, it seems, is privy to *Axel's Castle*; in his way, he is concerned with the total culture and the usefulness of art within it. American culture, he now realizes, is a "lousy" culture, with "no craftsmanship, no real ideas, no genuine integrity of spirit." These deficiencies answer his question, "How did we land here?" And so does Chet's remark:"The end of the jazz age — Gee Whiz! this is what it was all leading up to!"

At the end, having acknowledged his irresponsibility,[15] Beppo falls back on the "Puritan tradition of protest" as the "one sound thing we've got." In turning to Puritanism, he repudiates the twenties and returns to the old-fashioned values of character that Nick Carraway in *The Great Gatsby* locates in the Middle West.[16] He repudiates the broker and returns to the pioneer — not of course the pioneer to whom Bostock had appealed. "There's something in me," he says early in the play, "that still goes back to the West. . . ." The Mexico to which he will go is simply the West of his imagination, a place that helps him define the self-dependence, moral steadiness, and professionalism with which he would *retrieve* America. His solution is an American one, within the American experience itself, always, as Fitzgerald said of Gatsby's dream, "somewhere back in that vast obscurity . . . where the dark fields of the republic rolled on under the night."

"So still we turned West, as our fathers had done, for the new life we could still hope to find — so we sought to regain that new world which seemed still to be just at hand" — this apparently is what Beppo and Beth do. But these are the words of the narrator of *Memoirs of Hecate County*, an intellectual whose problem is similar to Beppo's. And having experienced more than Beppo — among other things the America of *The American Jitters* and *Travels in Two Democracies* — he gives us one of the summary recognitions of that time: "It was not really a new country any more; it was an old country: we had passed it in history. . . ."

---

[15] In this he is like the Beppo of Byron.
[16] Wilson's generation owes more than it has admitted to men of the temper of Paul Elmer More.

III

October 1930. The first voice we hear in *The American Jitters* is that of Dwight Morrow, the millionaire and former Morgan partner, who is campaigning for Senator in New Jersey. He speaks of the need for confidence (the International Association of Lions' Clubs has proposed that the week of October 19 be set aside as "Business Confidence Week") and of the fibre-strengthening values of adversity. He does not cite the statistics of the National Bureau of Economic Research that show that during the twenties two-thirds of the population lived marginal lives while a few were becoming very rich. He appeals to the moralizing that had once inspired Horatio Algers like himself. But the voice of this "nice little man" has been amplified, is loud and hollow, and Wilson, beginning his survey of depression America, hears in it "the great ventriloquial voice . . . of American capitalism."

At political headquarters in New York City on the night of election day, the Republicans are glum, the Democrats jubilant, the Socialists bitter. The Democrats, celebrating at the Biltmore, have eaten chicken croquettes and French peas; the Socialists at the offices of *The New Leader* on East Fifteenth Street have been drinking coffee out of paper cups. But only Dan O'Brien, the King of the hoboes, cooking his potato-and-onion stew in the little tenement room that is his headquarters, seems to have a concrete proposal. A follower of LaFollette, a veteran of Coxey's Army, the organizer of the first breadline in Washington, D.C., he hopes to lead the unemployed to the Capitol to petition President Hoover for work or unemployment insurance.

In Washington, the House committee investigating Communism interrogates William Z. Foster, Roger Baldwin, and others. For six months, Chairman Hamilton Fish and his colleagues have been looking into Communism. They still seem to be uninformed about the simplest things connected with it, and William Foster, the American-born Communist leader, uses the occasion not only to enlighten them but to spread propaganda. He tells them of the nine million unemployed, of the contradictions of capitalism, of the success of the Five Year Plan in the Soviet Union; and he compares the present revolutionary struggle to that of the American Revolution. He is competent and courageous; but his speech is full of the idiom of Russian Communism, and he is obviously re-

luctant to admit that he is in the pay of the Soviet Union. Roger
Baldwin, the "furious individualist" of the Civil Liberties Union,
is firm and direct, makes a good impression.

The misapplied functionalism of the new building of The New
School for Social Research declares "the lack of meaning for man
in the modern world" and "our helplessness under the industrial
system." The frescoes by Orozco are "overtense and disturbing";
in one of them we see the bald head of Lenin.

The small depositors of the Bank of United States, which
has recently failed, are in a bad way and some have come to City
Hall to appeal to Mayor Walker, who sends an assistant to see
them. A Mr. Littman says: "If this was an earthquake or a flood,
the city would float a loan right away. . . ." To which Mr. Kerri-
gan, the assistant, replies: "But an earthquake is an act of nature. . . ."

At the Metropolitan Opera House, the subscribers listen to *La
Bohème*, a diamond from the European mine of fine arts.

January 1931. The city officials will not permit the Communists
to speak from the steps of City Hall. Their demonstration becomes a riot and mounted police put it down. Bystanders are
unconcerned, clearing it from memory as quickly as the streets
are cleared. The Mayor's assistant offers to pay the one-way fare
to Russia of any ten of the delegation that has come to see him.

February 1931. Detroit, the representative industrial city, with
only one-third of its labor force fully employed. The industrial
process here is spectacular: the transformation of junked old
cars into the shiney models of the new. Various workers speak:
an Englishman named Bert explains the layoff and how one is
bled for Ford's famous wages of $5 a day; a woman tells of the
speed-up and the inevitable accidents; Fred Vogel, busy organizing the auto workers, points out the exploitation of the group
piecework system and cites the figures of the investors' undi-
minished returns. And there is James McRae, who has been to
Brookwood Labor College, but expects nothing from middle-class
movements, only from the Communists who, unfortunately, do
not yet "talk the language of the American worruker"; and Hen-
derson, an American electrician, whose absorption in technical
studies has made him classless. Much is to be learned about the
myth and reality of Henry Ford, the biggest man in town.

Supervising relief in the hill country of Kentucky, Miss Dabney of the Red Cross becomes skeptical about what can be done for ignorant people still taken in by a patent medicine salesman. The county agent tramps into the hills to see whether or not the starving Ingram children have eaten their fingers.

In the ballroom of the Hotel Carlton in Washington, Senator Norris, the old progressive, speaks to the Progressive Conference of the evils of the power trust and the wonder-working efficacy of public opinion. At the Fraternity Club in New York City, H. J. Freyn, an engineer who has been to Russia, tells the members of the Taylor Society, who are not pleased to hear it, that the Russians have put into practice the Society's ideals of humane and efficient management.

Flying from Washington to New York, the author meditates on the Progressive Conference: on the "mixed assortment" of people who were there; on the fact that John Dewey, president of the People's Lobby, was not admitted; on the comfortable circumstances of the intellectuals and the fact that they are afraid to say (as he had two months earlier in "An Appeal to Progressives") that "Capitalism has got to go."

On March 25, Otto Reich, a nineteen-year-old German waiter, unemployed; Irma Meyer, a Jewish housewife with derelict husband; and Mr. Dimiceli, a Sicilian skilled machinist, unemployed, attempt suicide.

With proper ceremonies and armed guards in the halls, the Empire State Building opens on May 1. Intended to be the triumphant expression of the new economic order, it mocks all it surveys and declares bankrupt "the planless competitive society, the dehumanized urban community. . . ." From its fifty-fifth floor, the show floor, the metropolitan region it drains spreads out before one, and over on the Passaic, which is in view, John Dravic, an unemployed worker, having carefully shot his three boys in their sleep, has killed himself.

The People's Lobby goes to Washington to petition President Hoover to call an extra session of Congress, during which, it hopes, appropriations will be passed for public works and unemployment insurance. The President refuses to see the Lobby, having already issued a statement which begins: "I do not propose to call an extra session of Congress. I know of nothing that would so disturb the healing processes now undoubtedly going on. . . . " At Valley Forge, the day before, he told the well-to-do of the "triumph of character and idealism and high intelligence" of the "naked patriots" of other times. Peter Romano, a Sicilian, who has lost almost everything in the crash, has just killed his importunate landlord.

The miners in the company town of Ward, West Virginia, are independent Americans who have been reduced to serfdom. Their victimization and distress is terrible. When they appeal to Governor Conley, they are told: "whatever conditions may be now, we have the best government on earth. We have eliminated all class distinctions. . . ." They had been organized in 1920, but had been deserted by the United Mine Workers' Union, and their own march had been stopped by federal troops. Once again they are eager to organize, and at an out-of-door meeting the officials of the UMWA try to woo them away from the National Mine Workers, a Communist-organized union, and the independent union led by Frank Keeney.

The semifeudal agrarian eighteenth-century world of Cousin Charles, the Tennessee tobacco planter, is attractive, but one can't preach away the evils of industrialism. "Engineers with the scientific imagination, statesmen possessed by principle" must be called in.

Nine Negro boys have been charged with the rape of two white girls on a freight train in Alabama, and are tried at Scottsboro. Eight are found guilty and sentenced to death. The International Labor Defense (a Communist organization) and the National Association for the Advancement of Colored People vie for the direction of the proceedings. The case will be appealed. Meanwhile the Communists' attempt to organize the sharecroppers creates unrest and bloodshed.

A million years ago the great valley in New Mexico through which the Jamez river runs was the crater of a volcano. After its eruption, life had to begin anew, and men appeared who found it "practical to live together" and who organized a classless community. The settlements of the new civilization are dying: eight people still live in the ghost town of Bellamy, two of them prospectors; and nearby, a lumber mill has shut down. The Indian communities survive.

The Indian corn dance attracts white voyeurs whose poverty is spiritual rather than material.[17]

At the Fourth of July celebration at Carlsbad, half of the fireworks display suddenly ignites, and the set piece, a large American flag, goes off prematurely.

The workers on Boulder Dam, a public works project handed over to private construction companies, can no longer stand the terrible heat of Black Canyon, the poor accommodations, and the "systematic skimping." Led by the Wobblies, they have gone on strike. Trusting the government, at its bidding they return to work. Payrates are reduced, and federal police now keep out labor organizers.

In Los Angeles, "the goofs hang like ripe fruit." Its people are "cultivated enervated people, lovers of mixturesque beauty. . . ." They have built all sorts of "god-boxes" and offer one "a thousand assorted faiths . . . from Theophistry to Christian Sirens." The ministers here have private radio stations, and a smut hound like the evangelical Rev. Bob Shuler has used his to become for Southern California the "veritable voice of God." Shuler has the politicians in his hands, and Aimee McPherson, broadcasting from her bridal chamber, has as many hearts and dollars. But Dr. Briegleb, Shuler's rival, is "handicapped by his education and by his Calvinist conviction that religion is authoritative, rigorous and grim!"

Sergei Eisenstein has come to Hollywood, the milltown of culture, at $3,000 a week. The producers do not like the morals of his scenarios. When his contract (and passport) expires, he goes to Mexico.

At the Coronado Beach Hotel, opened in 1887 (the year of the Apache revolt, the founding of the AF of L, and Henry George's campaign for the mayoralty of New York), the convention of the California Federation of Business and Professional Women's Clubs

---

[17] ". . . a most extraordinary population of rich people, writers and artists who pose as Indians, cowboys, prospectors, desperadoes, Mexicans and other nearly extinct species," Wilson wrote Gauss of the sights of New Mexico. "All bearing out my theory about Rimbaud!" He himself was taken with the landscape.

is troubled by the problem of how to use the $20,000 fund they propose to raise. In the hotel's summer house, a boy chalks on a blackboard the latest stock market quotations. Across the bay in San Diego, westward-tending Americans have found "a jumping-off place." The suicide rate of San Diego is the highest in the country.

John Anderson, Canadian wheat farmer, tells how the land was settled and used, and of the farmers, with 130,000,000 bushels of unsold wheat on their hands, who have been reduced to pauperism and to the terrible expedient of striking north into the brush.[18]

October 1931. Back East, winter weather and wage cuts, and 23,000 textile workers at Lawrence, Massachusetts are out on strike.

Mr. Southworth, the company spokesman who has just abruptly left a conference with the plant committee, is not one of "the best people" but their lackey, and the economic crisis has forced him, to his confusion, to become an arrogant master. Sam Bakely, newly graduated from Brookwood, "has Muste for a hero and the morality of socialism for a guide," and, having led the strikers in a march on Monomac Mills, is not surprised to find himself in jail.

The author explains his own case and point of view.[19]

The able-bodied and self-dependent man wandering in a daze along West Fifty-eighth Street is the representative American.

In the course of crossing the continent to do the articles he brought together in *The American Jitters*,[20] Wilson discovered America. "I came out here," he wrote Gauss from New Mexico, "by way of Virginia, West Virginia, Tennessee and Missouri, stopping off for various stories — and America certainly seemed a wonderful country. Its present sour situation is ridiculous." At the time he was doing the early installments, he was discovering Marx, who enabled him to grasp the dramatic aspects of a broken capitalism; and on his travels, he read the Beards' *The Rise of*

[18] Omitted in *The American Earthquake.*
[19] Omitted in *The American Earthquake.*
[20] The English edition was entitled, *Devil Take the Hindmost*, probably as a result of the following in "An Appeal to Progressives": "a system like ours in which everyone is out for himself and devil take the hindmost, with no common purpose and little common culture to give life stability and sense."

American Civilization, which, he told Gauss, "throws more light
for me on affairs in the U.S. than any other history I have ever
read." This reading, and certainly what must have seemed to him
in getting up this book the actual fulfillment of his resolution on
politics, contribute to the mastery that marks, as Gauss rightly
called it, this "adventure in realism."

   In *The American Jitters*, Wilson attempts to do the kind of thing
he appreciated in the work of Dos Passos: to make "a systematic
effort to study all the aspects of America and to take account of
all its elements, to compose them into a picture which makes
some general sense." (He wished to include an essay on Paul
Elmer More, but deferred to Gauss's advice.) As the work of a
bourgeois — one, he admits, who is doing rather well with his writing — it is also the record of the education that confirmed for him
the Marxian diagnoses. Like Steinbeck's *The Grapes of Wrath*,
which it anticipates in many ways and to which it is superior, it
is addressed to the bourgeoisie. By means of what Gauss called
its "realistic presentments," and by means of the subtle transfer-
ences of art, Wilson puts the reader in his own position and makes
him experience, as he has, the shock and indignation that reveal
within him those moral sentiments whose frustration is a source
of class animosity.[21] Contrast does the heavy work, reminding us
of a master who used it to similar ends, whose "Wragg is in cus-
tody" still rings in our ears; of Arnold, who may have taught
Wilson that "there is profit for the spirit in such contrasts . . .
criticism serves the cause of perfection by establishing them."
Everything in this panorama of the slump suggests that Marx's
prophecy is coming true, that the economy and politics and culture of capitalism are bankrupt; yet the book is not doctrinaire
because Wilson is not so much documenting contradictions as
using them to guide his own searching imagination. He is more
artist than propagandist, and one may say of him, without forcing
the comparison, what he says of Eisenstein: that he is "able to work
with the raw materials of life, and he succeeds in absorbing these
— people, landscapes, plants, animals, tools, furniture, clothing
and buildings — into his artist's imagination. . . ."

   [21] ". . . there is no hope for general decency and fair play," he says in
"The Case of the Author," "except from a society where classes are abol-
ished."

What counts most in *The American Jitters* is the effort to study out the land, its idioms and men. Cityscape and landscape are here, and various people, real and imagined, in their habits as they live; and we can hear their voices – it is a book of voices. Nothing in the book is of more importance than these people whom Wilson, as Gauss noted, has made "so simply reasonably human." The statistics of events and the small details that serve as historical landmarks – almost everything is refracted through them.

Toward composition, there is the obvious progression in space and time. This serves admirably the historical and thematic developments that give the reportage the continuity of a narrative. Thus, we move in the course of a year across the country and on the westward trek find that the West no longer provides an economic safety valve. (A Wobbly at Hoover Dam says: " 'Go West, young man!' – but what's the good of telling *me* to go West? I *am* West already!") Returning East, we find the bourgeois leadership still paralyzed and the situation worsening. Having searched the land for "creative statesmanship" and having seen the growing blight of poverty, we understand how the grapes of wrath – of class consciousness – are born. Of this, the great textile strike at Lawrence, Massachusetts is a portent, and although the strike is broken, we are not dismayed. We are not the baffled man in the street, for we have journeyed with the author, have felt the nudging of his art and been emboldened by the liberation from bourgeois ideology that he tells us he has been able to achieve; and we know that there is a direction in which we too can turn, one that seems to be an inevitable outcome of American history.

The articles in which Wilson reported the later and more harrowing stages of the depression were put beside the account of his trip to Russia in *Travels in Two Democracies* (1936). They are not composed in this way. Their coverage seems random, and they give one the sense of a disintegrating civilization. The opening vignette of Election Night, 1932, presents an Anglo-Saxon of fascist mentality, another man in the street whose bafflement has become resentment; the closing glimpses of the New Deal suggest a confusion of purpose in Washington. At the Inaugural of Franklin Delano Roosevelt, the people seem dreary and apathetic

— one feels "a numbness of life running out"; there are machine guns on Capitol Hill; and in the President's speech with its "old pulpit vagueness," one catches even vaguer suggestions of dictatorship. The bankruptcy of capitalism is evident in "Sunshine" Charlie Mitchell, the president of the National City Bank, "a man of low order," now on trial, and in the Buchmanites who evangelize in the ballroom of the Plaza. The desperation of capitalism is evident in the police-instigated violence that breaks the orderly protest march of the Illinois miners, and in the ordering of state troopers to quell the angry dairy farmers of Lewis County, New York. And its ultimate failure is evident in the appalling human detritus of the great cities — of Chicago, for example, where Hull House, founded in 1889 for the amelioration of social misery, can no longer even begin to accomplish its task.

Reading Wilson's reporting now may help one to define further its special strengths. One distinguishes immediately, as Nathan Asch did in the case of Dos Passos, between the reporter and the "artist-reporter," and notes that *The American Jitters*, in spite of its red binding and pulpy paper, is not a proletarian tract of the thirties. It is, as we have seen, a work of imagination and art such as might have been expected from the author of "The Men from Rumplemayer's." But only when one compares the reporting of the twenties with that of the thirties does one come on the element in the latter that contributes so much to its power: the fact that by finding himself in history Wilson found in history a point of reference. His previous reporting takes its significance from the personal relation to events that he invariably adopts, but having only this for its measure does not convey historical awareness so much as a sense of loss. Now, in addition to the personal, his writing has for reference his recently acquired Marxian views of crisis and history and the Beards' complementary account of America. He does not intrude but rather exemplifies these views in the writing, and he acknowledges them in "The Case of the Author." This biographical statement of how he came to Marxism provides both the personal and ideological reference for what he reports. "The Old Stone House" serves a similar purpose in *Travels in Two Democracies*, with this significant difference: the American history he recounted in the ideological portion of "The Case of the Author" is now assimilated into biography; it becomes the history of his family.[22]

And it is only when what Wilson reports has become history that one recognizes that the quality of imagination that keeps these reports alive has been from the beginning a historical one. No one has seen this so clearly as Alfred Kazin, who says of Wilson that he "is not a reporter but a literary artist driven by historical imagination — like Henry Adams and Carlyle." For reasons explained by the very biographical elements Wilson uses in his work, he is especially responsive to social change, and this has made him a recorder of the slightest as well as most cataclysmic tremors of our time. That he considered the crash an earthquake and the depression a social crisis of the magnitude of the Civil War is evidence of a mind both sensitive to the full impact of history and historically aware. The thirties provided a field for his historical imagination, one of the richest occasions for his kind of reporting — reporting, Kazin says, that gives "the impression of actual experience brought to white heat on the page" and, in the succession of its sketches, the "sense of history in motion." [23] Curiously enough, these comments describe the achievement in the writing of history that Wilson ascribes to Michelet; and it is interesting to note that by way of reporting, which quickened his historical imagination, he turned again, after dropping it years before, to

[22] Connected with this assimilation is the considerable wavering in optimism between the two biographical essays. He is no longer as confident of his social role as he was in "The Case of the Author."

[23] The reprinting of Wilson's documentary reports in *The American Earthquake* (1958) gave Kazin an opportunity to characterize the critic he himself — it appears from the dedication of *Contemporaries* — has chosen to follow. His discernment of Wilson's qualities is admirable. He notes Wilson's "instant feeling for the literary image that will convey the feeling of social crisis, for the scene that will instantly evoke a historical moment"; speaks of his instinct for culture and tradition which not only accounts for the sense of shock one finds in the work of this time but for the perspective that saved him later from the disillusionment that disabled writers who had no other background than Communism; finds in his willingness to search out subjects alien to his temperament the "secret of his durability" and in his "habit of willed attention, of strained concentration" the explanation of "the exciting luminousness and tension of his prose"; and, finally, points out the imaginative assimilation and personal accommodation required by the nimble art that keeps this kind of reportage from "relapsing into meaningless." "Edmund Wilson on the Thirties," *Contemporaries*, Boston and Toronto, Little, Brown and Co., 1962, pp. 405–411.)

Michelet's history. By August 1932, he had written for *The New Republic* an enthusiastic article celebrating his rediscovery of Michelet. With it, we may date the beginning of the preoccupation with how to write no less than with how to make history that led him to devote the remainder of the decade to the writing of *To the Finland Station.*

IV

The unity of *Travels in Two Democracies* is formal, not inherent. A prologue and an epilogue, whose moral is the overcoming of self-distrust by courage, and a story on the need for understanding between nations, mediating the American and Russian halves, bind it together. But the book does not cohere. The failure does not lie in the contrast between America and Russia — such a contrast, after all, was as inevitable in the thirties as political discussion — nor in the disparity between a faltering America and a purposive Russia, though one is disturbed by a treatment so obviously less than fair to the one and more than fair to the other. And this is not to say that the reporting is dishonest, but rather that the material of each part is different in kind.

Wilson is not the traveler in America we find him to be in Russia. In Russia, he is an innocent abroad whose naïveté delights us (we are glad for once to find him so much like ourselves!), a traveler who says of some six-winged angels in a Russian church what Huck Finn might have — that they give him the "willies." The Russian portion is a travel book where the American portion is, as we have seen, Wilson's special kind of documentary social reporting. And having no personal stake in Russian society and little saturation in her history, he has no definite way of measuring his experience. Russia, he confesses, eludes him; he is not admitted to her penetralia. The difference, accordingly, is one of initial and deeper social exploration, and in the former the feelings of the author displace the feel of the object they serve in the latter. But, finally, the motives of the respective "travels" are different, as Wilson indicated by reprinting the Russian portion in *Red, Black, Blond and Olive,* a book devoted to studies of national religions and myths. This is a proper disposition because in going to Russia he was above all making a pilgrimage to the tomb of Lenin.

The Russian travels were part of Wilson's preparation for *To
the Finland Station*, whose very title, settled on as early as 1934,
was the result of his response to that moment in history when
Lenin, returning from exile, arrived at the Finland Station in St.
Petersburg. ("Have you read any accounts of the extraordinary
scene that occurred?" he asked Gauss who had not appreciated
the title. "It marked dramatically the first occasion that a trained
Marxist had been able to come in and take hold of a major crisis."
And he wanted, he recalled more than twenty years later in a
passage still warm with enthusiasm, "to contrast this uninteresting
place, accidentally the scene of a climax in man's moral and political life, with the imaginary medieval castle of Villiers de L'Isle
Adam's *Axël*, which had given its name to an earlier book.") By
the autumn of 1934, when he had published under the title of the
book the installments on historians in *The New Republic*, he had
the three sections of the book clearly in mind; and he had begun
to prepare himself for a firsthand encounter with his materials by
learning German. He had also applied for a Guggenheim Fellowship in order to pursue his studies at The Marx-Engels-Lenin Institute in Moscow.[24] When the fellowship was granted in the
spring of 1935, he departed immediately for England, there to
take ship for Leningrad.

Wilson's account of traveling in Russia is as good as any, and
is superior, for example, to that of Joseph Freeman in *An American Testament*. Already, in this first of his travel writings, he
shows himself the insatiable observer — what James said of criticism as an opportunity for intelligence applies in Wilson's case
as readily to travel — and the master of candor who will take his
place among the best travel writers of the age. Travel writing
gives him a great stage, a society — later it will be Western civilization — and with its novel situations, the enthusiasms, hesitancies,
and questionings it occasions, permits him at the same time to
play a major role. All of his writing is self-revelatory, but none
in quite the publically direct way of the travel writing, where for
the sake of fidelity to his experience, and sometimes for the sake
of experience itself, he exposes himself. One thinks, of course, of
an amusing episode, the game of chess with Clavdia Dmítrievna,
the *blondínka* who manages the flophouse at the Ulyánovsk land-

---

[24] Suspected of Trotskyism, he was never admitted.

ing; and there is the more extensive report of the six weeks he
spent recovering from scarlet fever in an Odessa hospital, which
gives us fine glimpses of Wilson reading at night in the operating
room, playing with children and diverting himself with their
books (upon which he writes), and for the first time takes us into
the intimate life of a Russian institution. (We realize here, as in
the addition to the revised version dealing with the critic D. S.
Mirsky, that people more often than things lead Wilson into the
scene; this is an element of his success as a travel writer.) Yet in
speaking of his candor one has in mind something more easily
sensed than stated, something that may account for the fact that
even when his partisanship is evident, one does not, as in Freeman's book, take it for propaganda. Shall we say that for him
Russian Communism is finally not a matter of political logic but
of personal experience, that society must prove itself to him, and
that in travel writing, which he has made a form for treating
relationships of self and society, he has been willing in his own
person to stand in as a witness for mankind? In this, certainly, lies
the uniqueness and boldness of his work, and a challenge to candor as exacting as that of autobiography.

The burden a traveler such as Wilson carries to Russia is his
own expectation, to which is added there the weight of his ignorance. When he reaches his Finland Station he hopes to find a
Utopia that will satisfy his ravenous idealism; but even though
he is fortunate in coming during a season of fairly mild political
weather, there is much in this strange land to disturb him. Of
particular interest is his struggle to remain undaunted — the fact
that his only means of clinging to his belief in Russia as "the
moral top of the world" is the very vision of Lenin with which he
scores her failures.

He had first learned of Lenin in 1917, coming on brief reports
of the Russian revolution in the newspapers he had read while
awaiting at Southampton the embarkment of his army unit; and
Lenin, he realized later when speaking to a young Russian couple
who thought of him as a historical hero, had from that time
figured for him as a "great contemporary." [25] Now, aboard a Rus-

[25] Robert Morss Lovett writes of the postwar years that "only from Russia
was there light breaking on the world" and that "the Bolshevik Revolution
seemed at least one positive result of the war. . . ." (*All Our Years*, New
York, The Viking Press, 1948, p. 178.)

sian ship, he reads in Krúpskaya's memoirs of the terrible price Lenin's generation had paid to make possible the fine young men with whom he is traveling, and noting the Leninist phrases of their conversation he is amazed that "a single man should have impressed upon the thought of a whole people a conception of society and history which changed the very names of past events." To these casual comments much of the narrative of the voyage owes its point: the ship in Western society, and by contrast with its passengers, chiefly the English, the Russians come off very well.

The ship, of course, is bound for Leningrad, where, during his first evening, he sees at the opera a statue of Lenin, "the right arm and hand outstretched and in the eyes a look both piercing and genial, at once as if he were giving back to labor what it had made and inviting it to share in its heritage of culture, and as if he were opening out to humanity as a whole a future of which for the first time in history they were to recognize themselves the masters, with the power to create without fear whatever they had minds to imagine." With this salutation we enter Russian life.

In Leningrad, too, he visits the Museum of the Revolution, where one of the waxworks is a tableau of an official of the old regime at his desk with an album of police suspects before him open to the photographs and identifications of V. I. Ulyánov (Lenin) and Krúpskaya.[26] One photograph shows a young intellectual and idealist, the other a defiant *gamine* — "young people," he adds, "forced from their student days to make decisions and to act, to live out whole lives of thought, political organization, prison, before they are out of their twenties." [27] And he visits the Peter-Paul Fortress, to which Lenin's mother had come to see her son Alexander who had been arrested for taking part in a plot to kill the Tsar and whose execution had made a revolutionary of the younger boy.

Wilson is a sightseer in Leningrad, and the value of what he sees often derives from the imaginative re-creation of what he has read about the object before him. He has hardly anything to say about the Hermitage, though he gives in one sentence an impression of its clutter of valuable and poorly hung pictures. He observes accurately, but he sees best what he has already imag-

[26] Lenin's wife,
[27] The revision of this sentence intensified the original: "whole lives of thought" becomes "whole arduous lives of intellectual activity."

ined, the Peter-Paul prison, for example, where he tells us that in former times the guards had walked silently in soft shoes and men had gone mad in dark rooms and Kropótkin "had rapped out for the man in the next cell the history of the Paris Commune." A fascination of travel books, especially those by literary men, is just such matching of imagination with fact; and as fascinating here, where so much depends on what one imagines — not only the political value but the very interest of the book — is the increasing difficulty of doing this.

Having settled in Moscow and become more familiar with Russian life, he is troubled by the discrepancy between Leninist ideals and Stalinist facts. Sometimes, in the attempt to save Russia for himself, he makes errors of generous interpretation, as in his report on the Park of Culture and Rest. He sees the colorless "limbo" and the pale quiet people — their behavior, he suggests, is a carryover from their "old subhuman life of serfdom"; they had not yet discovered how human beings enjoy themselves. He is aware of the amusements that train them for aviation and war and the museum that exhibits for the edification of the young pictures of Nazi atrocities; he acknowledges the poor cultural fare. Yet he believes that these people have a new freedom, that their careful conduct is to be explained by the fact that they own the park and in them "a new kind of public conscience" has developed. He learns later, only to suppress it, that the simple explanation of what he has seen is fear; and having been to the Sokólniki Gardens, a resort of the privileged, he knows that the lack of social self-consciousness he finds in the Park of Culture and Rest has been achieved by exclusion — he knows what he confessed later he had "purposely soft-pedalled": that class stratification is already well advanced.

He does not, however, suppress his disgust with the apotheosis of Stalin. Glorification of the leader, he says, "is undoubtedly one of the things which affects an American most unpleasantly."[28] He may explain it as an almost inevitable result of the tradition of paternalistic government not yet left behind by the untrained

[28] In the revised version, Wilson tells of meeting Paul Strand, the photographer, in a travel agency and commenting in the presence of the office personnel in "our irreverent American way" on the difficulty of getting an authorization: " 'Comrade Stalin has just stepped out to the toilet'; 'Comrade Stalin is at home with a severe headache.' "

proletariat and what he considers the real identification of will between the people and their leader, but he wonders nevertheless if Stalin is wise "to allow this deification to be carried as far as it is." The cult of the leader, he insists, has "nothing to do with Marxism and is not justified by a socialist dictatorship." And for proof there is the example of Lenin: "Lenin was irreverent toward himself in the sense that he took himself seriously only as the agent of his cause. He cared nothing about power for its own sake; nothing about admiration. He always confessed and lamented his human errors of judgment. One cannot imagine Lenin, for all the popular devotion he commanded, allowing himself to be cast in a role such as that now assumed by Stalin. . . ."

With Lenin, Wilson beats down Stalin, and in the course of doing so exalts the humanity of the man he believes to be superior to Jesus. Reading in Suvárin's book on Stalin of the dictator's apprenticeship in denunciation, Wilson notes that Stalin "is certainly suspicious and intolerant where Lenin, through his own sincerity and his belief in the good faith of others, created that good faith itself." And examples follow, one of which seems almost scriptural: "Was not the young officer who came to kill Lenin so moved by the 'kind and simple face; face and eyes smiling at me, warm with tenderness and love,' that he could not bring himself to throw his hand grenade? — and did not Lenin laugh over the incident and have the man released?" Again, at the end of the section on Moscow, where Wilson discusses the hierarchical structure of Soviet society, he makes an occasion for this eloquent tribute to Lenin:

But Lenin himself had not only got outside class society, he had got also beyond the kind of society where inequalities of ability are unequally remunerated. I was told by the wife of a commissar of her calling on Krúpskaya in the Kremlin. There were no comforts in the apartment, she said; no ornaments, except pictures of Lenin. Preoccupied from her student days with workers' education and agitation, after a lifetime of meager and impermanent lodgings in all the countries of Europe, having lost long ago with Lenin, in concentration on their all-demanding vigilance for the fate of human society as a whole, any sense of her own right as a human being to beauty or recreation or rest, now, at sixty-six, her cause brought to victory, with those who had never had anything and whom she had labored to set free enjoying their little luxuries and amenities and herself at last lodged in security under the golden spires of the Kremlin, she seemed never to have noticed her furniture, never to have looked at her walls. To such a deliverance from material things the materialistic conception of history had led! It was characteristic of Lenin as of Marx — it was the mainspring of the whole Marxist system — that he was impatient of a world in which the things that men needed were reckoned in terms of money and went always to the highest bidder. And he insisted, in the very act of seizing power, that all he was doing was being done in the name of the day when neither capitalist dollars nor socialist rubles would have value. The Soviet Union are still far from that day; the people still work for money, and even the governing groups still work for more money than their neighbors. But they know that their state is not dedicated, as the capitalist governments are, to the mere preservation of the status quo in the interests of a propertied class. It is based on the bare walls and plain furniture of Lenin's and Krúpskaya's lodgings.[29]

The major incident of Wilson's "Volga Idyll" is the stopover he made at Ulyánovsk in order to visit the Lenin Museum; an unusual stopover, he explains in the revised version, made over the protests of his Intourist guide. Yet for some reason, he does not exploit the materials he has taken so much trouble to gather. In a few words, with the promise of more elsewhere, he describes the Ulyánov house, mentioning in a casual way the impression he was to make so much of when he painstakingly described the house in *To the Finland Station* — that it reminded him of "the houses of cultivated New Englanders as I used to see them in my youth." Perhaps he was depressed by the fact that here, forgotten and neglected, was the only thing in Russia with which he was able to identify; depressed in the presence of this house, at once the equivalent of the old stone house and the house of the eighties, by the anxiety he had recently felt on returning to Talcottville — depressed anew, with the example of Lenin before him, by his own halting course, his inability to leave the past behind. "So that is what it had been like," he writes, "the life of the educated middle class out of which Lenin had come — breaking out of the mold himself and leaving the old town where he had been bred . . . to disintegrate in the rain."

How deeply Lenin has stirred him! how much Lenin is in his mind! And when he casts up the sum of his impressions, balancing all that he finds wrong, in fact canceling it, is the phenomenon of Lenin. He will not have him venerated as a saint, yet he is awed

[29] See also *To the Finland Station*, pp. 417–418; Anchor edition, pp. 415–416.

by the queues of people that in all weather move toward his tomb under the Kremlin wall. And there, at the end of the travels, we find him moving with them past the exquisite and beautiful face and speaking the thoughts he would have them speak. "Here," he says, "has humanity bred, independent of all the old disciplines, the socialist whose study is humanity, the poet whose material is not images but the water and salt of human beings — the superior man who has burst out of the classes and claimed all that is superior which man has done for the refinement of mankind as a whole." Here is the fragile shell of the man who forced the world "to expand its conception of what man, as man alone, can accomplish. . . ."[30]

In its way this moving ending anticipates the strategy of the ending of *To the Finland Station.* Just as there we are not permitted to go beyond the moment of Lenin's arrival in Russia on April 16, 1917, so here, in this study of the most recent phase of the society Lenin had established, we are turned away from its actualities by the fervent praise of its founder. This, and perhaps the suppressions, are excusable when one realizes that Wilson's primary aim is not to introduce the Soviet Union to Americans but to change the minds of Americans about the possibilities of socialism. His task in the thirties, as he proposed it in "Brokers and Pioneers," is to be the "engineer of ideas" who takes down the old structure of thought and relays the foundations of the mind. He must go to Russia because only there can he have the experience of socialism, and for his purpose he must maintain, while noting the defects of some of the forms it has taken in Russia, a sense of its attractiveness. The gross contrast between the halves of his

[30] Consider the following description by E. E. Cummings of his experience at Lenin's Tomb as originally presented in his account of Russia in *Eimi* (1933): "On Saturday, May thirtieth, nineteen hundred and thirty-one, in the desolate city of Moscow, I glimpse an apparently endless line of unimaginably uncouth figures (each a tovarich or comrade; a soi-disant citizen of the subhuman superstate USSR) moving imperceptibly toward, and disappearing into, the tomb of their human god Lenin. . . . As the line unmovingly moves, I enter the tomb; I descend; I view the human god Lenin [the description in *Eimi*: "forcelessly shut rightclaw / leftfin unshut limply / & a small-not-intense head & a face-without-wrinkles & a reddish beard"]; I ascend; I emerge — and then (breathing fresh air once more) I marvel: not so much at what I have, as at what I have not seen." (*i: six nonlectures,* Cambridge, Harvard University Press, 1953, p. 99.)

Travels works to this end, as do the more subtle, not fully ex-
ploited notations of European travel and of his reading of Gibbon.
In London, the garbage scavengers remind him of depression
Chicago, and, returning to the West by railroad, he notices such
telltale signs as the Nazis' baiting of the Jews and the *rigor mortis*
of Paris. This helps to reverberate the comment, made in connection with Gibbon, that news of Hitler and of the Italo-Abyssinian
War had made him feel "very sharply that the existence of the
Soviet Union, with all of its slowness and rubbish . . . was
the only guarantee in Europe against another such ebb of civilization."

It is to his purpose also to rid Americans of the feeling of
strangeness that Russia evokes in them. He tries therefore to establish common ground between America and Russia: historically,
by representing Russia's present period as equivalent to our own
period of pioneering and her position in relation to "old systems"
and to the world as equivalent to ours after the American Revolution; geographically, by noting in scenes of Russian landscape the
likeness to the American wild. Both join in such a casual observation as "Log houses like America and not like Europe," and in the
reverie on characters from nineteenth-century Russian fiction in
which he says, "They had come back as we had done at home to a
straggling provincial civilization among prairies and wild rivers
and forests, bringing books and manners from Europe. . . ." He
visits a *dácha* "not unlike" the cottages on the New Jersey coast,
and unlike them too, and then again familiar because of what we
know of them from Chekhov's plays. The center of Moscow, he
finds, is like an American city.

But familiarity with Russia does not further this rather superficial kind of accommodation, and, as defects appear in the Russian system, Wilson uses them as occasions to point out—it is
his most cherished idea—that America, not Russia, provides the
better foundation for socialism. With Stalin for contrast, the president whom at the Inaugural he feared might become a dictator
is now "the humblest of public servants"; and when compared to
the docile and timid and manipulated Russians, the Americans,
readers though they may be of the Hearst papers, are critical and
self-reliant citizens who have, he claims, "certainly learned something about self-government. . . ." In Russia, he realizes as never

before that "being an American did mean something unique";
that "Americanism" is a valid concept — there were American attitudes, an American character, for hadn't F., the Slavic girl whom
he had taken to a Soviet film in New York, been embarrassed by
the Russian squalor and ashamed that her people had come from
the Ukraine? [31] Russia convinces him, as he explains significantly
in the paragraph preceding the account of his experience at
Lenin's tomb, that American republican institutions have "some
permanent and absolute value" and that they will not be destroyed
in the transition to socialism but will in fact make that transition
easier. For socialism, which in the simplest sense is a high general
standard of living secured by guaranteeing the people the benefit
of their labor, has everything to gain from a democratic system.
The case for socialism, he maintains, "could be made out in the
United States on the basis of the American tradition and com-
monly accepted principles," and from this point of view it would
appear that "the socialist ideal is more natural to us than to the
Russians."

At the beginning of the Russian travels, Wilson admonishes the
American who is "likely to have a vision of the Soviet Union as
simply the United States plus one's ideal of socialism." One lesson
of the travels is that Russia is not like that; another lesson, it seems,
is that the new society will be.

V

To the Finland Station, Wilson's most substantial
effort toward redirecting the bourgeois mind, is neither the systematic account of the writing of history that Gauss, his mentor
in matters of history, hoped it would be, nor, as Wilson himself
knew and critics were quick to point out, an adequate account
of the philosophical background of Marxism. Like so much of his
work, the book was the product of personal education — of the
need at the beginning of the thirties to reorient himself by mastering a new body of thought and of the need at the end of the decade
to salvage from the ruin of radical politics what was precious in it.
The writing of history which began in his own historical investigations of the origins of socialism was, it turned out, a way of

[31] F. is the prototype of Anna in *Memoirs of Hecate County.*

doing this; for by writing history he made, as he said of Michelet, "the centuries of the dead keep him company and lend him their strength and their faith that he might wake strength and faith in the living."

Three years after the publication of *Finland Station* in 1940, Wilson spoke in "Thoughts on Being Bibliographed" of its place in the program of his journalistic work. He considered it a part of the double task that the cultural situation in America had required of the critic: that he explain the difficult new art of the time (which he had done in *Axel's Castle*) and that he "bring home to the 'bourgeois' intellectual world the most recent developments of Marxism. . . ." But in speaking in this way he submerges his education in its public context and thereby asks us to forget his intense engagement in the thirties; and he startles us into an awareness of the fact that a few short years, by disturbing the continuity of culture, have given him the perspective of a lifetime.

Though some of the contents of the book had been printed serially in 1934, 1937, and 1938, it remains an irony of its publication that it appeared too late to do the work he had, at least at the start, expected it to do. That it appeared when it did accounts for the imprint on it of both the enthusiasm and disillusionment of the Left in the thirties. Gauss defined the character of the book at its inception when he called it a *"Discours de Combat* to intellectuals," and the enthusiasm that drives through its pages is explained by a remark in "Thoughts on Being Bibliographed": "The young intellectuals of the thirties *did* want to join Marx and Lenin in their great field of intellectual historical action." There, too, one finds an explanation of the disillusionment that pressed upon Wilson the necessity of saving Marxism from the doctrinaire Marxists: "within the decade . . . the young journalists and novelists and poets who had tried to base their dreams on bedrock, had the spectacle, not of the advent of 'the first truly human culture,' the ideal of Lenin and Trotsky, but of the rapid domination of Europe by the state socialism of Hitler and Stalin. . . ." That the book appeared at all testifies to Wilson's doggedness; even more, to an unwavering faith in a humanistic tradition of which for him the achievements of the pioneer Marxists are a continuation and a great vindication. To keep alive this tradition will increasingly become his work. He dedicates himself to it in "At Laurelwood," written during the composition of the book, and in "Mr. Rolfe," written a few years afterward.[32] Excursions into the past will kindle his faith in it, but none will give it, as this one does, an intensity so glowing. For here, in history which might without paradox be spoken of as contemporary, his whole being is moved by his master passion, the passion for justice.

There are other books whose treatment of historiography or of Marxism is more serviceable; few so singularly personal and in-spiriting. Meyer Schapiro's brilliant review of the book in *Partisan Review* locates one source of its power: "the revolutionary per-sonality," which, Schapiro says, is the book's real subject. And it is true, as he points out, that Wilson's primary interest is in the heroic personalities who devoted themselves to the revolutionary task, that his sympathy for creative and disinterested minds is unfailing, and that the most memorable parts of the book are the accounts of the men — those masterly characterizations which "impose themselves by their concreteness, finesse and sympathy, and by the intelligent correlation with the documented actions and words of these men, like the great fictional characters of litera-ture." *Finland Station* is a revolutionist's Plutarch's *Lives*.

Biography is the foundation of the book. The lives of men pro-vide the perspective of events, and this is why, with Wilson, psychology accompanies history. The psychological approach is essential to one who believes, as Wilson does, that men make history as they make works of art — out of psychic travail; and it supports his philosophically idealistic notion of creativity as well as his insistence on the work of individuals. (The pioneers of so-cialism in his history are all great individuals.) But this approach is most important to him because it contributes to the process of identification by which he moves into his subject and because only in this way can he find in his own experience the materials with which he reconstitutes the life of the past. Michelet taught him these necessities of the *reconstitution intégrale du passé*, and he will say of Taine, when judging his accomplishment against Michelet's, that though he "can read all the documents on a great social struggle as he can read any other books, there is nothing

---

[32] They may be considered installments of what Gauss suggested might become his "Pilgrim's Progress."

in his own personality or experience which enables him to re-create in imagination the realities these documents represent." What there is in Wilson's personality or experience that enables him to bring to life the portion of history he presents is explained in part by Schapiro's observation that in *Finland Station* "the condition of intellectual work becomes as concrete, as unforgettable, as the moments of action." He knows the arduousness of the intellectual life, and the actors in his history are mostly intellectuals. Yet, as we shall see, he is enabled by more than this; that he "turn[s] himself inside out in his books" is as true of him as he believes it is of Michelet.

Lifted from the text, many of the individual portraits — those of Michelet, Lassalle, Bakúnin, Engels, Trotsky, Lenin, and especially that of Marx, the most searching and detailed — could be placed in *The Wound and the Bow*, where Wilson studies the relevance to art of the psychic wound. But in the text, they work in behalf of history, so that in these lives we have a chronicle of the major crises from the French Revolution to the Russian Revolution. And what better windows could we have for looking out on this history? Professional historians, familiar with events, may overlook the chronicle in their fascination with the character drawing; to the common reader, however, the chronicle is also a source of lively interest. Psychologically, Wilson makes much of the relativity of character, of the technique, common to both Michelet and Proust, of presenting a character at different stages of his career; and in organizing the book he makes much of a few significant events — the most important structurally is the Paris Commune of 1871 — which figure in the lives of many of the characters. Though the first section on the French bourgeois historians has a retrograde movement, the remainder of the book moves forward with ever-quickening pace, and the movement of events, so necessary to the reconstitution of the past, is not lost in the portraiture. We acquire a sense of what is happening in France, Germany, and Russia, the major scenes of action; a sense of the miseries and ugliness of industrialism, especially as Marx and Engels knew them in England; and even some acquaintance with the communitarian experiments that are being tried in America. And all the while we are being moved by the spectacle of human aspiration, the very pulse of this history; by the nobility of these men, so full of the energies of thought and action, who are learn-ing in response to events to become their masters in the future.

But if we attend more closely, we find that we are also being moved by the historian who, as a consequence of his psychologi-cal method, has himself become implicated in history. We are told by Eleanor Perényi, in a recent sketch of Wilson in *Esquire*, that in writing of Marx's tribulation with boils he was himself similarly afflicted. Throughout the history we feel this power of sympathy: that by identifying so closely with the men Wilson has identified as closely with their cause,[33] has as intensely experi-enced their struggle as he has Marx's boils, and has therefore earned the exaltation of the moment when Lenin, at the Finland Station, takes history into his hands. It is just because of this iden-tification that at times the history becomes a personal and con-temporary parable and that Wilson takes issue with men and ideas in such a personal way.

The book, of course, had its occasion in the contemporary social crisis. As Wilson explained to Gauss, the purpose of the first sec-tion was "to show the dying out of the bourgeois revolutionary tradition as a prelude to presenting the rise of Marxism" — a pur-pose also served at this time by his own social reporting. And one of the things he said he wanted to do in the chapters on Renan, Taine, and Anatole France was "to disarm the bourgeois liberal reader's objections to Marxism by reviewing the various liberal attitudes — exemplified by these French writers and stated as eloquently as they can be stated, all attitudes which are still cur-rent today — and by showing their relation to social class and to fear of socialism." He addressed *Finland Station*, as he had some of his most aggressive articles of the early thirties, to the tem-porizing liberals, and by means of a few points of reference re-minded them of their experience since the war. The moral of the German Social Democrats who voted for war credits was clear enough, as was that of the French bourgeois intellectuals who had withdrawn from politics. And there was Babeuf, with whom Wil-son began the account of the origins of socialism, whose defense in court was fashioned by him to recall that of Sacco and Vanzetti; there was even the not altogether far-fetched comparison of the young Marx and Engels to Mencken and Nathan. So by shaming

[33] The identification also works the other way.

the liberals, then arousing their sense of justice and setting before them noble exemplars, he summoned them to that action on which his heart was set.[34]

Yet the book may have appealed most to liberals in just those places where Wilson, again as a result of contemporary events, was forced to address the Marxists. His case histories of the revolutionary personality are not always attractive. We feel his weight most in his insistence on judging the moral qualities of men and the moral consequences of ideas; and he judges men and ideas not by any "revolutionary" standard of pragmatism or Realpolitik but by the "absolute" standard of the bourgeoisie. As he presents them, these revolutionists are not strange, they are very much like ourselves. They have formed their characters in bourgeois households and have mounted their revolutionary thought on bourgeois culture, and in leading the proletariat they have no intention of bringing about the subversion of cultural standards that Ortega meant by "the revolt of the masses." They are not of the breed of contemporary doctrinaire Marxists who have abandoned bourgeois moral principles for the "myth" of the Dialectic and who, on this account, may be said to have betrayed the ideal of the first truly human culture. To be accurate in speaking of Wilson's revolutionary personalities, we should add the modifier "bourgeois." They are bourgeois revolutionary personalities, men of the middle class who transcended their class by becoming, as Wilson indicated in the title of the series that contained his first article on Marx, "critics of the middle class."

The dialectical structure of *Finland Station* is amusing in view of Wilson's attack on the Dialectic, but it is not important. If it owes something to Hegel and Marx, it owes more to Wilson's inveterate habit of staging discordant encounters — to the liberal

[34] The subtitle of the book — "A Study in the Writing and Acting of History" — describes more accurately Wilson's personal theme and directive than the substance of the book. He adumbrates the subject, and there is not, as he would have us believe, either dialectical necessity or historical development in his presentation of the movement from writing to acting. His is simply the case of another American scholar who, in having had too much contemplation and too little action, chooses action in order to claim for intellectuals a more direct power in the determination of affairs. In doing this, however, he has consulted his idealism rather than his gifts for statesmanship. He is not a "doer" but a "sayer" who by saying does most.

tradition of discussion, seemingly peaceful, in Justice Holmes's phrase, a "free trade of ideas," yet not without combativeness, as Holmes made clear in speaking of it as "the competition of the market." The dialectical turns of the book are simply a part of its rhetoric; their function is polemical.

What is important in considering the book is the fact that Michelet and Lenin enclose it. Jules Michelet, the son of a Parisian printer who had been ruined by Napoleon's suppression of the press, and Lenin, the son of a Russian civil servant whose liberalizing educational work had been undone by Alexander III; Michelet, the writer of history *par excellence*, Lenin, his peer among the actors of history; Michelet, upholder of Enlightenment thought and fierce partisan of the unfinished French Revolution, Lenin, a man of the Enlightenment also, and a maker of revolution — these are the greatest of Wilson's great men. And Michelet, with whom he begins the book so exultantly, gives him the two major themes so splendidly embodied by Lenin: that humanity creates itself and that the truly superior man is he who most completely represents the people.

Wilson is excited by the rediscovery of Michelet — it is as much an advent in his life as the discovery of Vico was in Michelet's — because he finds in him the assumptions of his own thought. He too believes that human society has an organic character and that to reconstitute its past is to bring it before us in all its fullness and living complexity. (If he notes the fact that life overflows the containers of written history, it is not to lament the historian's impossible task but to pay tribute to the life he himself pursues and whose diminishing depresses him.) Also his is Michelet's view of history as " 'the war of man against nature, of spirit against matter, of liberty against fatality' "; a view of human destiny which may serve as a summary statement of the deepest conflicts in *Discordant Encounters* and of an idealistic faith whose basic article is not the denial of matter but rather an acknowledgment of man's struggle with it and, in that unending struggle, of the creative agency of ideas that makes it meaningful and progressive.

Lacking such an idealistic faith, Renan, Taine, and Anatole France seem also to lack the power of reconstituting the past. In Renan's hands, history becomes a skeleton of ideas; in Taine's, a categorizing that squeezes from it the living drama; in France's, a pursuit of the essences of periods, an exercise in historical imagination. From participation and faith to withdrawal and skepticism — this is the course of decline from Michelet's revolutionary ardor traced by these historians. Academics (Renan and Taine are "members of learned castes"), confined to the library and the study (France is no longer quite the exemplary public man Wilson had made of him only a few years before), they are counterparts of the Symbolists of *Axel's Castle* who once more appear to bring this section on "foreclosures" to an end in the present. Like the Symbolists, they have lost an organic connection, have "completely dissolved . . . the relation between the rioter in the street and the scholar in his study. . . ."

There are other historians in the nineteenth century with whom we could plot a less dismal curve, but neither this nor the fact that the historians in question did not provide a dialectical foil for the Marxists, is to the point. The climate of opinion represented by these historians did — and continued to — exist; and Wilson's primary purpose was not to explain the logic of history but to dispel a gloomy by a brighter weather. He appeals, finally, to our desire for spiritual health: he presents two movements from the same period of history, two psychic curves, one morally and spiritually downward to passivity and despair, the other morally and spiritually upward to activity and exuberance. The show of dialectic is sleight of hand, and in what he actually does we detect something of the diabolic-idealism he attributed to Marx. Above all, he would have us feel as Michelet tells us he felt, that "'Action, action! action alone can console us! We owe it not only to man, but to all that lower nature which struggles up toward man, which contains the potentiality of his thought — to carry on vigorously thought and action.'"

With Babeuf, Wilson is able to return to the French Revolution and begin anew at the pitch of passion. The Directory had frustrated the ideals of the Revolution and arraigned Babeuf, who, after Thermidor, had insisted on its original aims. His defense in court, artfully rehearsed by Wilson, is, as he says, "a summing-up of the unrealized ideas of the Enlightenment and vindication of their necessity." It is, in addition, a prototypal situation: the self-defense that in turn arraigns an entire society, a dramatic moment in the life of a revolutionary and one that seldom fails to stir our sense of justice.[35]

But with Babeuf condemned, we seem to be condemned to the long and painful workings of the Dialectic. Already familiar with those historians who followed Babeuf and who lacked the will to change the world, we must now meet the Utopians, among the more prominent Saint-Simon, Fourier, and Owen, who had the will to change the world but not a historical understanding of the real mechanism of social change; meet them before we can come to the Marxists who command the scene because they have both the will to change the world and the historical understanding of how to do it. The chapters on the Utopians are the least satisfactory just because the Utopians have no genuine dialectical historical necessity. Saint-Simon (added at Gauss's behest) and the others seem only to point the moral of the futility of generous idealism spent on private schemes and small social enterprises. But there is a current of nostalgia, especially in the discussion of American community experiments, that suggests personal reasons for their inclusion.

That so many Utopians tried their experiments in America subtly supports Wilson's feeling that Europe is beyond redemption and that America is the proper field for socialism. And his reminiscence of the phalanstery at Red Bank provides a fixed point in terms of which, perhaps unconsciously, he orients himself in history. "Here," he writes of the community at Red Bank, "was the center of that pastoral little world through which, as one of the Fourierists said, they had been 'desirous of escaping from the present hollowhearted state of civilized society, in which fraud and heartless competition grind the more noble-minded of our citizens to the dust'; where they had hoped to lead the way for their age, through their resolute stand and pure example, toward an ideal of firm human fellowship, of planned production, happy labor, high culture — all those things from which the life of society

---

[35] Foster did not forget its possibilities when confronted by the Fish committee. Wilson himself enacts a similar role in his defense of Dorothy Perkins. This situation may be considered the representative anecdote of revolution and it compels his imagination because in every case it is a moral victory of the underdog and the individual. It is the kind of situation that one, thwarted by a boy with the pony-cart, might imagine for consolation.

seemed so strangely to be heading away." And here, one might say, is the vision of society most congenial to him, a society not of the proletariat but of the noble-minded such as he found later at Degániya in the desert waste of Israel; a society, moreover, for whose foundation something at once more wonderful and less mysterious than the Dialectic is needed, the very thing in fact that moves through the dialectic of humanity — the spirit of creativeness and endurance of man himself.

This is the point Wilson makes by placing his criticism of the "myth" of the Dialectic within the framework of his portraits of Marx and Engels. We are not to forget that thought is projection and that this is both its glory and shame. Thought arises in the mind of man: this makes it suspect, yet keeps it human. Those very portraits which disclose for us the peculiar germ of a seed of thought are not intended so much to discredit thought as to summon our respect for what man can do. And it is Wilson's purpose, as Schapiro notes, to show that the revolutionary movement is the result of the peculiarities of men; that the whole human being is involved in thought and action, and that historical effectiveness therefore depends on moral qualities as well as on intellect or will.

Wilson admires in Marx the strength of character that enabled him to break all bourgeois ties and the intellectual powers that he brought to the service and defense of primary human rights. But his bourgeois sense of decency is offended by what Marx made others pay and do for him. He finds inexcusable Marx's demands and insensitivity in his friendship with Engels; the poverty Marx forced his wife and children to endure pains him; and though he sees the necessity, he does not condone Marx's tactics with Proudhon and Weitling. The Marx whose Promethean-Satanic impulses Wilson uncovers in his youthful writing is later revealed as hateful and revengeful, anal and sadistic, a spirit who denies — in his later years he was familiarly known as "Old Nick." He is a man of infirmities, of neurotic traits; a relentlessly misanthropic man whose sneers, Wilson says, "are the true expression of his nature. . . ." By contrast there is the steady and genial Engels, the revolutionary writer who also runs a factory in Manchester and enjoys such delights as horseback riding. With him it is easier to identify, as Wilson does in recounting the walk through France to Switzerland during which Engels repaid the hospitality of the villagers by drawing caricatures for their children; it is easier to identify with a man as "complete" in his way as the ideal man of the Renaissance. But the closer because deeper identification is with Marx who, Wilson says, made up for what he lacked of Engels' practical ability and athletic skill by "the immense range of his mind." One finds in Wilson similar diabolic-idealistic traits,[36] though not in the extreme forms they take in Marx, and time will reveal in him the Old Testament prophet he finds in Marx. And finally it is with Marx that he dwells longest and tells most completely the story of the generations that means so much to him. He is aware of what a family line is called upon to pay for "genius" — of Heinrich Marx's anxieties for his son, the erosion of Jenny Marx's nerves in her life with Karl, the dreadful furies that pursued his children. For him the single sentence he placed in isolation on the page at the end of this family chronicle — "Such pain and such effort it cost to build a stronghold for the mind and the will outside the makeshifts of human society" — for him this sentence most fully acknowledges his awareness of the broader human base that supports the great men who, in his account, are the moving force of history.

Wilson upholds this hard-won humanism by attacking the "myth" of Dialectic. He stands with Proudhon who told Marx: "let us not set ourselves up as leaders of a new intolerance, let us not pose as the apostles of a new religion. . . ." His attack, however, is not directed towards Marx and Engels, who after all never worked out the implications of the Dialectic, but towards the Marxists of the present who have joined the "Church" of the Dialectic — the Stalinists for whom the Dialectic is the established creed. It is this that accounts for his inordinate attack: he places all the blame for the inconsistencies and errors of Marxism on the "evil" Dialectic, discounts it by attributing it to the German proclivity for metaphysics (he regards metaphysics as "the poetry of imaginative people who think in abstractions instead of images"; metaphysics and German thought are two provinces he has not inhabited), and ridicules it by tracing its triadic character through the Trinity and Plato and Pythagoras to the male sex organs. Under attack Marxism becomes for him the monolithic

[36] See "Morose Ben Jonson," *The Triple Thinkers* (revised edition).

system Calvinism was for Oliver Wendell Holmes, and he hopes by destroying its keystone to see it collapse like the Deacon's "One-Hoss Shay."

The grounds of his disapproval as well as limited approval are humanistic. He approves of the Dialectic insofar as it represents "the idea that the human spirit will be able to master its animal nature through reason"; and he stresses the reciprocal interactions of its process because this makes an opening for the agency of ideas. What he disapproves of most is the fact that under the "disguise" of the Dialectic, history has become History, "a semi-divine principle . . . to which it is possible to shift the human responsibility for thinking, for deciding, for acting. . . ." At no point is he more adamant than where he insists on the absolute evil of lying and killing, actions (means) whose moral value those armed with the Dialectic would defer for judgment until the working-out of History. For Wilson history is dialectical, if not Dialectical; it is a process, but its end is not assured; nor is it certain that the proletariat, the chosen instrument of the Dialectic, will serve to advance it. The process whose relentless movement Marx did nothing to humanize is not attractive to him. The imperfectly realized brotherhoods of the Utopians mean more to him, it seems, than the human brotherhood that he says Marx put off until the coming of the Dialectical millennium.

The chapter on "The Myth of the Dialectic" appeared in the Fall 1938 issue of *Partisan Review*, where it was followed by a rejoinder by William Phillips entitled "The Devil Theory of the Dialectic." Phillips' criticism of Wilson's views, which anticipated Schapiro's verdict of "crude autopsy," did not prompt him to reconsider the chapter. Instead, in what immediately follows, he adopts a deceptive mildness. By showing how an understanding of the Dialectic made Marx a penetrating social critic in those books which make his reputation as a historian, by praising the flexibility of his mind and his love of learning for its own sake, he turns his praise into censure of the narrow-minded and the doctrinaire. And then, in his treatment of Marx as the "poet of commodities," he resumes the attack.

His strategy here is to consider *Das Kapital* as a work of the imagination and, as Schapiro complained because it proved unflattering to both, "to find resemblances between theory and

character. . . ." No one takes seriously Wilson's curious notions
— that Engels' lucid prose was due to his French Protestant blood,
Lenin's diligence to his mother's German blood, Marx's system-
breaking to his Jewishness and his severity to the Old Testament.
But this is not to say, as Schapiro would like to, that there is no
necessary connection between the obsessed Marx of Wilson's portrait and his book. There is a moralist as well as an economic historian in *Das Kapital.* And it is the historian and not the moralist
whom Wilson believes to be mistaken: the historian with his Labor
Theory of Value, his crude class psychology, his misplaced faith
in the proletariat, and his ignorance of American democracy, not
the moralist drawing from the Enlightenment faith in human
rights and equality and from his own tormented spirit the acid of
his indictment of the age. That psychological criticism so often
lends itself to debunking is reason enough to be wary of it, but
Wilson's criticism, even in *Finland Station* where it replaces gods
with men, is not of this kind. Marx's trauma is not only made
the sign of his common humanity but the experience that empowered the prophet. "His trauma," Wilson says, "reflects itself in *Das
Kapital* as the trauma of mankind under industrialism; and only
so sore and angry a spirit, so ill at ease in the world, could have
recognized and seen into the causes of the wholesale mutilation
of humanity, the grim collisions, the uncomprehended convul-
sions, to which that age of great profits was doomed." Might we
add that only someone who for similar reasons was sore and angry
in spirit and ill at ease in the world could have so brilliantly portrayed this Marx?

And now, with Marx dead at his desk and the roll call of deaths
that brings his story to a close, we turn to the men whom other
family chronicles have prepared to be the soldiers who take up
the weapon he had forged. We turn first to Lenin — to the boy
Vladímir Ilýich Ulyánov in the provincial city of Simbírsk, to the
bourgeois household which, by contrast with the impoverished
households of the Marxes, seems so bright and good. The low
frame house is the one Wilson had visited and whose atmosphere
he had found "perfectly comprehensible and familiar"; a house,
he says, such as one might enter in Concord or Boston: orderly
and clean, with mahogany furniture almost exactly like "the sort
of thing you would find in your grandmother's house," and potted

rubber plants, embroidered pillows, lace tablecloths, a grand piano, and, in Vladímir's room, some butterfly nets and a bound magazine containing installments of *The Adventures of Tom Sawyer*. In all of the details of furnishings and life within it, this house represents the bourgeois culture which the Marxists wish to supercede but which Wilson makes out to have been for the revolutionist a school of austerity, industry, and devotion — virtues of the disciplined life that he associates with the "New Englanders of the plain-living and high-thinking period."

One feels the closeness of identification in the way Wilson assimilates Lenin's childhood environment and in a variety of details both trivial and important. There is, for example, Lenin's red hair, a detail as irrelevant to the purposes of this book as the fact that he excelled in the classics and history and not in the sciences. But then there is his father's professional humiliation, the traumatic force of which Wilson does little to measure, though his narrative of subsequent events suggests some connection between it and Alexander's terroristic activity and thus with Lenin's revolutionary career. Of Lenin's lack of success as a landlord of a small estate, Wilson's only explanation is one that applies equally well to his own revulsion at the incident of the pony-cart: "He evidently considered abnormal any relationship that took on the character of the relation between master and underling." He cannot identify with Lenin's revolutionary activity nor with Lenin's own identification with the dispossessed, but he can with the professional aspect of Lenin's work — with the fact that Lenin followed his calling in a disciplined way. And certainly of personal significance is Wilson's remark that Lenin "is imaginable as a statesman of the West, developing in a different tradition."

With Trotsky, for whom Wilson's sympathy is not as great, the identifications are fewer and of less importance. Trotsky's father, who established a successful farm and operated the only gristmill in the region, suggests the pioneers of Talcottville. The literary boyhood, the student magazine, the confession that "authors, journalists and artists always stood for a world that was more attractive than any other world, a world open only to the elect" — these, of course, remind one of Wilson himself. He honors Trotsky-the-writer, the revolutionary of unusually wide culture, and yet he does not warm to him. Trotsky's admirable traits are

needed, it seems, to depict the complete revolutionary personality, and even more to bring out the nobler lineaments of Lenin,
whom Wilson, even in the chapter devoted to Trotsky, manages
to give greater prominence.

The imbalance represents an assessment of character, and the
basis of this assessment is clearly established by the verbal play
of the titles of the two following chapters. One runs: "Trotsky
Identifies History with Himself"; the other: "Lenin Identifies
Himself with History." We are back with the Dialectic. In the
chapter on Trotsky, Wilson explains his antipathy to fixed systems.
He says of Trotsky: "He is . . . far from the exploratory spirit
that distinguished Marx and Engels; and, being essentially a writer
and a doctrinaire rather than like Lenin an inspired worker in the
immediate materials of humanity, the implications of this dog-
matic Marxism are all the more clearly exposed in his work." In
the chapter on Lenin, the selfless inspired worker is at work ("the
imagination for history has been transferred to practical politics"),
and in the next chapter, he reaches the Finland Station.

An accurate subtitle for *To the Finland Station* would be "On
Heroes, Hero-Worship and the Heroic in History." Lenin, of
course, is the greatest hero, his life the success story of someone
of Wilson's class who went from the study to the street, or, to
justly characterize his achievement, the epic of the intellectual
who takes over the direction of history. Regardless of what happened in Russia after the Revolution, the arrival of Lenin at the
Finland Station remains for Wilson the peak moment in the history
of Western humanism. This humanism consists of an awareness
of the fact, as Wilson says in his own version of the content of
Marx and Engels' vision, that "the human spirit is always expanding against predatory animal pressure, to make larger and larger
units of human beings, until we shall finally have realized once
for all that the human race itself is one and that it must not injure
itself." And it is sustained by the belief that man himself, without
God, must create his own future. Such a humanistic spirit moves
through this book and is the most notable thing about it. The book
celebrates the human will to overcome the injustices of existence.

four

The Culture of Hecate County

I

Memoirs of Hecate County (1946), on which Wilson was already working in the late thirties, grew out of a disillusionment and demoralization even more profound than those he had experienced in the twenties. This disillusionment and demoralization was the end of a trajectory of experience, the result of the "peculiar course" that "the progress of the Communist faith" took among intellectuals during the depression. The peculiar course, as he explains in speaking of Hemingway in *The Wound and the Bow*, was due to "the exaltation of the Marxist religion" which seized the intellectuals like a "capricious contagion or hurricane. . . ." "In the moment of seizure," he says, "each one of them saw a scroll unrolled from the heavens, on which Marx and Lenin and Stalin, the Bolsheviks of 1917, the Soviets of the Five-Year Plan, and the GPU of the Moscow trials were all a part of the same great purpose." Later, he adds, "the convert, if he were capable of it, would get over his first phase of snow-blindness. . . ."

He was capable of it early, having already been disturbed on his Russian travels by the oppressive atmosphere of fear and suspicion that followed the assassination of Kírov[1] and by the "effort to outlaw Zinóviev and Kámenev" from the histories and albums of the Revolution. After 1936, he could not, with his discernment and idealism, grant that Russia was the moral top of

---

[1] He reported that the official statements were "certainly extremely implausible. . . ."

the world; nor could he, having all along been suspicious and critical of Communist Party tactics, accept, as he censures Hemingway for doing, the embrace of the United Front. The difficulty of that time can be seen in the argument of *To the Finland Station*, the writing of which dragged on as the terrifying events of the later thirties defiled his hope — the hope for a new art of man which he did his best by means of this book to keep from foundering on the rock of Stalinism.

The intensity of his idealism may be gauged by the intensity of his revulsion from Stalinism: the way in which it has rankled and driven him reminds one of the torments of Captain Ahab. If nothing else had, the astringent bitterness of "Karl Marx: A Prolet-Play" (1938) would have shown that he was no longer one of those who, as Gauss said in 1934, had achieved serenity by believing in the Dialectic. He was to say later that he had been betrayed to this religion by his residual Protestantism, but his apostasy did not bring him comfort. It forced him into the position of standing alone. Dr. Stockman of *An Enemy of the People*, a man who exemplifies Ibsen's great theme of "the conflict between one's duty to society as a unit . . . and the individual's duty to himself" and who in the end vindicates the social conscience in his own individualistic way, now attracts him.[2] So does John Jay Chapman, who was disillusioned by his experience of organized political reform and was "thrown back on the individual conscience." And they help him in *The Triple Thinkers* (1938) to define the new — the old — hero, the artist who in his art is above politics yet because of his art a moral force for the redemption of society.

Wilson is not abdicating politics — he is critical of Chapman's withdrawal. He is not retreating to the simple alternatives of art and politics and, finding political action bankrupt, escaping to an aesthetic realm. Social commitment is not abhorrent to him, but rather, as he says in the central essay on Flaubert, "the idea that the soul is to be saved by the profession of correct political opin-

[2] In *To the Finland Station*, Wilson also writes: "There sometimes turn out to be valuable objects cast away in the rubbish-can of history — things that have to be retrieved later on. From the point of view of the Stalinist Soviet Union, that is where Trotsky himself is today; and he might well discard his earlier assumption that an isolated individual must needs be 'pitiful' for the conviction of Dr. Stockman . . . that 'the strongest man is he who stands most alone.' "

ions." The greatness of Marx, Engels, and Lenin lay, among other things, in their ability to rise above class, to become moving forces because of this advantage; and this advantage of the intellectual remains in his definition of the artist as a triple thinker, for it secures the possibility of bringing to bear on society the uncorrupted truth for which the artist lives. Wilson reminds the Marxists that great artists have understood the economic and social forces of history and have in their art contributed to social change; in Emerson's words they have worked "silent revolutions of thought." They have been led to do so, he maintains in *The Wound and the Bow* (1941), where he is still defending his new position, not by anything so simple as class origins but by deeper, more complex psychic stresses. And they are able to do so because art, as John Jay Chapman said, is a conductor of moral energy — it works, Wilson explains, according to the law of "moral interchangeability."

What the political decades of the thirties and forties came to for someone like Wilson can be seen in Mike Gold's *The Hollow Men* (1941), where, in a chapter on renegades, Wilson is characterized as "ascending the proletarian 'bandwagon' with the arrogance of a myopic, high-bosomed Beacon Hill matron entering a common street-car." To have ascended and alighted were common experiences; so was the name-calling. Not so common was the fact that he did not ascend the patriotic bandwagon of men like Archibald MacLeish. Having lost faith in Russia did not mean that he had gained faith in America. He was not appeased by the New Deal, even though it had enacted much of the program proposed by the writers on the left in the heyday of *Culture and Crisis* (1932). The American social reform which he had envisioned had not materialized. At the end of the thirties, he was bereft of politics, caught between conflicting ideologies, and very much aware of the fact that Stalinism might not be a Russian phenomenon only, but the phenomenon of our time, the phenomenon of brutal power.

In "At Laurelwood" (1939), the essay in self-recovery in which he describes the incident of the pony-cart, he confronted in his family's history the "two kingdoms of force"[3] which were competing once more for the dominion of the world. Against the power of darkness ("the lethal concentration on power"), he pitted the

[3] Henry Adams' phrase.

"instinct to give light and life. . . ." He had arrived at the position that had always been his — that had in fact impressed him, a champion of justice, into political service. To repossess this position now was as much a homecoming as the recognition of Dr. Stockman; it was to find oneself supported in a lonely calling by the knowledge that all men who had fought for the "Human Idea" — as Fitzgerald defined Wilson's concerns in the thirties — had done so as heroes of light and life. In the memoir of Mr. Rolfe, written during these darkening years, he reaffirmed the humanistic tradition of self-reliance that flowed through Emerson and John Jay Chapman to him. "I myself," he said, "have been trying to follow and feed it [this tradition] at a time when it has been running low. Its tradition antedates our Christian religion and has in many men's minds survived it, as one may hope it will, also, the political creeds, with their secular evangelism, that are taking the Church's place." [4]

In personal matters as well these were difficult years, the "devilish" years of middle age, as Rosenfeld called them. Margaret Canby, whom Wilson had married in 1930, died in an accident in California in 1932. In 1931, he had given up his post on

[4] The humanism that Wilson has in mind was brilliantly defined during these years by Erwin Panofsky, who also set forth the difficulties of holding this attitude. Humanism, Panofsky explains in "The History of Art as a Humanistic Discipline" (1938), can be defined as "the conviction of the dignity of man, based on both the insistence on human values (rationality and freedom) and the acceptance of human limitations (fallibility and frailty). . . ." From this, he says, "two postulates result — responsibility and tolerance." "Small wonder," he adds, "that this attitude has been attacked from two opposite camps whose common aversion to the ideas of responsibility and tolerance has recently aligned them in a united front. Entrenched in one of these camps are those who deny human values: the determinists, whether they believe in divine, physical or social predestination, the authoritarians, and those 'insectolatrists' who profess the all-importance of the hive, whether the hive be called group, class, nation or race. In the other camp are those who deny human limitations in favor of some sort of intellectual or political libertinism, such as aestheticists, vitalists, intuitionists or hero-worshipers. From the point of view of determinism, the humanist is either a lost soul or an ideologist. From the point of view of authoritarianism, he is either a heretic or a revolutionary (or a counterrevolutionary). From the point of view of 'insectolatry,' he is a useless individualist. And from the point of view of libertinism he is a timid bourgeois." (In *The Meaning of the Humanities*, ed. by T. M. Greene, Princeton, Princeton University Press, 1938, pp. 92–93; reprinted in Panofsky, *Meaning in the Visual Arts*, Anchor Books, Garden City, New York, Doubleday and Co., 1955, pp. 2–3.)

The New Republic in order to pursue his own writing, but the impression one has, especially after his wife's death, is one of restlessness, of the need for movement and action. His life is unsettled, stabilized primarily by his devoted care of his daughter Rosalind. He married Mary McCarthy in 1938, and in need of a larger income consulted Gauss about the possibilities of teaching. He taught summer school at the University of Chicago in 1939, and returned to *The New Republic* in 1941, only to leave after a few months because its backers, the Elmhirsts, were using the magazine as a vehicle for British propaganda. He had no permanent position until late in 1943, when he took over the literary editorship of *The New Yorker*, a job, he told Gauss, which wasn't of much interest to him but "which [he] needed the worst way."

The shadow that falls over these years and becomes noticeable at the end of the thirties is the shadow of time, the most implacable moralist. The younger generation has become an older generation and has behind it a record of achievement and failure. Wilson was acutely aware of this in "Thoughts on Being Bibliographed" (1943), where he relates the history of his generation and speaks of the "break in the literary movement" of which it had been a part. It is a sad chronicle, for the conditions of the literary life have disintegrated. Those few writers who have not succumbed to Henry Luce or Hollywood and have kept alive their "small fire while the cold night was closing down" find themselves, as he does, willing to bridge the abyss to the creativity of another generation but faced with the risks of "poor remuneration or complete lack of market, public disapproval, self-doubt." And as he traces the phases of this disintegration — those cultural discontinuities he will soon depict in reviewing the career of Paul Rosenfeld [5] — he finds himself a stranger in the present, one of those who belong "to a kind of professional group, now becoming extinct and a legend, in which the practice of letters was a common craft and the belief in its value a common motivation."

"Thoughts on Being Bibliographed" and "Paul Rosenfeld: Three Phases" were an issue of the stocktaking he had begun in *The Triple Thinkers*, *The Wound and the Bow*, and his novel-in-progress. Every generation reaches the stage of appraisal, and in the case of Wilson's it was publicly announced in 1940 by

[5] Rosenfeld died in 1946.

Fitzgerald's death. Fitzgerald's uncollected and unfinished work was left to him to "point and punctuate," as he says in the time-haunted dedicatory poem of *The Crack-Up*, the volume he put together and published in 1945, and properly named after the title of Fitzgerald's own confessional essays. For crack-up was the inescapable moral, one that the surviving members of the genera-tion were not permitted to forget.

It was relentlessly driven home by "The Moral of Scott Fitz-gerald" (1941), an essay of Glenway Wescott's which Wilson reprinted in *The Crack-Up* and which undoubtedly contributed to his own stocktaking and confirmed him in the kind of novel he was writing. No essay on the crisis of this generation is so memo-rable, so honest, direct, intent on prescribing a course. The moral of Fitzgerald's death, indeed the very awareness of death, is used in a "warlike way" to "enliven the rest of the regiment" and to call them back to "particular literary virtues." Viewed in the light of death, which Wescott also saw "boding on all the horizon," the separation of the private and the public, the literary and the real life, was no longer possible. (So Wilson, developing the theme of individual conscience, cited this prescription of John Jay Chap-man's: "If you are not strong enough to face the issue in private life, do not dream that you can do anything for public affairs. . . . You must say what is in your mind. It is the only means you have of cutting yourself free from the body of this death.") What was needed now, it seemed to Wescott, was the very candor that made Fitzgerald great. The line to follow was that of the self-expressers, of Thoreau and Whitman, who knew the economy and power of the personal pronoun "I." In a time of "awful political genius run-ning amok and clashing, migrations, races whipped together as it were by a titanic egg-beater, impatient sexuality and love of stimulants and cruelty, sacks, burnings and plagues" — in such a time the artist's duty was to give the "naked truth about man's nature. . . ." Wescott proposed that the artist stand before his mirror and reveal himself not as he thinks he is or wishes to be but as he is. Thus, after a century of dishonesty, and now when the practice of the "deliberate lie" prevails, the artist would give his countrymen "little examples of truth-telling; little exer-cises . . . to develop their ability to distinguish truth from un-truth in other connections when it really is important." Like

Wilson in *The Triple Thinkers,* Wescott recalls the writer to his vocation and ventures "a higher claim for literary art than is customary now." With good writing, let the artist build a dyke and, like Faust, keep the devil waiting. This is the course to follow, the next step, if his generation is "to age well." Otherwise, the devil, whom he sees "standing worldwide in the decade to come," is "bound to get some of us."

That Wilson confronted public and private demoralization in the mirror of *Memoirs of Hecate County* may explain why it is his favorite among his books. It is, to be sure, a more accomplished work of fiction than *I Thought of Daisy.* But even though reviewers recognized the advance in art, they did not rate it so highly as he did when it was reissued in 1959, nor see in it, as Robert Warshow did, the supremely honest testimony of the period. Malcolm Cowley, reviewing it with care, found its weakness in neither skill nor technique but in its lack of "animal faith"; the stories were held together by "a single mood of revulsion" and, as in *The Waste Land,* "the storm never breaks and they [the characters] are all left wandering in Limbo-by-the-Sea." In an equally searching review, Diana Trilling, noting that of all the critics Wilson was the most "torturedly alert to the social-moral disintegration of the last two decades," complained that he had not mastered the contemporary despair as an intellectual should — had not maintained "amid disorder, some principle of private order from which a principle of general order could be induced. . . ." It is true, as Mrs. Trilling says, that the Wilson persona is the "egoist among the bedeviled" described on the dust jacket of the book: no previous persona is so cold-hearted and contemptible, so concerned with saving himself in the seas of his social milieu. Reviewers at the time, however, were adrift in the same seas and may have found the testimony unbearable. The remorseless satire of the commercialization of literature in "The Milhollands and Their Damned Soul" put in question every writer's integrity; and the unflinching portrayal of the dilemmas of an intellectual, all the more convincing because the author was an intellectual easily identified with the narrator of the book, undoubtedly disturbed someone like Mrs. Trilling who in reviewing one critic's novel was giving advance notice of another.

Memoirs of Hecate County belongs with those works which Wilson calls night thoughts. It is the product of the dark depressing nightmarish world, the hades, usually kept from public view, in which he sometimes wanders and where his tightly reined emotions break loose in furious demonism. There are times when, like Ishmael, his splintered heart and maddened hand are turned against the wolfish world. His demonism, however, is not in its nature antisocial, as it is in those toward whom it is directed. It is best characterized by the destructive (and self-destructive) rage of the narrator of *I Thought of Daisy*, who, having found the fabric of human decency rent, is ready to slander humanity by satirizing it. It is the reflex of his idealism, and its personal and public use is purgative.

That the narrator of *Daisy* partially resists the temptation to satirize mankind and eventually finds a way out of despair is an indication of the distance that separates the worlds of *Daisy* and of *Hecate County*. Now the narrator, who has lived through the twenties and is simply the narrator of *Daisy* grown older, cannot find in the public world the kind of support represented by Professor Grosbeake. He still cherishes Grosbeake's humanism, but can preserve it only by withdrawal. With the failure of the social enterprise to which he had dedicated himself in *Daisy*, he cannot resist satire nor even spare himself. He reminds one of the morose Ben Jonson of Wilson's later psychological study: a sensitive, aloof man who does not yield to intimate fellowship and who satirizes all the negative values because he "is tormenting himself for what is negative and recessive in his nature." This further note to his own relentless self-criticism, Wilson added to the record in the second edition of *The Triple Thinkers*. Jonson, like the narrator of *Hecate County*, is redeemed only by his love of his discipline.[6]

The Triple Thinkers is perhaps the best source to which to go for the principle of private order that Mrs. Trilling finds lacking in *Hecate County*. The narrator flees Satan and the nightmare world; he returns to his "buried stone house" and to his work — to his "old solitary self, the self for which I really lived and which

[6] By drawing this parallel, I do not wish to suggest that Wilson is to be equated point by point with Jonson, whose anal-erotic traits he discusses. I wish to indicate that there is very little that is adventitious in his work, that to some extent everything he does — and when he takes it up — is a personal index.

kept up its austere virtue, the self which had survived through these trashy years." For all of his difficulties, he manages to complete his book, just as Wilson himself, at the cost of depicting his revulsion, managed to strengthen the dyke by the honest writing of his novel. By writing this novel, and even more by taking the inspiration for it from Flaubert, he realized for himself the conception of the triple thinker.

The model he had in mind was undoubtedly Flaubert's *L'Éducation sentimentale*, a political novel as searching in its way, he says, as Marx's analysis of the Revolution of 1848, and one therefore that justified Flaubert's belief that the artist lost nothing by ridding himself of "social convictions." At first one is not inclined to see more than a general likeness, but Wilson's discussion of the novel points up those aspects that reveal the extent to which it provides the scenario for his own. And one is advised to see it in this way by his confession that the book is better appreciated when read in middle age, when one has "had time to see something of life and to have acquired a certain interest in social and political dramas as distinct from personal ones."

The hero of the novel, Frédéric Moreau, is the prototype of the narrator of *Hecate County*, especially as he comes into full view in "The Princess with the Golden Hair." Moreau is a young man, moderately well-off, intelligent and sensitive, but lacking stability of purpose and emotional integrity. "He becomes aimlessly, willlessly, involved in love affairs with different types of women," Wilson explains, "and he is unable to make anything out of any of them: they simply get in each other's way till in the end he is left with nothing." One of these women, Mme. Arnoux, the wife of "a sort of glorified drummer," is the counterpart of Imogen Loomis, the princess with the golden hair; another, Rosanette, Frédéric's mistress, is a girl of the working class, and his liaison with her, like the narrator's with Anna Lenihan in *Hecate County*, "is a symbol of the disastrously unenduring union between the proletariat and the bourgeoisie. . . ." Frédéric's education covers thirty years (almost the span of time in *Daisy* and *Hecate County*) and leads him into many corners of society; and it teaches him that he himself is as shoddy and lacking in principle as any of the representative social figures he has met. To follow him, Wilson says, is to acquire an idea that one can never get rid of: "that our middle-class society of manufacturers, businessmen and bankers,

of people who live on or deal in investments, so far from being
redeemed by its culture, has ended by cheapening and invalidat-
ing all the departments of culture, political, scientific, artistic and
religious, as well as corrupting and weakening the ordinary human
relations: love, friendship and loyalty to cause — till the whole
civilization seems to dwindle."

The tragedy is not Moreau's any more than it is the narrator's
in *Hecate County*. It is for Wilson the tragedy of "the poor human
race itself reduced to such ineptitude, such cowardice, such com-
monness, such weak irresolution — arriving, with so many fine
notions in its head, so many noble words on its lips, at a failure
which is all the more miserable because those who have failed in
their roles have even forgotten what roles they were cast for." The
narrator of *Hecate County*, however, will remember the role for
which he has been cast; will remember what Wilson had written
long before of art for art's sake in reviewing Upton Sinclair's *Mam-
monart*: that it "means simply that the artist has the right to
practice his art with a view to the perfection of his own kind of
product — that he should not be expected to meet the require-
ments of specialists of other kinds." To keep the enemy at a distance as Flaubert had done by "heroic application to mastery of
form" is the course that he will follow. When he had reached bot-
tom in *Daisy*, he had impugned literature itself; now he no longer
believes that art is imposture because it imposes a deceptive order
on the chaos of life. Indeed, by means of the order of art he will
not belie the chaos but reveal it for what it is.

The "memoirs" of the title is related to Casanova's *Memoirs* and
indicates the spirit of the book. In writing of "Uncomfortable
Casanova" (1941), Wilson spoke of the "courage of an individual
point of view" and the "capacity for feeling" required by a writer
like Casanova who rendered "the passing glory of the personal
life," especially the "ups and downs of middle age when our character begins to get us and we are forced to come to terms with
it. . . ." He recognized as more important than Casanova's vanity
the fact that he did not spare himself; "fidelity to truth" was one
of his admirable traits, and he did not write to glorify himself but
to tell "an astonishing story that illustrates how people behave,
the way in which life works out." To have written the *Memoirs*
was, he believed, an exemplary act, "a real victory of the mind

and spirit"; for it represented the possibility the artist always has of falling back on his intellectual resources. "One can still test one's nerve and strength," he wrote, "by setting down an account of life as one has found it, with all its anti-climax and scandal, one's own impossible character and all."

II

Wilson hesitated to send his *Memoirs* to Gauss probably because their correspondence at the time was about Fitzgerald's *The Crack-Up* and the good dean was disturbed enough about the fate of his young men. Much that others would have missed, all that made it "hair-raising" for Wilson, he would have recognized. Even in the Hecatean shade, the landscape was familiar to him — it was the landscape of Red Bank and Princeton, of Manhattan and Stamford, Connecticut (where Wilson had lived in the thirties in a wild and secluded place called Trees). He knew some of it intimately, some from letters; he knew its history and a good deal about its spiritual weather. It is unlikely that he would have been shocked. He had always insisted, in his lectures on Byron, that a writer is not immoral if he gives, frankly and indiscriminately, the good and bad of his life. Yet sons spare their fathers the intimate details of their lives, and Wilson wished to spare Gauss the agony of witnessing what Beth had desired in *Beppo and Beth* — the puking up of experience.[7]

The presiding deity of the *Memoirs* is Hecate, herself ambiguous, having in the course of becoming a popular goddess acquired both good and evil powers, and being represented, as in the illustration Wilson uses for the frontispiece, by three women, each with a special attribute, standing back to back. Triune goddess of night thoughts! she announces, as does the epigraph from Gogol's *Viy*, the overwhelming descent of evil.[8]

The moral atmosphere of *Hecate County* is fixed, as Malcolm Cowley noted, by the first story, "The Man Who Shot Snapping Turtles." It introduces us to the Manichaean world of Asa Stryker, an older man vaguely associated with the generation of Henry

[7] *Beppo and Beth* is a dramatic, if different-keyed, companion piece of *Hecate County*.

[8] The epigraph is an oblique tribute to another presiding genius, Wilson's friend Vladimir Nabokov.

Clay Frick, who in his obsession to create a "paradise" for wild ducks disturbs the divine economy by warring on the enemy, the snapping turtles. Unable to destroy this evil, Stryker, a moralist of absolutes, eventually adopts the suggestion of Clarence La-touche, a Southerner with pragmatic and Darwinian ideas: he exploits the evil — "Let the turtles create economic, instead of killing aesthetic, value!" He establishes a turtle farm and a canning factory and, with the help of Latouche's advertising skill, success-fully markets turtle soup. And he becomes a captain of industry, a hard paternalistic one, whose career of exploit, in which he him-self acquires the predatory nature of a snapping turtle, is ended by what to all purposes is a self-defensive murder at the hands of Latouche.

The story of Stryker may have been suggested by "The Good Neighbor" of Wilson's Stamford poems, but he has made of it a parable of American history, of the Calvinist temper as it has been converted — he even hints at the Civil War — to capitalistic ends. Perhaps this is why Stryker's situation, which seems ready at any moment to give way to parody, is not funny. Its closest analogue is Sherwood Anderson's "Godliness," the story of Jesse Bentley; and, in setting the stage, it serves to remind us, as Wilson will remind us again in *Patriotic Gore*, of the genesis of those attitudes that have darkened the course of our history. Hecate County has become Hecatean in time; its fields and woods, the pristine wilder-ness of the discoverers the narrator recalls in the last episode, have been morally as well as economically despoiled. Wilson knows, as Hawthorne did, that the morality of Calvinism is itself devilish. The lurid landscape is not simply a projection of the narrator's distemper, a night scene by El Greco such as Nick Carraway imagines in *The Great Gatsby*; it is also substantive.

The narrator observes Stryker from a distance, but he is in-volved to the point of anguish in "Ellen Terhune," where he enters the haunted landscape of his own past. If the story of Stryker is Hawthornesque, the story of Ellen Terhune is Jamesian, forcing the narrator back to the Jamesian America of the 1880's and 1890's. Ellen Terhune is a gifted composer whose story is both a case history of the artist's difficulties in America and an example of the theory of the wound and the bow. She belongs to the narrator's social class — in many ways her background is fabricated from

Wilson's, as it might be in a story in which the atmosphere is dominated by a house of the eighties. The story tells of Ellen's self-
vindication and release from deathly repression through art, and
in this respect is also Wilson's story, one that enables him to ex-
piate the sins of his father's generation and justify the vocation he
has followed. The terrible, subtle family antagonisms that burden
him are here; and so is the terror of the irresistible pull of the past,
of the desire to know it for oneself, and, in knowing it, of becoming emotionally responsible for it. For, although the actual present
of the story is 1926, the narrator finds himself on visits to Ellen's
house involved in decisive actions of successively earlier stages
of Ellen's life. And it is impossible for him to cast good and evil
in the simple Manichaean terms of the pioneer exploiter of nature:
they have become an inextricable psychic web of past and present.

"Ellen Terhune" is also a confession of guilt and an act of atone-
ment, a story by means of which Wilson tries again to right his
relations with Edna Millay. Many details confirm the identification of Ellen and Edna, but the guilt of the narrator, the compulsive need he feels to help her in her "terrible eclipse of the
spirit" — the phrase is from Wilson's memoir of Edna Millay —
this is conclusive testimony, awesome and beautiful in its pre-
science. In this story of the twenties, this story of his own neurosis,
Wilson imagines a situation whose psychic truth will be re-en-
acted, not only in 1948, when after an absence of nearly twenty
years he visits Edna Millay at Steepletop,[9] but in 1950, when, not
knowing she had died the day before, he had dreamed of her because, he explains, he had had "the impulse to console her . . .
for the neglect she . . . had been suffering." The story of Ellen
Terhune belongs with these actual events because, like them, it
was prompted by "the kind of sympathetic sense of the rhythms
of another's life that may sometimes persist in absence, as I had
had, in 1944, the feeling that she needed support, at the time of
her nervous breakdown."

The power to imagine the situation so intensely is an indication
of his need to confess the guilt he feels as a result of knowing her
desperate creative impasse and the extent of her artistic conquest
and the long years of silence during which he had, like the nar-

[9] Ellen's Vallambrosa is an inversion of this "densely green tree-grown
hill."

rator, been only polite in commending her gifts and helpless in aiding her to achieve her victory. This victory is imagined: it comes with the narrator's full realization of Ellen's past, at the moment when, sitting with her mother in the old house — her mother is not yet married, Ellen's life has yet to begin — he hears the completed sonata whose hideous theme he had actually heard in his first interview with Ellen, and which Ellen herself, at that moment in a lonely hotel room in New York, had not been able to finish because in her fierce struggle she had succumbed to a heart attack.[10] This episode is imaginatively successful and thematically right. The author does not flinch, as Malcolm Cowley believes he does, by avoiding a final encounter with Ellen. By means of his art, he wishes to tell Edna that "she had triumphed . . . to assure her . . . that I at least understood and applauded" (the words are the narrator's); but he wishes also to face the truth of his behavior: that he had been in a Jamesian world of ghosts — of psychic presences — and that because of whatever it was that made him incapable of extending this tribute when it was needed, he himself, in the terrible doomed sense of James, had been a ghost. To have it otherwise would have been to spare himself.

A similar determination on truth can be seen in the brutal self-caricature of "Glimpses of Wilbur Flick." As a social document, this story, covering the years from 1912 to the late thirties, provides a gauge of morale for the historical moments of the novel. For the author it serves other purposes: to recover the past in order to confront what, with the slightest wavering, he might have become. Wilbur Flick ("Ducky") does not seem, as so often is the case in Wilson's work, to be sketched from someone he knew — the details of his residence at the local inn (the Nassau Tavern at Princeton) were imagined and later substantiated by Gauss. Like Gandersheim in *The Little Blue Light*, Flick is a double of the author, a buried self.

The important fact about him is that he is an outsider. From his days in college when his English affectations and *fin de siècle* literary interests had put him outside college life and America, he has been unable to grasp the reality of his time or — it is a part

[10] Ellen's sonata suggests Edna Millay's "unfinished Erebean poems . . . her last fierce struggle. . . . "

of the problem — to find a serious role in society. He is the artist
without courage or stamina, or better, the aesthetic temperament
without a purchase, a dilettante, a collector; and his morbid conscience is the result of his having been cheated of his work in
society. After the crash of '29, he acquires a mansion (another
house of the eighties) in Hecate County, takes up Catholicism for
aesthetic reasons, and adopts rightest social views. By the mid-
thirties, having become addicted to drugs, he ends up in a sanitarium. Here he revives an early interest in magic.[11] At first, like
the narrator of *Daisy* in his disquisition on literature, he considers
magic a "big-sell" for human inadequacy; later, having discovered
its "classical" forms, he makes it his discipline, and his confidence
is restored. And at last he finds his role as a magician in a night
club. Witnessing Flick's triumph, the narrator tells us that it has
been earned — that Flick had found the necessity in himself and
had mastered a craft. Magic, he explains, is like art, a manipulation in behalf of the illusion of harmony, the art of putting something over on other people, an exhibition of superiority. By means
of imagination and dexterity Flick achieves his deepest wish, to
"astonish people." [12]

Unfortunately Flick is undone by the jealousy of others and the
difficulty of his situation as a worker — and by his paranoia. In
our last glimpses of him, he is on the road to self-betrayal and
degradation. At the time of the Spanish Civil War, he gives fund-
raising parties for the Communists, having, without abandoning
his class and the desire for power, found an elite with which to
identify. Later he joins a WPA theater project and uses his magic
to parody the claims of capitalism.

Now to some extent during the early thirties, Wilson had used
his art for similar propagandistic purposes. Robert Cantwell has
noted the differences between his social reporting of the twenties
and of the thirties by contrasting his article on Dorothy Perkins
with articles such as that on Foster and Fish, from which Wilson
himself, in a footnote added later, cites an example of the "capacity
of partisanship to fabricate evidence." But Wilson was not self-
drugged, as he feels Hemingway was in the thirties. He was not

[11] Wilson is an amateur magician.
[12] Is this also the narrator's deepest wish? the author's? Is this why the
narrator, in need of an audience, never makes a new life elsewhere?

taken in tow by the Stalinists; he did not raise money for the
Loyalists, nor make a speech at a congress of the League of American Writers, nor hunger for violence and, by reverting to Stryker's
kind of morality, launch a "rabietic fury" against the Fascist "bas-
tards" — Flick calls them "those rats." That he might have was one
of the terrors of the years following the crash, when, as he says
in explaining the barometric accuracy of Hemingway's stories,
one felt "the apprehension of losing control of oneself . . . and
the fear of impotence which seems to accompany the loss of social
mastery." There is evidence enough in *Hecate County* to show
that he was demoralized by the weather of the time. His sensitivity
to social "pressures" is one of the most impressive things rendered
in the book; for in it there is no firm line between self and society,
disintegration in either being recorded in the other. This may explain the exorcistic necessity of the book and help us recognize
that the narrator, detestable as he is, is still not as detestable as
Flick, the prototype of certain "independent" intellectuals of his
generation, or any of the Milhollands, the prototypal bookmen of
our time.

One does not fix one's impression of the narrator until "The
Princess with the Golden Hair." In the first three stories, he is
either an observer whose point of view we might easily take or a
haunted mind with which we might sympathize. We do not see
him in his habit as he lives, and when we do, in the clinical narrative of "The Princess," we find an uncomfortable man, as Wilson
said of Casanova, who in turn makes us uncomfortable. We are
distressed, not so much by the analytical description of sexual encounters (which immediately brought the book the wrong kind
of celebrity and the penalties of legal proceedings), but, as Mrs.
Trilling was, by the narrator's "unrelenting heart," by the gap
between his sensations and emotions and his inability to alter for
the better the lives of either of the women he pursues. With this
impression in our minds, we find it difficult to credit him with
any saving virtue. We fall back on our own sense of the primary
reality of personal relations, forgetting the equally primary reality
of our relations with the world — those relations explored in the
following stories where the narrator's determination not to yield
to the general chaos is not without heroism. For the intellectual

whose role is in jeopardy ("I know now," Wilson wrote at the end of the thirties in "At Laurelwood," "that the tides of society can give a new configuration to all but the strongest personalities, if they do not sweep them away"), for the intellectual whose role also commits him to gauging the social health by means of his own responsive self, social nightmare may too easily become private nightmare.

The extent to which the unstable society of the thirties has unsettled the narrator is shown in "The Princess." In this story, personal indecision is the result of political indecision: the narrator is an uncertain ideologist wavering between two women who for him are not only sexual spoils but representatives of the class struggle he is waging in his own mind. If his sexual relations are abhorrent, it is because of the cast of mind that prompts him to see human beings as ideas. This is his unpardonable sin, the sin of a time of ideologies, as he learns when he discovers that his ideas do not fit the reality of his experience. In those very episodes that make us cringe for him, he is with cold honesty showing us both the ineffectualness and degradation of the intellectual who, while still bound to his inherited bourgeois ideology, attempts to find a fulcrum in Marxist ideology. It is significant that when he assesses his experience with Imogen and Anna he finds the key to its value in his passion for art — in his awareness of immediate experience. "It was Anna," he says, "who made it possible for *me* to recreate the actuality; who had given me that life of the people which had before been but prices and wages, legislation and technical progress. . . ." The passion of the artist had made it possible for him to break through "the prison of the social compartments," to rise above class and ideology, and to find, with Anna's help, "the true sanction for life." Set in the years from 1929 to 1932, the years during which Wilson turned to Marxism, the story rehearses the difficulties of ideological allegiance. At the end, where the narrator becomes aware of his failure and finds in art a superior allegiance, it points to the solution Wilson arrived at in *The Triple Thinkers.*

Mrs. Trilling, justly but too simply, compares the situation of the intellectual in *Daisy* with that of the intellectual in "The Princess." The former had broken through his isolation by turning from Rita's aesthetic world to the sanction of actual life to be found in Daisy's common America; the latter, finding in Imogen, the upper-class fairy tale princess, the neurotic stigmata of the malady of the ideal, and in Anna, the proletarian heroine, a malady of the real — an actual disease of the reproductive organs — is doomed to isolation by impossible alternatives. In both cases the alternatives may be categorized, in Mrs. Trilling's way, as idealism and reality, and used to indicate the sad turn in the intellectual's travels on the road to social mastery. But we must remember that, in spite of the author's dichotomizing habit, these are stories of different times and places and that the counters in the one are not the equivalents of those in the other. Rita does not represent the values of Imogen, nor Daisy, whom the narrator can only break through to when he has placed her in the background of his class, the proletarian values of Anna. The intellectual's need to find a place in society by committing himself to the reality of his time is the same, but the realities are different. To overlook this — to suggest, as Mrs. Trilling does, that the diseased alternatives of the thirties indicate only the perversity of the author, that the sad turn is only his — is to fail entirely to appreciate one of the most stubborn facts of intellectual life in our time: the cultural discontinuities, the kaleidoscopic alignments, themselves signs of social instability and sickness, that have made sustained intellectual work a perilous undertaking.

The narrator in *Daisy* does not confront political realities, but finds a position from which this will be possible, and, like the author of *Axel's Castle*, announces his willingness to do so. In "The Princess with the Golden Hair," the most clearly ideological story in the novel, the narrator is in the presence of political realities and is possessed by them. What are these realities? Their contents are the lives of the rich and the poor, the lives of Imogen Loomis and Anna Lenihan. For the narrator finds the anatomy of society, as Wilson said of Dickens, by "working always through the observed interrelations between highly individualized human beings rather than through political or economic analysis. . . ." This is also Wilson's method, whether in criticism, political journalism, or historical writing, and the imaginative grasp required by it accounts in large measure for his literary success. One might say that in "The Princess" he tried to body forth in the Loomises what he had already sketched in the scenario of "Mr. and Mrs. X," and in Anna the undeveloped character of June Macy, the night-club girl of *Beppo and Beth.*

Ralph and Imogen Loomis represent "the better element," those upper-class people who consider themselves members of the governing class, but who in fact are careerists used by "an enormous machine for money-making. . . ." Ralph, an advertising agent, serves the industrial powers, while Imogen, a perfect illustration for Veblen's *The Theory of the Leisure Class,* minds their pseudo-Elizabethan countryhouse. Their lives are sterile — they have no children — and they sustain themselves by a romantic social fantasy as neurotic as Imogen's spinal disease. (Wilson does not bait Ralph as Lawrence does Sir Clifford in *Lady Chatterley's Lover,* a novel he had praised for its depiction of social realities and its demonstration of the necessity of understanding sexual relations as part of larger emotional situations. He has too much of himself at stake, even though in characterizing Ralph he is declassing himself. Instead, he suggests the crippled society of the Loomises — a society in which the narrator is not a master — by describing Imogen's inadequate, self-determined sexual response.) Anna Lenihan, dancehall hostess and waitress, figures in the narrator's experiment in misery, his initiation into lower-class life — and it is life, grotesquely, stubbornly cancerous in its vitality. She is modeled on Dorothy Perkins, the Maggie of the Lower West Side whose trial in the twenties was for Wilson a personal *cause célèbre.* The narrator's relation with her suggests Friedrich Engels' double life with Mary Burns, the Irish girl who worked in his factory in Manchester. The gonorrheal infection he acquires, necessary here to indicate the misfortunes of the productive class as well as its inability to help itself, was probably suggested by Casanova's *Memoirs.*

The narrator aggrandizes his sense of superiority by both relationships. For Imogen, he is an "intellectual," an adventurer in the underworlds of bohemia and Communism, a courtly lover and a desired conqueror; for Anna, who prefers that he keep his social distance, he is a representative of an attractive upper world. Loving neither passionately enough to meet the full demands of her life — having in fact used each as a stay during his interrupted relationship with Jo Gates — he is demoralized by his failure to fulfil the responsibilities entailed by his involvement. For he feels responsible to both, and, as an intellectual, to both "classes" — to both he might be the needed enlightener and leader. But he casts his lot with neither. Having lived within the iridescent bubble of Imogen's world, but unwilling to sacrifice his work for the money-making that would make him master there, how should he presume? And what can he do for Anna who does not consider herself proletarian and does not wish her lover to renounce the bourgeois world for what he imagines will be a proletarian romance in Brooklyn? The narrator's problem — a problem of the book on the socio-economic bases of art that he is having difficulty finishing — is the old one of highbrow and lowbrow in a form not amenable to Marxist solution. He wishes to have the best of both worlds, to create a new world. "No," he tells Imogen when, after speaking of his desire to vindicate the humanity of the poor, she asks if he is a Communist. "No, I'm not: I wouldn't do as a Communist; but I can certainly see the necessity for a sounder society than the one we've got, and for some kind of better life than this life that we all live!" And so, in his vascillation, he finds himself in the mid-world in which he prefers to remain, yet unsatisfied, guilt-ridden, and homeless because the discordant encounters of the thirties had made it a no-man's-land.

What can he do? Should he become a Wilbur Flick, a pawn of every available ideology, an other-directed intellectual? Should he renounce the professionalism that he believes to be the intellectual's heritage for the panderer's world of book clubs, Hollywood, and TV, to become another of the Milhollands' damned souls? Or should he, having already seen in the case of Stryker how easily an ideology of the elect can be made to serve the Devil, forget what Mr. Blackburn, the Devil himself, tells him of Hitlerism and Stalinism, only to accept as more humane the revival of religion that the Devil finds necessary for his work? These alternatives may be the three faces of Hecate, or the three assaults of the witches that the philosopher in Gogol's *Viy* did not finally have the courage to withstand. And the demonism of the concluding stories, no longer Hawthornesque or Jamesian but Wilson's own, may be an answer. For the demonism not only enacts the final assault in *Viy*, but represents the narrator's contempt. The demons boil up from his own bitter self; they are real people, neighbors, familiars with whom he transacts business and drinks cocktails; yet, twisted by the times as he has been twisted, compromising themselves with each turn of the business of the day as he with the last fibre of decency refuses to be, they have become devils. To see them as such, to name them, to flee them is to break their insidious charm, and to find again within oneself the strength of one's long-cherished love of excellence and good.

The ideological issues of the twenties involved the ethos of a puritan-commercial-industrial civilization. Those of the thirties and early forties were economic and political. Now, within the framework of the cold war, they are cultural, arising from the problems of mass-culture. Every ideological conflict has its devil, but the devils of the earlier conflicts lose their horror as they fade into the past. All of them appear in *Hecate County*, but the one who now frightens us — Wilson recognized him before most of the social critics — takes the form of the man who manipulates and degrades our minds. In *Hecate County*, such devils are represented by the Milhollands, who direct a variety of interlocking literary enterprises, and by the Blackburns, whose instrumentalities remain mysterious but whose resemblance to the Luces establishes the nature and scope of their work.

As early as 1930, in a Joycean parody called "The Three Limperary Cripples," Wilson assailed "the Book-of-the-Munch-Club" (also "Bunk-of-the-Bunch Club") and the "chewer[s] of books for choosy readers with bad buy custards. . . ." By the forties, however, only the demonic satire and burlesque of "The Milhollands and Their Damned Soul" was up to the task of dealing with a literature that, in the hands of the Milhollands, had become an industry, like Hollywood, feeding "'back to the public its own ignorance and cheap tastes.'" Warren Milholland, an instructor in English who turned to journalism in the twenties, runs the Readers' Circle and controls the magazines, whose favorable reviews he needs, and the publishers, like Flagler Haynes, the damned soul who takes his risks. By the mid-thirties, the narrator explains, "there was such perfect coordination [collusion between book club, publisher, magazine, and newspaper review] that one could be quite sure, any given week, of finding the same new book featured in all of these papers." Meanwhile, Spike Milholland, a romantic literary Marxist in his college days, becomes "'a barker for Parnassus.'" On the radio and in his newspaper column, he promotes literary haberdashery; and by the forties, when publishers are following "the current fashion of celebrating the national culture," he finds a more powerful place on television and becomes a spokesman for "the national propaganda bureau that had continued, since the end of the war, to work on public opinion at home as well as abroad." [13]

This literary situation is the end result of the arrogation by ideologists of the popular art that in the twenties had seemed to promise a healthy culture. It is the point at which the literary movement described in "Thoughts on Being Bibliographed" has arrived — a kind of crossroad such as Hecate might choose to guard. The narrator himself has been compromised by it. He is somewhat in the position of Beppo who, when admonished not to sell out, exclaims that he must practice his art in order to live. Rather than doing the life of Eakins he prefers to do, he chooses to do the short survey of American painting that his publisher wants to market "in the drug stores, the cigar stores and the railroad stations." And it may be that he has taken this step because he lacks the courage of his friend Si Banks — is unwilling to pay the price and incur the particular kind of demoralization of taking "the incorruptible line." His problem, like the author's, is to maintain himself as an intellectual and to secure the place he has always had in the publishing world.

Si Banks, once a poet and an editor of an *avant garde* magazine, now a publisher's agent of sorts and an alcoholic literary derelict, is another double, not a Wilbur Flick but someone to oppose to him, a composite of the incorruptible author of night thoughts and, one suspects, the incorruptible Paul Rosenfeld. Like the

[13] These shots are not random. It is evident that both Van Wyck Brooks and Archibald MacLeish are targets. Of Spike, Wilson writes: "He had complained, in his earlier phase, about what he called the 'betrayal' of his generation by writers like Eliot and Pound whom he had at one time enthusiastically imitated; and it now seemed that this generation had also been treacherously 'betrayed' by the Marxists whom he had admired later." The best commentary on this turn in the cultural situation is Dwight Macdonald's "Kulturbolshewismus & Mr. Van Wyck Brooks," printed in *Partisan Review* (November–December 1941) and reprinted in *Memoirs of a Revolutionist*. Macdonald notes that Brooks, in his speech on "coterie" literature, had remarked that Edmund Wilson "partially agrees with me." This shocked Macdonald and probably Wilson, who seems to have used this story to make his position clear.

author, he stutters, indulges a demonic outlook, and writes corrosive maxims. (Among them: "Marxism is the opium of the intellectuals"; "All Hollywood corrupts; and absolute Hollywood corrupts absolutely.") Like Rosenfeld, who was strong enough to stand free of the ideological snares of the thirties and who was broken by the literary situation of the forties, he upholds the highest responsibilities of literature. The narrator, employing Wilson's touchstones, speaks of "the purity of his love of letters and his stubborn insistence on his right to judge the actions and values of the world." And though he appears at the end as a jackdaw of Rheims, his presence is inspiring, reminding one of what Wilson would say of Rosenfeld — that "he remains for me, looking back, one of the only sound features of a landscape that is strewn with deformations and wrecks: a being organically moral on whom one could always rely, with a passion for creative art extinguishable only with life." Rosenfeld had always fought against the corruptions of literature that are the commonplace of popular art, and Si Banks speaks for him when he establishes the incorruptible line of the book: "in literature, just as in anything else that's serious, nothing's really any good at all that isn't based on the recognition of the very best that's ever been possible. . . . The most immoral and disgraceful and dangerous thing that anybody can do in the arts is knowingly to feed back to the public its own ignorance and cheap tastes." And Rosenfeld was an implacable as Si Banks, who does not accept the narrator's ready excuses for accommodating oneself to the system. " 'He did it for the wife and kiddies' — that's an excuse that doesn't go in the arts."

Si Banks, living out a solitary, destitute life in the Village, paying the price, is the character whose example the narrator would like to follow. He dominates the story of the Milhollands, in point of time the most recent episode, and he appears in the narrator's dream at the most crucial stage of "Mr. and Mrs. Blackburn at Home."

In this, the concluding story, the narrator, following his affairs with Anna and Imogen, has returned to Hecate County and, still undecided about the course he should take, has deferred a decision by adapting himself to the social life there. Among the people with whom he now feels comfortable are the Blackburns. These powerful people belong in an American demonology be-

cause the narrator finds them "at home," and they are especially
horrifying to him when he discovers who they are because he has
all to easily been "at home" with them.

The Blackburns live in an enormous house of the kind that
might have been built by the millionaire of "At Laurelwood," a
house in the bad taste of the 1900's, with an enclosed court, a Rap-
pacini's garden, containing hideously exotic plants tended out of
season. Blackburn, who keeps up this perverse custom, is in type
a descendant of the old moneymakers, and the devilish meaning
of his life is suggested by the narrator's reflections, which frame
the story, on the pristine American landscape and the possibilities
of the West. The devils are those who have corrupted the American dream, who have despoiled the "heroic America," leaving it
an "old country," where, as the narrator learns, one can no longer
possess a West; they are men whose vision is Manichaean, who do
not understand what the narrator means by evolving one's own
morality, and who, like Blackburn, purposely seek their ends, the
same old ends of power, by fostering a revival of religion. Blackburn is the enemy Wilson had first encountered in the episode of
the pony-cart, one of the masters of the tides of society that he felt
might sweep him away.

The lurid atmosphere of the narrator's experience at the Blackburns' party and the accompanying sense of dissolving personality
are brilliantly conveyed. (We have since become more familiar
with the maimed scenery of intellectual life; it has, for example,
been painted on the large canvas of Doris Lessing's *The Golden
Notebook*.) In his drunkenness and confusion, the narrator tries
to accommodate the virtues of the old America — the virtues that
were still intact in *I Thought of Daisy* — to what he finds in this
upper-class suburban hell. Later, he inquires about a job in Hollywood and brutishly attempts to take Jo Gates; but finally, becoming aware that he is acting the part of the host, he rushes from
the party to the haven of his old stone house.

He has found his way directly to the heroic America that the
narrator of *Daisy* had found with the help of Professor Grosbeake;
or, rather, he has found its nucleus in the forgotten integrity of
his own self. Still possessed by nightmare, he dreams that he is
talking to Si Banks of his childhood, of their common enthusiasm
for the *Ingoldsby Legends*, one of the books that stirred his de-

monic imagination; he feels, as never before, the bond, the love of letters, he shares with Si; and as he remembers that in childhood he had been "silently in love with excellence and unable to take quite seriously the respectable pursuits of my elders," he realizes that his childhood is still with him, that "it had come to me in dear little Si — to reassure me, entertain me, renew me." Yet the desire for identification with the ideal represented by the actual Si demands too much, and the narrator, in consoling his drunken and demoralized friend, is suddenly frightened by a suspicion of homosexuality, and turns away.[14]

In his dream, the narrator manipulates a toy-devil, but on awakening he is still bedeviled by evils he can neither control nor exorcise. Blackburn had predicted the purges and genocide of our time, evil pervasive and monstrous, no longer restrained by moral sentiment. This, the narrator, a man of good hope, had refused to believe. But the world he enters after 1934, the time of the story, substantiates it — there are intimations of it in the stories of Flick and the Milhollands. Now the devil is not the puppet he had played with in childhood nor anything as amusing as Larry Mickler's electric sign of Mephistopheles: he is dehumanized mankind itself, mankind run amuck, possessed by the fury of hate that triggers the little blue light. The narrator, who is having difficulty completing his book (for Wilson, it was *To the Finland Station*), has been reading Spengler's *The Decline of the West* (by the time Wilson published *Hecate County*, he was preparing for the press *Europe Without Baedeker: Sketches Among the Ruins of Italy, Greece, and England*). History itself has destroyed his dream of man. In turning West at the end of the book, he finds, as Wilson had in the early thirties, the ruins of the heroic America, evidences of decline.

The sentimental education of the narrator may be called the education of an old-fashioned liberal. Like Wilson, he wishes to advance the Human Idea, those humanistic, liberating values of freedom and reason, that long-standing Western tradition of independent men extending their freedom, making their own lives,

---

[14] Homosexuality is used again in *The Little Blue Light* to represent both the desire for unification in the self and its difficulties — the inevitable split between the ideal and the real.

by the exercise of reason. In the twenties, he had fought the enemies of man by upholding the new spirit in art. In the thirties,
he had looked to socialist reform to place humane ideals on a
sounder economic foundation. The socialist key unlocked the
door of history, but the door, in America as in Russia, did not open
on the vista he expected. The landscape revealed to him was that
of Hecate County, and there he found the agents of the new mass
society. And what made their work more diabolic than anything
he had ever known, was the cynical determination to destroy the
very keystone of the liberal hope for man — the rational power
of mind and the moral power of independent spirit that under-
write all human progress.

Is it not fashionable to call such a faith sentimental? to see in
Hecate County intellectual bankruptcy rather than the honest
revulsion of a man who is willing to bear witness to his faith? The
run of intellectuals, like everyone else, prefers ready-made solutions. But as Isaac Rosenfeld wrote in *An Age of Enormity*, a book
devoted to the themes of this time, "It is the mark of all genuine
faith that while affirmative choice is made, the struggle toward
it is great and uneven, and the adversary is not slighted. All the
rest is complacence." The narrator, a representative intellectual,
has not fared well because the social continuity necessary to his
role is gone; more than ever, he is an outsider. But he has not lost
faith in excellence, and he knows, as C. Wright Mills said in "The
Social Role of the Intellectual," an essay of 1944 which brilliantly
illuminates the sociology of *Hecate County*, that "the independent
artist and intellectual are among the few remaining personalities
equipped to resist and to fight the stereotyping and consequent
death of genuinely lively things." Could we follow him beyond
his *Memoirs*, we would find that he has been sustained by an
awareness of the continuity of the human spirit. He finds compa-
triots wherever he can, in the true artists and intellectuals, in the
triple thinkers, who have always been spokesmen for the spirit of
man. He has been able (as Wilson advised in "American Critics,
Left and Right," a policy statement of 1937) to make up his mind
in what capacity he is going to serve, to work in good faith in his
own field, and to maintain the discipline, the aesthetic and ethical
standards, of his craft. The *Memoirs* itself is the earnest of his
choice.

III

In spite of the fact that Wilson published seven books and more than one hundred articles in the forties, these years for him were "bleak and shrivelled." Cultural impasse and impoverishment characterized them. The end of an era had come: a time of uncertainty, of displacement (to us a word that now figures in his writing). Unlike *Axel's Castle*, the work of the twenties in which he plotted his course for the thirties, *To the Finland Station*, his work of the thirties, did not provide any direction for the forties. It spoke eloquently for a tradition of social aspiration at a time when those at home and abroad who claimed to represent it were unwilling to further it. And for Wilson, who had already defined an independent position in *The Triple Thinkers*, it was a farewell to reform. *The Wound and the Bow*, published in 1941, upheld this resolution on independence, and with these psychological studies Wilson reclaimed his place as a literary critic.

But *The Wound and the Bow* is very much a book of the times, addressed to the times. Its manifest intention is to explain the way in which the artist works out his trauma, follows the curve of his art, and, by doing so, serves society. But the story of Philoctetes, in terms of which Wilson exemplifies this theory of art, had special relevance for him as it had for John Jay Chapman, who had translated the play. The psychological aptness of the myth is not so much to the personal point of the book as the fact that the myth speaks for a wounded man who feels that he is needed for a "cause" yet is grieved by betrayal and banishment. *Philoctetes* is a fable of political intrigue discovered, undone, corrected. In the case of the wily Odysseus, it tells a familiar story of political expediency, and in the case of Neoptolemus a counter-story of a young man who becomes an "independent" thinker. Neoptolemus learns the absolute value of decency — "Everything becomes disgusting when you are false to your nature and behave in an unbecoming way." Caught in the tragic dilemma of choosing between the political claims of country and the claims of humanity represented by a single person — the theme is a variation on that of *Antigone* — he chooses the latter, with the happy consequence of thereby winning Philoctetes to the cause. The fable does not explain adequately the psychology of art, as the critical debate that Wilson provoked by advancing it indicates; but it does explain the terms on which the artist will serve. His wound and his art have their own claims and are best put in service when this is understood and sympathized with. We learn from Philoctetes of the artist's suffering and endurance and "principled obstinancy."

Of the books that were published in the remaining years of the decade, *Europe Without Baedeker* is perhaps the most significant example of the intellectual role Wilson found for himself. *Note-Books of Night* (1942) brought together the poetry and sketches he had written since *Poets, Farewell!; The Boys in the Back Room* (1941), a brief study of the California school of writers, reproved writers who had sold their talents short; [15] *The Shock of Recognition* (1943), an excellent anthology, was, it seems, an attempt to reorient himself and others in relation to the American literary enterprise — to renew a sense of the ardors and responsibilities of letters; *Memoirs of Hecate County* (1946), his finest achievement of these years, was, as we have seen, a memoir primarily of the thirties, a casebook of lessons for the intellectual, including the new lessons he would have to learn if he were to survive in the forties. During these years, Wilson himself was living at Wellfleet, keeping the stream of his writing flowing, holding fast to the discipline of his craft; and though all he wrote had its bearing on the times, it did not have, as he did not have, the kind of centrality that had made *Axel's Castle* and *To the Finland Station* such important books. One need only compare *Classics and Commercials*, the chronicle of the forties, with *The Shores of Light*, the chronicle of the twenties and thirties, to realize how much the issues of art and politics that had crystallized the earlier writing had been dissipated in the sands of the war years.

Unable to find financial backing for the magazine he felt was needed to promote the new literary activity he looked forward to after the war was over, Wilson joined *The New Yorker* and used his position as literary editor (he replaced Clifton Fadiman) to foster the cultural health. Most of the articles collected in *Classics and Commercials* were written for *The New Yorker*. Reading them reveals the accuracy of the title, for it leaves the impression that Wilson's choice was limited to classics or com-

[15] Perhaps it was his way of revenging Fitzgerald.

mercials, to those serious books that represented the continuities of his thought or popular fare like Lloyd Douglas' *The Robe* which prompted him to say that the reader "cannot live by bilge alone." [16] One feels in all he wrote at this time, even though much of it is slack, that he writes with authority and uses the office of reviewer to judge the current intellectual life. *Classics and Commercials* begins with Archibald MacLeish's misuse of language — with his attempt to bring writers into line with the present national purpose by branding as "irresponsibles" the writers who had written honestly in the period following World War I; it ends with a memoir of Paul Rosenfeld. This framework suggests the discordant encounter of the chronicle, not only that of commercials and classics, but the underlying one of betrayal and intellectual integrity. The purpose of the articles is to define in a time of bad writing the nature of good writing and literary integrity; to hold writers to their best, even if at times he must instruct them and use the blue pencil. The spirit that informs them is expressed in the declaration he takes from Katherine Anne Porter:

In the face of such shape and weight of present misfortune, the voice of the individual artist may seem perhaps of no more consequence than the whirring of a cricket in the grass, but the arts do live continuously, and they live literally by faith; their names and their shapes and their uses and their basic meanings survive unchanged in all that matters through times of interruption, diminishment, neglect; they outlive governments and creeds and societies, even the very civilizations that produced them. They cannot be destroyed altogether because they represent the substance of faith and the only reality. They are what we find again when the ruins are cleared away. And even the smallest and most incomplete offering at this time can be a proud act in defense of that faith.

The articles in *Classics and Commercials* are a defense of this faith at a time when Wilson felt the ineffectuality of the old humanistic point of view and the helplessness of the disinterested intellectual to bring about change in an almost totally disordered world. Though most of those he reprinted treat literary subjects, they were originally installments of a wider survey of the contemporary horizon. Something of that search finds expression in them: his despair of the possibility that the death of society may paralyze our responses to experience; his fear of police states,

[16] Among his feats of disgust are his articles on bestsellers and detective stories.

mechanized warfare, and pressure groups; his anger with intellectuals who take refuge in national glorification or religion; his unwavering reliance on intellectual courage, humanitarian socialism, and education rather than manipulation of the masses; his determination to search, as he says in an essay on Aldous Huxley, for "the earthly possibilities of human life."

Admittedly a literary chronicle, *Classics and Commercials* indicates the literary exhaustion. It is not, however, as representative of Wilson's efforts to inform himself and Americans about what they must know and the responsibilities they must accept as the considerable number of essays he did not choose to reprint. These essays are closer to the pulse of the decade. Like Dwight Macdonald's essays in *Politics*, they are not run-of-the-mill journalism, but serious attempts to sound contemporary experience, to understand the new life and realities of a world at war. In them Wilson forces his readers to consider the unspeakable atrocities of the death grapple of nation-states, the reduction of the human spirit and the withering sense of life which almost make impossible the human rebuilding that must follow the destruction of civilization. He tours the fronts in the war diaries he reviews; he investigates the diplomatic mind; he searches in the latest books on the warring nations for clues to the attitudes that will shape the future. And he questions American policy — what he called in an essay on Puerto Rico, a feeble halfway imperialism that neither rules nor intelligently helps; dismisses as formulas incapable of commanding the refractory realities of the present the liberal and radical suggestions of men like Carl Becker, Norman Thomas, and Alfred Bingham (the essay is entitled, "World Federation and the Four Fidgets"), and reminds us that Europeans lack faith in the possibility of a new order in Europe, especially one made by Americans. His own proposals for the future include the federation of Europe — to be established by the Europeans themselves — and "collectivization" at home. And his major effort is to reorient us to these possibilities, especially the first, by making us aware of the dimensions and profound effects of what is going on, thereby shattering our "Never-Never Land" conception of Europe and adjusting the "dangerous discrepancy" between the fairy tale and the actuality of "absurd, anachronistic nationalisms and unequal stages of social development tearing one another to pieces."

These essays provide a commentary on *Europe Without Bae-deker: Sketches Among the Ruins of Italy, Greece, and England* (1947), the travel book in which he records his firsthand impressions of Europe and which, in turn, binds together in a work of considerable unity the themes of his previous journalism. The power of this book, dismissed at the time as the work of a prejudiced and provincial literary man, comes from Wilson's refusal to yield the personal point of view and from his passion for spiritual and moral values and his devotion to culture when, in the debacle of culture, such values have almost been snuffed out. The title of the book recalls the grand tours of the confident years when Baedekers had been reliable guides to "culture"; and the subtitle recalls a long tradition of sketchbooks in which ruins had been a source of delight in the picturesque and not, as now, the everpresent rubble of a wasteland. And it is just because he is a literary man aware of these perspectives and in his own person suffering their ironies that the book assesses costs and suggests the kind of rebuilding that the sociologist and political analyst failed to consider. Their work — he had reviewed much of it unfavorably — was not quickened by personal response to concrete experience or by attention to the small details of everyday existence that make the sum of the quality of life. Nor were they so much the possessors, so steeped in the heritage of human thought, that they saw with the eyes of history a ruin that would have made a Gibbon weep.

Wilson visited Europe in the spring and summer of 1945, during the last days of war and the first days of peace. He wished to see what liberation meant and whether, as Dwight Macdonald said when noting in America a lack of leadership towards social progress, "it is to Europe above all that we must look at present." Certainly the "spun sugar" of Archibald MacLeish's speech on the need for waging peace by creating common understanding, with the report of which Wilson opens the book and announces one of its themes, was discouraging evidence of official American talk. ("The Atlantic Charter," Wilson said, "is not much better.") There was, he found, no common understanding among the Allies and insufficient understanding, sympathy, or respect for the nations they had "liberated." England had formulated the policy for Italy and Greece and was adroitly making America serve it, and both, fearful of playing into Russian hands, had turned away from the possibilities of the new order the liberated nations hoped to build for themselves.

The lack of understanding, exemplified by England, is due primarily, he explains, to national traits, to survivals of old virtues and ways of thinking. These account for England's strength in the war and for the maintenance of her customary civility, but also for the determination to create in Europe a balance of power to her advantage. The former, especially the civility which contrasts with American hysteria, Wilson admires, but the latter awakens his virulent Anglophobia: he would remind America of this haughty nation "intent on keeping up face," this little island where "every penny counts," and he would, as he sometimes does when baiting Englishmen in conversation, remind England that she is no longer a first-class power who can bully her way in the world. (We remember that the Englishman in *Beppo and Beth* is named Longbroke.) His attitude, justified to some extent by what he saw of British policy, goes back to American sources that make it possible for us to consider his work a note on Emerson's *English Traits* or the latest confirmation of the condescension, so wounding to American pride, that almost every American, even Anglophiles, had felt in England. He explained his antipathy to "*la morgue anglaise*" in his study of Dickens, and now, in an England that for him brings to life his reading of the nineteenth-century novelists, he closely observes the conventions and manners that Pound before him had called "a system of defense."

Brutal rudeness and class snobbery defend property, social privilege, inherited advantages. But this is an old American criticism, easily brushed off, and not so telling as the analysis that discovers their nurseries in the public schools. If these institutions are praised for instilling the sense of excellence that even in time of war has kept up aesthetic standards, they are also damned as part of the tradition that Churchill, on the occasion of refusing to seat in Parliament a representative of the Scottish Nationalist Party, upheld for adding to "our dignity and power." The code and glamor of the upper-class world survive, anachronistically for Wilson; the old virtue has gone out of them. They simply fill the social vacuum left by the failure of the middle class, the generation of

Wells, Bennett, and Shaw (which had nurtured him), to build a lasting civilization. The present generation of writers, he says, tends "to creep back into the womb of the public schools." (And some of them, in turning to religion, were already, as he was to complain later, "crawl[ing] into cracks to avoid disaster.") The middle class no longer seems articulate, and the laboring class, regimented by the war and Americanized by movies and pulp, does not seem capable of providing leadership.

The "defense" may be observed in a pure form in the field. American and British troops do not mingle, and whenever they are brought together, as in the Allied Commission, the British, even when fewer in number, manage to gain control. Many of the British officials whom Wilson meets are self-important blusterers, like Sir Osmond who is politically ignorant and parades his classical learning in order to disguise his imperialistic aims, or bullies, like the Irish major who boasts that he has beaten natives in the East. Even Harriet, the British UNRRA worker whom he compares with Mattie, her American counterpart, is a product of the system.

In a fictionalized account of relief work in the Abruzzi that dramatizes the difficulties of sustaining life in war-pulverized Italy,[17] Wilson points up the differences between English and American traits. The English, he commented earlier, using *The Wings of the Dove* by way of example, were desperately materialistic, the Americans disinterestedly idealistic. And here is Harriet, so grimly British, punctilious and cold, straightened by a provinciality that does not admit her learning the language or taking notice of the culture and preserves the sense of superiority that makes her treat her wards as conquered people; and Mattie, capable and warm, eager to learn, to sympathize and fraternize. Harriet and Mattie are not extreme types, even though they are characters in one more discordant encounter; they are recognizably human and in their peripheral work exhibit the kind of misunderstanding and cross-purpose to be found at every level of Anglo-American effort.

Wilson explains these differences in national traits as the consequence of geographic and historic factors. The tight insularity

[17] In method it is similar to "Red Cross and County Agent" in *The American Jitters*.

of England does not permit the informal ways of continental America — the comparison contains a taunt similar to the old one of Thomas Paine; and England is a *nation* ("an entity which perpetuated its local breed and had to compete and perfect itself among entities of other breeds") where America is a *society*, a more advanced system joining together diverse people in the interest of constructing a "way of living." In England, accordingly, the defense of the national existence makes self-criticism an act of treason. Whatever the truth of these rough distinctions — they exclude, for example, the fact that "societies," in defense of their ways of life, treat criticism in the same way — it is Wilson's purpose, especially because of the long-standing refusal of the British to understand America, to understand them, and to put them down. Coming to Europe, but most of all his intercourse with the British, has made him defiantly American. Like Crevecoeur's Quaker minister, he looks westward, away from the ruins, to those green fields were civilization begins anew on a better plan. In striking back at the British, nothing he says is so devastating as the remark that "the real English social revolution occurred, not in England, but in America. . . ." Some well-read Englishman may have remembered that a century earlier Emerson had commented on the trim hedgerows of England and the ample nature of America and had told the British that the true Englishmen were the Americans. Yet Wilson is neither advocating isolation nor working up an undeserved national esteem. He is telling us why we should refuse to be treated like colonials and should take the lead.

Towards Russia, the other power we must understand, Wilson's attitude is unequivocal but not erinaceous. Even though he did not visit Russia or confront her officials, he focusses attention on her by reporting on some Russian exiles in Rome and on Alexander Barmine's autobiography. This chapter (and what he says of Malraux and Silone) rehearses the history of his disillusionment with Russia and ends with comments on the "satrapship of Stalin," the lack of civilization indicated by his regime, and the impossibility of international understanding between "a state run by political police and a state run by independent citizens." These comments, however, seem to set conditions for possible accord, seem to appeal to those Russian traits that he finds similar to the American.

As early as "Dostoevsky Abroad" (1929), he had associated America and Russia by noting their common position as provincials in relation to Europe, and he pursues the same line of thought here, adding the recent developments that have reversed the relationship between "the larger societies" (Russia and America) and "the little European nations, among which England must now be counted. . . ." Like America, Russia is a society, not a nation. The social engineering this implies still remains to temper his response to Russia; in fact, this is the element of Marxism that he believes Europe now needs and that some of her intellectuals, either having passed through a disillusionment with Stalinism similar to his own or coming, after the blackout of the war years, to Marxism and Leninism afresh, wish to possess.

To confuse with Stalinism the social aspiration stirring anew in the liberated nations is the mistake of ignorance or policy that Wilson finds so disheartening in the Allied government of Italy and Greece. One cannot, he feels, disregard or discount the profound experience of Marxism, for it still kindles the social vision and the quest for the meaning of man of the most searching European minds. These "pilot-minds," as Margaret Fuller once called the leaders of thought in her generation, are now rare. Wilson little feels as Keats did in the Romantic Age that "Great spirits now on earth are sojourning": the greatest casualty of the war has been the ruin of thought. Men like Santayana, living in the Hospital of the Blue Nuns in Rome, still making it his business "to extend himself into every kind of human consciousness," or M. Platon, the curator of Minoan ruins in Crete, pursuing his work throughout the war, exemplify the personal discipline and endurance that maintain civilization. Their virtues are Wilson's, but he identifies more readily with men of his own generation whose experience of Marxism has been similar to his and who, as artists, are doing most, he believes, to create a better future. Malraux and Silone, he says, "stand today almost alone in Europe as writers of first-rate talent who have continued to take imaginative literature with the utmost seriousness and who have never lost their hold on the social developments, larger and more fundamental, that lie behind national conflicts." He calls them "survivors" — they have survived "the intellectual starvation" and "the spiritual panic of the war." But they are survivors in another more impor-

tant sense: they still believe in art, in Malraux' words, as "'a recti-
fication of the world . . . a humanization of the world.'" For
Wilson they are the most encouraging signs of life.[18]

His own modest book is a work of art in which the instinct for
the human survives. He travels in behalf of the human spirit.
Wherever he goes he calls attention to surviving works of art, not
in the interest of art history, but the better to impress us with the
fact of six years of war that most appals him: the "wholesale negation practiced by man on man," a negation made possible by man's
increasing insensitivity to a massive technology of destruction. He
does not, as many contemporary artists do, try to match the horror
imaginatively. Instead, with his even, low-keyed exposition he
evokes, in the presence of the ruins, those monuments of former
human achievement, a world — even ours of yesterday — which
was built to human scale; and with his gift for significant detail,
he introduces us to ordinary human life now. Human history
spreads out before us, and we finally become aware of what man
has wrought when we realize how easily civilization itself and
the human qualities that create and sustain it can be effaced. The
ruins on the Acropolis, he finds, "still transform the world where
they shine"; but to the British Basutoland troops, who use the
Forum for their rendezvous with prostitutes, "the splendors of the
Caesars, Italy, Europe itself, cannot mean very much more than
they did to Attila's Huns." "We've had it!" a catchphrase used for
"such everyday situations as the exhaustion of PX supplies or the

[18] In the mid-forties, one might describe Wilson as a composite of Malraux,
Silone, Orwell, and Sinclair Lewis. With the exception of Lewis, whom he
thought of as a "national poet," all have been seriously involved with Marxism. Malraux came to it through "disgust with the bourgeoisie" and "the
motivation of a very strong sense of what non-Communists call 'human
decency.'" Silone has tried to merge the ideals of primitive Christianity and
modern socialism; Wilson's acceptance of Silone's Christianity prefigures another special case — that of Pasternak. Orwell, whom he first reviewed in
1946, attracted him for just those qualities one would attribute to him: he is
a student of international socialism who remains irreducibly British (for
Wilson, read "American") and is not free of provincialism; his virtues are
"old-fashioned" — he thinks for himself and speaks his own mind, deals with
concrete realities rather than with theoretical positions, has a disciplined
prose style; he never satisfactorily formulates a position, but his impulses,
though often in conflict, point to what he wants and doesn't want and are
a reliable guide, suggesting "an ideal of the man of good will . . . still alive
in a benumbed and corrupted world."

end of sorting-out of the mail," is now, he notes, applied even to "the downfall of Western Civilization."

The art of the book is in touches as casual and small as these. Previous trips with Baedeker measure the present: he journeys by air and Europe unfolds a new landscape. We are reminded in Milan of Leonardo, Stendhal, and Mussolini; in Rome, of Hawthorne's *The Marble Faun* and Douglas' *South Wind* (and of the superior moral vision of the first), of Goethe, Keats, and Gogol, and of such living artists as those who have just produced *Open City* and Leonor Fini whose paintings need not exploit Surrealism because Surrealism itself has been caught up with and overtaken by actual life; in London, of *Peter Grimes*, and in Crete, of *Arsenic and Old Lace* — new works that capture the psychological temper of the time; in Naples, of *Lili Marlene*, the pathetic song, originally German, that expresses the feelings of soldiers everywhere. Every level of human life, the official and the private, the high and the low, is sensitively presented: we share for a while the life of an upper-class Greek family whose connections provide a spectrum of the intellectual and political situation; we watch Harold Laski, making a political speech, appeal to a "craning gray-faced chicken-eyed woman" who for Wilson is a type of wartime Europe; we learn about the blackmarket, the ways of street boys and prostitutes. No response in the entire book is secondhand or perfunctory, and among the finest touches in the book are those in which Wilson certifies his own humanity. He tells of his discomforts and revulsions, of the jumping mouse trick with which he sometimes amused children, of women to whom he brought gifts and women simply noticed in passing who restored for him the delight which in itself is a keystone of civilization.

The climax of the book and perhaps its best section is the account of a brief visit to Crete. On this terribly war-scarred island, we are back in Minoan and Homeric time, among a "primitive" people of great courage and independence. Visiting the museum at Heracleion and the ruins of the palace of Minos at Knossus, we learn of a civilization that "has come and gone without leaving the key to its secrets"; on the occasion of a memorial service at Anogeia, near Mount Ida, we attend a "Homeric" banquet, and at the ceremonies for the dead are moved by the traditional threnody of the women. And with all this stirring within us, we are quickly

transported to Athens, where the G.I.'s know nothing of civilization and care less, asking only if they can get ice cream and dough-
nuts and beer.

The common cause that Wilson would foster, the cause of
civilization itself, seems unlikely to succeed in a world of national
animosities and ignorant good will. Europe for him has been
declining since World War I; now she has had it. In America,
there is not much to hearten him. With his homecoming the book
trails off into reflections that are important as clues to his despair
and hope but that mar its artistry. He expatiates on themes that
will figure even more prominently in later work: on *careerism*,
which at this time he considers a phase of national growth that
we have fortunately passed through, thus becoming the most
politically advanced nation — the last fifty years, he feels, have
been, artistically and socially, a great creative period in America,
and he is still undisturbed by the careerism of the new white collar
class; on *the compatibility of socialism and democracy*, especially
when responsibility is distributed and self-dependence is not im-
paired by centralized authority; on *eugenics*, the breeding of
better human beings, a desperate hope, but the very sum of the
humanistic faith to which he clings; finally, on *the anthropoid
apes* whose "human" capacities hold out the possibility of improv-
ing man's animal nature.[19]

Wilson found himself on his return from Europe in a disoriented
state similar to that which he had experienced in the twenties. He
could not, he explains, find the values he had known and on which
he depended, and he felt that he had to resume his role and contribute to creating them. His reflections are his immediate contribution — just as the needless introduction to *Patriotic Gore* is a
contribution. But the books they mar themselves contribute more.
The logic of his art is always superior to the compelling logic
of the moment, and it brings *Europe Without Baedeker* to a fitting
close. He tells of a visit to Norman Kemp Smith, a former professor of his at Princeton, now in Edinburgh, who fortifies him in

[19] Writing on "Zoölogists and Anthropologists" in *The New Yorker* (September 10, 1944), Wilson reports an experience that recalls Emerson's in the
Jardin des Plantes: "I remember walking one day through the prehistoric
section in the Natural History Museum . . . and feeling, in the presence
of this record of the forms of life focussed here by man's creative vision, an
excitement and exaltation such as I got from literature and music."

much the same way that Professor Grosbeake did the narrator of *Daisy*. Life for Kemp Smith in Edinburgh is not as abundant as it was in Grosbeake's time — he is older, alone; the world is bleaker — but the life of his mind is as intense and rich and his faith as inspiriting. He speaks of God, as the Whiteheadean Grosbeake did, as a way of accounting for "the life that was in us and the coherence of the universe"; and he renews Wilson's faith, first spoken in *Daisy*, in those qualities he finds godlike — "vigorous physical persistence . . . rectitude in relations to others and to one's own work in the world, and . . . faith in the endurance of the human mind."

five

Passage Home

I

The critical role Wilson has chosen to play is defined best by the resolution of *I Thought of Daisy* and by what he said in "Dostoevsky Abroad" (1929): "we must try to stick close to the realities of our contemporary American life, so new, and so different perhaps from anything that has ever been known, that, if we cannot find out for ourselves what we want and where we are going, it is impossible, with Europe declining, that anybody else can tell us." He has gone to European art and thought, yet he has always been intransigently American — *Europe Without Baedeker*, a classic form for rendering the complex fate of the American, may have first made readers aware of this. The value of certain American principles and traits has increased for him with his commerce with the contemporary world; and America, in spite of so much to dismay him, remains for him a challenging experiment. It is significant that on his return to America in 1945, he speaks of role in a legitimate sense: "the old drama in which you figured will not get underway for you again unless you go back into your role. You have now to contribute, yourself, to creating interest and value. . . ." And it is significant that the first occasion of these remarks was his salute to an old American landmark — to Sinclair Lewis, who, he was pleased to find, was still at work in his role of "national poet," facing the new.

It was not easy for Wilson to resume his role when he returned to "peace torn" America (the phrase is one with which Gauss greeted him), for the drama was not the old one, or, if it were, the scenery was being shifted, and one's familiar lines seemed strange. More and more — it is the most drastic alteration in his career — he seems to be speaking from the wings and even at times from the darkened stage of an empty theatre. He manages, however, to continue in his old role while he prepares to play another. He returns once more to current literature: when new evidence comes in he fills out the portraits of those writers who have long interested him or adds to the appraisal of his experience of Marxism. He remains intellectually *au courant*. But there is no literary cause to arouse him, only a book here and there, like Malraux' *Psychology of Art*, Orwell's *Animal Farm*, or Pasternak's *Dr. Zhivago*. Frequently he looks back to the twenties, in part to recapture a sense of vitality, in part to recall the world of his own exciting performances — *The Shores of Light* and *The American Earthquake*, chronicles of a society in creative ferment, also make it possible for him to play his old role again.

Nor is there much to excite his political ardor. "The United States, with its great role to play in the world," he told Gauss in 1945, "was not contributing much intellectual leadership — merely the atom bomb." The present — it was now a time of witch hunts, state encroachment, rabid nationalism, and atom bomb diplomacy — the present, he said in 1951 in reviewing a book on bees, "is not one of the great ages of the self-dramatization of man. It is no age of authentic leaders in departments of statesmanship or thought. . . . Nor is it an age of great ideas. There is little left even of Marxism save a mask for a civilization that recalls the hive. . . ." At this time, he also reviewed two books on the lives of those who had been imprisoned for refusing the draft because he wished to inform his readers, in view of the possible advent of totalitarianism in America, about ways of adjusting to prison life.

He did not, at least not in the way he once had, report on current events, and one might assume, as he himself leads one to believe in *A Piece of My Mind* (1956), that he had followed the narrator of *Hecate County* into withdrawal and, as he says, retreated into old fogeyism. Yet all the while, beginning in the mid-forties, he is at work on *Patriotic Gore*, a book welling from the deepest springs of his life and bearing directly on the political and literary problems of the present — of its many applications perhaps the most important, in respect to what he said of our insect civilization, is to press the fact that today "we resemble less the prophets and saints of the Old and the New Testaments, the heroes of Plutarch's 'Lives,' or even the characters of Shakespeare, all self-conscious individuals, than the relatively undistinguished members of those insect species. . . ." His other work during these years — his plays, *The Little Blue Light* and *Cyprian's Prayer*; his studies of the Zuñi and the Iroquois, of Haiti and Israel; his reflections and interviews — is political in a way peculiar to our time. It is concerned with the endurance and survival of the individual and of minority societies, with the persistence of varieties of life; and it aims to restore our sense of the human scale, of genuine human needs, and of the power of the human spirit in the face of forbidding nature and human tyranny to fashion and maintain worthwhile disciplines and cultures.

In attacking current events from the periphery, as in his accounts of the Indians and the Haitians, or from a greater distance in history, as in his study of Genesis, Wilson is not trying to escape the pressure of immediate issues: he is simply eternalizing the point of view from which he considers them. The curve of his career, following so closely the curve of recent history, has forced him to play a role which is less that of the Dr. Johnson or Sainte-Beuve in which it is customary, on superficial acquaintance, to cast him than that of the prophet; and this may well be the role for which he had originally been chosen and for which all of his previous work has prepared him. He has become a spokesman-at-large of the human spirit. He seeks now its deepest sources in history, and he tries now to awaken it within us in order to combat present-day fanaticism and exclusiveness. In his plays, especially in *The Little Blue Light*, he gives us his apocalyptic vision; when he speaks *in propria persona*, as in the introduction to *Patriotic Gore* and in *A Piece of My Mind*, he exhibits a capability for wrath. And at times it is possible to think of him — and not without admiration for the expense of spirit it has cost him — as a latter day Essene Teacher of Righteousness, bearing with him the scroll whose very title announces the struggle in which, from the time of the incident of the pony-cart, he has elected to engage: *The War of the Children of Light against the Children of Darkness*. In the postscript to *Red, Black, Blond and Olive*, he says, in explaining the common theme of his studies of Russia and Israel,

"Again I am announcing the supremacy of moral force and human will over the adventitious aspects of life, the material encumberments of earth." For him the moral of his experience in Jerusalem and Moscow is the same — that "spiritual power resided, not in temples or altars or tombs, but in the person of the man who possessed it." In affirming this power, we feel that he possesses it and that, like M. Dupont-Sommer, the French scholar whose independence he praises in his book on the Dead Sea scrolls, he belongs with the "great secular seekers for truth," who, he goes on to say, "as well as the Teachers of Righteousness may establish their lasting disciplines."

In the new forms which he has chosen to employ one discovers him in his new role. The kind of reporting he did so well in *The American Jitters* and *Travels in Two Democracies* has been superseded by a kind of travel book, equally objective and artful but reflective in a different way. In the one, reflection serves the immediate interests of the social engineer; in the other, it is set free to range the eternal-present of man's experience. One sees the difference in *Red, Black, Blond and Olive* (1956), a collection of studies in civilizations, where the earlier work on Soviet Russia (originally part of *Travels in Two Democracies*) sets off the recent work on Zuñi, Haiti, and Israel; and one may already have noted it in *Europe Without Baedeker*, the transitional book in this development, which begins in the documentary rapid-fire way of the travels of the thirties, but seems impelled to form itself into larger and more unified wholes, until, in the superbly wrought chapter on Crete, it arrives at the prototypal form of the later work. The transition here is especially crucial because it is marked by a loss of hope in immediate reform. No social machinery seems available to raise the curtain of darkness; even the survivors have turned to the ultimate questions of man's nature and justification and have begun the investigation of civilization itself so characteristic of our time. And Wilson, too, has turned from the machinery of society to the spirit that puts it in motion, to moral forces within civilization — to rectitude, justice, fellow-feeling.

The transformation may be imperceptible — and on that account all the more remarkable — because from first to last Wilson's prose style has remained pretty much the same. But now one realizes that what at first was stiff has become supple. The authority with which it first invested him has been earned, and it has become a voice, a personal instrument of great flexibility and resonance. This style is so much his that for the most part it does not adjust readily to the dramatic and fictional uses to which he puts it; it is the language that seems awkward here, not the management of form. In fact, his identity with the style may explain his use of such forms as the fictionalized memoir or the fact that in his plays the vehicle doesn't speak as much as those portions of himself he has set on the stage. But in the travel studies he has found a form which his style can mold, and he has made it a genre recognizably his own.

As he explains in the postscript to *Red, Black, Blond and Olive,* the travel studies are more than the result of simple curiosity or the desire to indulge in historical perspectives. They are reflections on the central political experience of his life — on his blindness to the mythic, religious, and Utopian elements of Marxism. (Perhaps this is why, even though he had already acknowledged these elements and his own susceptibility to them in *To the Finland Station,* he reprints his observations on Soviet Russia and restores materials that he had suppressed in 1935.) He had, he says, found his eighteenth-century tradition in Marxism, only to discover later that he had "gone to live in a myth." What he calls his "atavistic Protestantism" had to some extent led him astray. And now, by putting together his studies of "national religions," he would show us that, valuable as they sometimes are "for social cohesion, for dynamic purpose, for moral discipline and contemplative ecstasy," they are after all limited and limiting "human projections" which "must come into competition with other such myths and inevitably prove misleading and dangerous." This is the idea that possesses him and that he will go on to develop fully, and in respect to America, in *Patriotic Gore.*

Yet one feels that these studies provide him a welcome excursion into religious experience. (One thinks of John Stuart Mill turning for emotional sustenance to the Romantic poets.) Vehement against religion as he has always been, he is nevertheless of a religious disposition, and when religion is a wholly individual affair, as in the lives of John Jay Chapman and Pasternak, he is sympathetic with it. He turns to it now to sustain his ever more hard-pressed belief in the sufficiency of human agency; for religion, in its sources so close to art, is, as he makes us feel, a human projection that testifies to the greatness of the human spirit. He wishes to explore the mysterious depths of consciousness empowering this spirit and to relive the stages of religious development. He would find that which exalts man, but as a partisan of human progress, also dismiss religion as anachronistic.

Perhaps the discordant encounter that he finds in the history of Western civilization between time and eternity, practical worldliness and transcendent principle, is his own. In reading his account of the sacred dances of the Zuñi, one remembers his early work, *Chronkhite's Clocks*, where the mechanical rhythms of the modern office are contrasted with the needed organic rhythms of a "primitive" Negro. But now, when he is entranced by the miracle of human energy evoked by the Zuñi dances, he feels that he must resist their spell. The great Shálako bird is after all only a young man in a ten-foot mask, and, cheerful and benign as the Zuñi religion is, how can he, a Protestant who has "stripped off the mummeries of Rome," turn back to a "primitive Nature cult?" In another connection, he tells us that the Zuñi have no sense of the clock, but this is apropos of the fact that a letter recalling him to his "own urban world" finally distracts him from the troubling vision of the Shálako.

The nature cult of the Zuñi, in which "the power of the natural elements [is] made continuous with human vitality"; the Voodoo of the Haitians, offering the therapy of possession; the Biblical Judaism of Israel, telling so much about man's intercourse with God and his awakening moral consciousness — all these are grand. But all are "primitive," and in every case — in the fierce resistence to outsiders of the Zuñi, the presence of a UNESCO experiment in Haiti, the sectarian snarls of modern Israel — we are made to feel the insistent demands of the present. Wilson recognizes the psychological values of transcendence, but he accepts neither transcendence as an end in itself nor the theology that makes it a "religion." The moral energy acquired in the experience of transcendence must turn the wheels of history. He admires most in Haiti the vigorous practical Protestantism of Pastor McConnell, for a Protestant, he says, "must demonstrate virtue" and "a really fine example of Protestant practice is to me a good deal more impressive than the giving oneself up to God of either the Voodoo-worshipper or the Catholic." And in Israel he admires most the intellectual pioneers of the *kvutzót*. Their work, inspired by Zionism and a Tolstoyan socialism and associated in his mind with the Essene community and the Utopian communities of America, seems to him the best realization of the moral impulse within three thousand years of history. With the community at Degániya, he concludes both the study of Israel and the studies in civilization.

The matrix of these studies is history, the temporal world of man. Religions are placed as occasions in time and considered developmentally as human responses to natural and political landscapes. The reading of Genesis in the Hebrew is also a historical exercise, for philological matters introduce one to a different time and place and mentality (and more is gained for humanistic inspiration than lost for religion by this reading of it). The importance of the Dead Sea scrolls — their discovery is the only major event of the atomic age that Wilson has chosen to report in detail — lies in the fact that they force one to ponder the origins of Christianity and to entertain the provocative idea that man himself evolved it. Viewed in this way, the miracle of revelation becomes a miracle of human genius — and the "special genius" of Jesus is of the miraculous order of Shakespeare's. But perhaps the miracle most significant for us is that man himself has been able to reconstruct his own history and by doing so to transform gods into men. This new evidence of man's agency, Wilson hopes, will mollify sectarian animosity and thereby bring to an end the religious war of Western civilization. And his own investigations serve a similar purpose: to discount (not debunk) "religions," to disencumber them of all that makes for exclusiveness and fanaticism, and, at the same time, to point up by means of them man's will to persist.

It would be truer to the affirmative intent of these studies — indeed, of all of his recent work — to think of them as studies not so much of the evil of national religions as of the good of persistence and art. That man must persist and that art (in the most inclusive sense and always as the polar term for ideology) enables him to is the message of his prophecy. In society-at-large as well as in his personal life, he feels intensely the need to summon for survival the powers of endurance. He himself turns to the past because it gives him what the future withholds: lines of continuity, extensions of his own endurance. He turns, for example, to the Indians, not only because he feels the cause of imperiled minority groups to be his own, but because they plant him more firmly in America. He is deeply sympathetic with the nature cults of the Zuñi and the Iroquois — of literary critics writing today, he is one of the few both responsive to and informed about nature. But, finally, what attracts him is a desire, like Thoreau's, to know the American environment. The Zuñi take him back to "a piece of prehistoric America." And the Iroquois, his neighbors at Talcottville, serve as a "backward extension" of his own history, their remarkable "force to persist" compounding his.

When he considers the ceremonials of the Zuñi and Iroquois in terms of art, he is able to identify with the participants and make the ceremonies stand for his own work. The sacred dances of the Zuñi may be mummeries, but the dancer, "by his pounding . . . generating energy for the Zuñis; by his discipline, strengthening their fortitude; by his endurance, guaranteeing their permanence," is doing what Wilson believes the artist should. So with the Little Water Ceremony of the Iroquois, with its theme of death and resurrection: "The members of this medicine society [who perform the ceremony] really constitute a kind of élite, and they are making an affirmation of the will of the Iroquois people, of their vitality, their force to persist. These adepts have mastered the principle of life, they can summon it by the ceremony [by art] itself. Through this they surpass themselves, they prove to themselves their power. Ten men in a darkened kitchen . . . make a core from which radiates conviction, of which the stoutness may sustain their fellows."

But the Indian world in which he imaginatively participates is nevertheless alien, time-bound and place-bound. The Indians have survived by maintaining, with small concessions, the past in the present. He must reach back to them, for the continuity is outside of rather than within the stream of history. With the Jews, it is otherwise. Their tradition has come forward in time (and in many places) as a part of the progress of Western civilization itself. It is the Jews with whom he most closely identifies, for with them he comes home.

What he identifies with is the moral genius which he believes to be the characteristic genius of the Jew.[1] When he first developed this idea in *To the Finland Station*, this moral genius was attributed to the germ plasm! "It was probably the Jew in the half-Jewish Proust," he says, "that saved him from being the Anatole France of an even more deliquescent phase of the French belletristic tradition."[2] Jewishness is used to explain the differences in the views of Freud and "the more purely Germanic" Jung; and it would seem that because they were Jews, Marx, Freud, and Einstein possessed their moral authority and were system breakers. Even Jewish readers were put off by this curious line of thought, and it is understandable that readers of the chapter on the Jews in *A Piece of My Mind*, in which Wilson expatiates on the "Judaism" of New Englanders, might take it for the crotchet of an old man.

The tenability of these ideas is of less importance than the fact that they are a piece of his mind. The clue to the first is to be found in its context. Wilson is considering Marx as the "poet of commodities" and concludes that historical evidence alone "cannot necessarily convince people that the progress of human institutions involves a process of progressive democratization. . . ." "You can only appeal to them," he says, "by methods which, in the last analysis, are moral and emotional." The clue to the second may well be the remark addressed to assimilated Jews in his proposal for Judaic studies (*A Piece of My Mind*): "to cut oneself off from one's forebears is likely to produce bad effects: it sets up strains and repressions. . . ." In his list of eminent Jews, he is obviously extending the prophetic tradition to which he feels he belongs. To find that tradition very much a part of the mind of his forebears not only establishes continuity with them, and through them with the Biblical Jews, but better validates his own claim.[3]

In the chapter on the Jews and in the opening paragraph of "On First Reading Genesis" where he tells of how he came to

[1] To some extent he identifies with the Jew's marginal position in society.

[2] The idea was first advanced in the discussion of Proust in *Axel's Castle*. There Wilson said that "there remains in him much of the capacity for apocalyptic moral indignation of the classical Jewish prophet."

[3] It also explains associations for which New England is the link. For example, Lenin, a gentile, comes from a "New England" household in Simbírsk.

study Hebrew, Wilson explains the heritage, once neglected by him, that he now wishes — and has taken considerable trouble — to possess. The Puritan, the Mather, side of his genealogy is now something of which to be proud; now we are told of John Jay Chapman's identification with the Jews ("They are the most humane and strongest people, morally, mentally and physically," Chapman wrote. "They persist. I'm glad I'm a Jew.") And though the Judaizing of the New Englanders explains much that he disapproves of — the American sense of "mission" and the zeal of the Abolitionists — it also explains, as one sees in what he has written on Justice Holmes, the intellectual basis and moral inspiration of the Brahmin aristocracy, the elect with whom he feels he belongs because in his own role he has maintained the family tradition of professionalism. Lawyer Holmes, like Wilson's father, looks back to the minister, the minister to the prophets; and in their callings, all have done the responsible work Wilson has undertaken to do.

The studies of Israel and the Dead Sea scrolls, both products of Wilson's journey to the Holy Land in 1954, constitute the record of a pilgrimage to the sources of moral inspiration. Like Melville's pilgrimage, Wilson's results in historical awareness and wonder at the paradox that these barren hills have produced a gospel so fertile; but unlike Melville's pilgrimage, which did not restore his religious faith or kindle a humanistic faith to replace it, Wilson's strengthens his faith in man. For him the Bible peoples these hills with men fiercely concerned with the survival of the family; [4] and these men, Abraham, Isaac, and Jacob, live in a world — not the world of Zuñi or Voodoo — in which Jehovah is all too human and derive their authority from personal intercourse with Him. In these encounters, often discordant, Wilson discovers the developing moral consciousness and those notions of rectitude and justice that, with the claims of fellow-feeling added by Christianity, define his moral conception of "God." In working through the stories in Genesis, one feels that he is permitting himself to walk with God; he has left history for a moment of eternity, the better to experience the permanence of these moral values. And one of the results of this experience can be seen in his spokesman for these values in *The Little Blue Light*, the Wandering Jew, whose legend,

[4] Always family-minded, he has himself become something of a patriarch.

he explains in the chapter on Genesis, "is an attempt by Gentiles to synchronize the Jewish eternalness with the vicissitudes of their own intensely temporal history."

Between the families of Genesis and the community at Degániya, there has been a never-broken moral current. As he observes modern Israel, where remnants of the past, like the Samaritans, and curious products of the Diaspora, like the Guardians of the City, still go their exclusive ways, and barbed wire tells of the violence of Arabs and Jews — as he sees all this in the perspective of "the running down and falling apart" of Europe, the rebirth of Israel seems to be a recurrence, the result of one of those long cycles of history which, at least imaginatively, makes history timeless. The moral values given to the world in Genesis have now made fertile the Palestinian wasteland; where all once began, the work of reintegration is once more beginning; the wandering Jews have come home to make good the inspiration of centuries. And especially in communities like Degániya, that collective of self-governing responsible people, it is possible to see an enterprise of our time not unlike that of the Essenes, an enterprise of survival and endurance, neither exclusive nor fanatic, morally equal to the world, indeed a dispensation for civilization.

Of all the religions Wilson considers, Judaism seems to be the most compelling. He prefers its remote nameless God to the Shálako or Grandmother Erzilie of Voodoo or Christ. The God of the Jews, he explains, "has no go-between but the prophets, and these are human beings, whose words one uses in praying but to whom one does not pray." The Jew lives with God in an empty room, in the synagogue where the words on the wall "declare the power of the spirit, the authority of the moral sense." His faith is in "the power of the human spirit, in touch with its divine source," a life-giving faith that works through the intellect and spirit and needs for its habitation only the soul of man. This moral conductivity is the reason for the survival, not of the Jews alone, but of mankind everywhere. "The heart of the world is Jewish," Chapman said; and whenever one worships God, as Jesus says in John 4, "in spirit and truth," whenever one speaks in spirit and truth, he finds that heart and becomes its prophet. The faith is universal, its prophets many, its instrument the word.

II

We look to our artists and critics, as the Zuñi look to their dancers and the Iroquois to their medicine society, to keep us in cultural health. By their serious discourse, these "intellectuals" (among others) keep open the communication by which a culture lives. They give us, as Lionel Trilling says, news of ideas; and by altering our sensibilities to its rhythms and by radiating the conviction needed to confront its problems, they help us meet our age. In offering these notions of the functions of the intellectual, one must add that not all who go by this name subscribe to these functions or consciously undertake them. To those, like Wilson, who do, those who do not are "careerists," no saving remnant but a part of an intellectual bureaucracy. And as this bureaucracy, a corrupting agency in a corrupt society, takes over, it becomes ever more urgent that the intellectual be recalled to his proper work, to the high responsibility of serving society by using the word in spirit and truth.

Wilson has much to say about contemporary reality, for his studies in civilizations inevitably point to our own. In telling the story of Lot, for example, he is fully aware of the menace of genocide; and in treating the Essenes, he describes a political climate similar to ours, even in respect to such matters as oaths of loyalty. He considers Haiti as an instance of the possibility of mixed cultures and the Indians, especially the Iroquois, as representative victims of the centralized bureaucratic power that he feels is overtaking all of us. But in the face of this reality, he has more to say to the intellectuals. It is clear that he thinks of the intellectual as a prophet upon whom depends the salvation of society. Yet it is equally clear, as one sees in "The Messiah at the Seder" (*A Piece of My Mind*), that he disclaims the fanaticism that usually accompanies the messianic impulse. He is not about to establish an orthodoxy like that of the Marxists or the Freudians or, in his own specialty, the Leavisites. He has no doctrine, unless what he says of Lenin, the intellectual he admires most, contains doctrine: "The moral triumph of Lenin was to make himself part of the people, to identify his interests with theirs, to energize them with his own drive and to guide them to construct . . . a workable human society." And he has no explicit method or discipline.

His only requisite is that the intellectual be an individual who demonstrates moral and spiritual power by contributing in his work to what he calls "realistic perception."

Of this, he is himself an example in these studies, although in them he points out others. In the study of the Zuñi, there is Frank Hamilton Cushing, an "adventurer scholar" and man of letters who lived with the tribe and became a Priest of the Bow; in the study of the Iroquois, William N. Fenton, the leading Iroquois scholar who has brought to his work "an intelligence at once scrupulously scientific and humanly intuitive"; in the study of Haiti, Pastor McConnell, whose practical grasp of the Haitian situation has turned him to the basic work of education; in the study of the Dead Sea scrolls, David Flusser, a Jewish scholar of independent and audacious mind. All of these men have been passionately devoted to their work and have given their lives to it; none is academic, institutional, sectarian, or bureaucratic in his way of understanding. Cushing was an anthropologist of the old school whose object was to understand the Zuñi as human beings and not, as Wilson says of Ruth Benedict, to make patterns of culture at the expense of the complexity of life. One recognizes here Wilson's personal quarrel with academia, but it is more than that: it is a quarrel with every restricted form of intelligence, with the "objectivity" and the professional jargon which are the results of habits of mind that have serious consequences because they keep objects at a distance, blur the sharpness of the local and the concrete, and preclude human understanding. Such habits of mind may lead a team of experts who have not been in the field to write a long report in a "pompous, polysyllabic and relentlessly abstract style," a report like that of the UNESCO mission to Haiti from which he maliciously quotes, and to expend more on the report than on the mission itself. Or they may support the tyranny of centralized authority, for example, the dealings of the New York State Power Authority with the Iroquois; may permit the engineers and bureaucrats, whom he likens to beavers because of their indifference to the landscape and their compulsive, often gratuitous building, to go ahead with their projects.

Of his recent studies, *Apologies to the Iroquois* (1960) is the most explicit example of realistic perception — of what might be called an independent, decentralized, local intelligence confronting contemporary reality. Wilson himself is involved: the Indians are his neighbors and he, too, has experienced the power of the state, having had to fight both the highway builders and park-planners who would dispossess him of property on Cape Cod.[5] He writes to a specific issue, formulating the problem, as C. Wright Mills suggested that the intellectual should, by stating "the values involved and the threat to these values"; and he thereby awakens in us "the felt threat to cherished values . . . that is the necessary moral substance of all significant problems of social inquiry. . . ." This explains the importance of a book dealing with back-page news items, and it explains the fulminous reply of Robert Moses, the chairman of the New York State Power Authority. "The struggle to restrain these projects," Wilson says, "is undoubtedly at the present time one of the principle problems of American life."

It is the problem, in a later phase, of what Benton MacKaye called the metropolitan invasion of the indigenous environment, and in this phase represents a conflict that is worldwide — the conflict, Wilson says, of the "individual with the forces of the centralized state." In *Apologies to the Iroquois*, the resolute individual seems still to have some chance of restraining these forces.[6] But this is not the case in the plays in which Wilson gives us an apocalyptic vision of the struggle. In *The Little Blue Light* and *Cyprian's Prayer*, the individual is overpowered, conspired against and killed or forced to withdraw.

Both plays dramatize the problem of the intellectual in our time. Like the earlier plays, they are installments of Wilson's personal history, of the chronicle of his involvement with the problems that in each stage of our recent history define the role of the intellectual. But they differ from the earlier plays by being courageous public statements, examples of what the gardener — the Wandering Jew — in *The Little Blue Light* means by fighting with words ("I can only help to fight with words. It is forbidden me to fight with

[5] At this time he was in the midst of difficulties over his income tax, and his feeling of harassment by the government finds its way into the book.

[6] Since the writing of this book, however, the Kinzua Dam project forcing the Senecas off their land has gone through.

weapons."). These are the plays the Hungarians have chosen to translate.

A sense of evil of Manichaean proportions pervades both plays, but *The Little Blue Light* is the shriller, more hysterical and apocalyptic. It was produced in Cambridge and New York in 1950 and 1951, at the beginning of the McCarthy era. In it, Wilson says, he is treating a phase of American history more "desperate" than those he chronicled before, a phase he chooses to place in the "not remote future," one easily imagined and made credible by following out the logic of current events. The play depicts the demise of the liberal, the Enlightenment tradition. Nothing much has changed in the physical aspect of the external world — the terror is not that of Huxley's or Orwell's preview of worlds to come, for the environment is familiar — but the inner world has been eroded, leaving men who are satisfied with a security maintained by lies and secrecy, by mindlessness and brutality, by a secret bureaucracy (a power elite) working within the public bureaucracies.

This state of affairs has a very recent history. It dates from the end of World War II, when one of Wilson's personae, Gandersheim, had gone to Europe to live. Now, having been dismayed by the struggle for power there, he has come home. The European nations, he reports, are "just clustering like iron filings on these big concentrations of power." And the United States, he says (as Wilson had in *Europe Without Baedeker*), backs the reactionary movements, movements that use the methods of fascism. In fact, it was because of what he learned in the war, and later in America, that Luke Teniakis, the Greek whose Relief Bureau has become the controlling power in America, abandoned his idealism. He had fought in the Greek Liberation Movement that "was put down by the British with U.S. tanks"; and in America he had learned the methods of power employed by political machines and pressure groups.

In America, the most important fact of the last ten years, according to Frank Brock, the liberal spokesman of the play, has been the disappearance of the two-party system. Government is now only a matter of the spoils of power "scrimmaged" for by competing pressure groups. The political spectrum reminds one of Van Wyck Brooks's chapter heading in *From the Shadow* — "Infra-Red into Ultra-Violet." "First of all," Frank explains to

Gandersheim, "you have the Reds — they're the extreme Right:
they want to institute state slavery, abolish civil rights altogether
and have the country run by an oligarchy. Then you have the New
Federalists — they want to restrict the vote to big employers of
labor and incomes in the upper brackets. Next come the Constitu-
tionalists, who are the nearest thing we've got to a Left: they
want to keep the Constitution. All of these have political programs. . . . But that doesn't tell the whole story, because there
are all the other groups that function without programs but work
for their group interests. The strongest one now is Labor. . . .
Then there are the Children of Peter, with their religious organization behind them. Actually the objectives of the Peters are just
about the same as the Reds', and their methods are about the
same. . . . Last and most disgusting perhaps is the new group of
Yankee Elitists, our indigenous variety of fascists. . . ." As a liberal, Frank believes that all these groups are directed by ideas and
can therefore be confronted in the intellectual marketplace, but
Judith, who has gone over to Teniakis, informs him of the end of
ideology: "The old groups haven't got any real ideas. The Reds
haven't believed in their Communism since sometime in the early
thirties. The so-called faith of the Children of Peter is something
no decently educated person — with the exception of a few panicky
poets — has been able to take seriously since the seventeenth century. And as for the Yankee Elitists, with their talk about the
Founding Fathers — if even John Adams turned up today, they'd
denounce him as a dangerous demagogue." All want power, Judith
says, and Teniakis, having had enough of ideologies, "is simply
concentrating on power. . . ." In this struggle for power, freedom
of the press and of speech and the Bill of Rights are ignored; journalists no longer uncover the news but accept handouts from the
publicity departments of pressure groups; poll-taking is rigged to
produce the required public opinion; and mechanically processed
mass-culture supplies a debased intellectual food — "kennel food,"
according to Frank. Yet America is still freer than Europe: it is
still possible for a courageous individual like Frank to publish an
independent magazine.

Frank Brock speaks of himself as "an obstinate oldtimer . . .
a journalist who still takes journalism seriously, an American who
still believes that this country has a great contribution to make

to the progress of civilization. . . ." He is a Westerner — for Wilson, as for Whitman, the West is the locus of democracy. He grew up in a small Western city where his father had run an independent newspaper and managed to survive as "a ring-tailed gyascutus of Populism from the heroic Bryan period. . . ." And now he runs the *Spotlight* on the old-fashioned liberal principle that "everybody's got a right to look at the world from the corner he's sitting in — and to yell about anything he doesn't like"; he assumes that what interests him from his corner will interest other people. His magazine, however, prints factual articles that do not draw conclusions (in the department of special American problems he is planning to print an article, "Can the Apache Be Saved from Extinction?"), but the cultural climate is such that the magazine is considered controversial, and in order to avoid the pressure groups he has had to remove the editorial offices to the country. Like Wilson, whose journalistic faith he shares, Frank gives us a considerable piece of his mind. He, too, believes that we can only be saved by having the "guts" to "think for ourselves and act on our own ideas." He sees himself as a defender of "the decencies against the gangs that don't give a damn for them" and believes that "the whole turn against tyranny depends on just one man who dares to speak." What he suggests for his epitaph — *"He died for American journalism!"* — the play makes good.

Frank is a quixotic figure because the world in which he lives has in fact been reduced to the Manichaean terms of Gandersheim's vision. Gandersheim, the author of the Shidnats Slyme stories, has a demonic imagination and represents the part of Wilson that is overwhelmed by the evil in the world. Shidnats Slyme, the principle of evil, is Gandersheim's equivalent for Belial, Moloch, Kali, Nobodaddy; and his forms are many, whatever force that blights or kills.

Having fled this evil in Europe, Gandersheim has returned to the countryhouse of his boyhood, another house of the eighties, "the only place," he says, "I really belonged." He has rented the house to Frank and now stays on as his secretary. In the course of the play, he explains to Frank what the reader already suspects, that he and Frank are aspects of the same person. "I am an Easterner," he says, "an aesthete, what's usually called a dreamer — I've travelled, become cosmopolitan; while you're very much the

Westerner and rugged practical man: you stick by the country and its *mores*. And yet both of us represent the same old American thing: an individualistic idealism. We're two faces of the same coin—and it was written that we should land up here, in this silly old house of mine, working on the same brave project." The two faces of the coin might also have been called highbrow and lowbrow; and since between them Frank and Gandersheim are said to embody the traditions of Thomas Paine and of Melville and Poe, the coin itself might be called the liberal imagination.

Gandersheim's real name is Myles Standish Ferguson. In prep school, he was nicknamed "Froggy" (a variant of "Bunny"). His background is more recognizably Wilson's than is Frank's—indeed his appearance is closer to Wilson's, and some of his attitudes, especially his glorification of his Puritan stock and his hatred of parvenus, are Wilson's, admitted here, one should add, in a way that belittles them. Gandersheim is not an attractive character, having been drawn with the same brush that drew Wilbur Flick; he is even demeaned by being a homosexual. Yet he is a partisan of good and loyally supports Frank whom he believes to be the power that works against Shidnats Slyme. Although his vision of evil was born in this house—it is the result of his boyhood Calvinism and the shock of the status revolution—the forces of good are identified with the house itself. From it, they wage a war of enlightenment. As the gardener, a chorus character who speaks for history, says: "There's still some hope in a house like this."

The gardener, the doomed rabbi or Wandering Jew, has himself turned for shelter to this "stranded" house. Always speaking with the calm proper to his sad and infinite wisdom, he utters "a few old platitudes"—the variety of dialects he speaks may give them new currency. He admonishes Judith, Frank's wife, for the idea of perfection which makes it impossible for her to bear the slightest taint of evil. "To make de beauty from de tings dat are damaged," he tells this female Stryker, "dat is the greatest triumph for de man"; and he advises her to use the agencies of love and art. With Gandersheim, he acts as an analyst, explaining that the myths of the psyche have some truth in them and "teach us what to expect." When Gandersheim tells him of his vision of evil as a little blue light, he turns on the light in the darkening room, a gesture that Gandersheim, with his conspiratorial mentality, interprets as a sign that he controls the forces of evil. But the gardener is the upholder of light, not an agent of Teniakis', only "God's agent," and not the agent of Gandersheim's Puritan God, the hanging judge, no instrument of righteousness. The gardener represents the forces that men have forgotten but that will prevail because, like the gardener himself, they cannot be killed: the forces of the spirit, of "the godlike imagination that recreates life through art." That is why he fights only with words and repudiates hatred and violence which, he says, only make more evil. He believes that "only through love, can evil be turned away." At the end, when the little blue light has done its destructive work, he appears from the darkness, a Hebrew prophet, to speak of his long wanderings, to question and yet to affirm man's power to be the bearer of Light. "The Light," he says, "will not wholly fail — I shall bear it, though the Heavens be darkened. . . ."

If there is any consolation in his prophecy it lies in the fact that history is still only history, that this darkened moment is not the end of the world — the wheel of time still turns. (The little blue light, a flashlight in size and appearance, is not in its effectiveness an atom bomb, though it is our assumption of something like this that contributes to our sense of terror. The bomb is never mentioned; indeed, in a play dealing with our not remote future, it is notably absent.) Yet for the moment of history chronicled, the play is Wilson's equivalent of Shaw's *Heartbreak House*: it closes out an era, not however with any suggestion that things will be the better for it. There is no question of Frank's being silenced eventually by Teniakis. Should he publish his exposé, the bright light of publicity would not be enough, as he assumes, to change the state of things; his needed act is at best a significant gesture. In any case, the secret, conspiratorial power he fights has betrayed him in his own house. The forces of evil that he confronts are not so much public as private; are psychic forces within the heart — those "brooding frustrations and disillusions, childlike hurts and furious resentments," as Wilson says of Shaw's play, which "rush suddenly into . . . utterance. . . ." The little blue light is triggered by emotions of hatred, fear, grief, by unpleasant emotions generated in the relationships of individuals; and the play is concerned primarily with these relationships.

The feeling of terror conveyed by the play has genuine sources in the political situation of the time[7] but it is created for the most part by the abrasive relationships of characters. These relationships, by far the most unsatisfactory and the most spiteful in any of Wilson's plays, allow him to express his frustrations and resentments. Gandersheim, for example, allows him to express not only self-disgust but the furious resentments of his childhood — they seem to be directed at his mother — and Judith, the last of several characterizations of the new woman, his resentment, presumably, of Mary McCarthy. He has never been comfortable with the new woman, accommodating her where he can in his imaginative work to his own domestic ideal; and now — it is a major area of concern, as one sees in his remarks on sex in *A Piece of My Mind* — he has Gandersheim speak his mind: "that's what's short-circuiting the world: the woman that won't be a woman, the woman that men can't depend on! . . . what good is a woman, for pity's sake, if she doesn't want to make *men*?!" Judith has neither domestic nor maternal virtues. She is a new woman of the type Wilson noted in Lewis' *Cass Timberlane*, one who competes with men without learning a trade, is rebellious at marriage yet unwilling to take a job; and she, too, leaves her husband but doesn't stick to her lover. Judith's brief affair with Ellis, Frank's secretary, makes a "careerist" of the young man who had been trained for public service. And it is Judith, whose unstable emotions set off the flashlight, who finally betrays Frank.

Aesthete, journalist, prophet — of these personae, only the prophet remains, alone and friendless. His gospel, derived, he says, "from the conscience, the courage, the insight, by which men of a chosen race asserted their superiority," is unavailing now that the traditional disciplines have been replaced by the "new one of electronics" and men trust only the "brute vitality of the universe." "What use for me to continue today if my words cannot influence the action? What use to play commentator merely in a world I can no longer guide?" — his questions are the complaint of the intellectual, who, as Wilson says of himself in *A Piece of My*

[7] See Isaac Rosenfeld's "The Meaning of Terror," *Partisan Review* (January 1949), especially the concluding paragraph: "So who is alienated? We are the prophets and inheritors of the present world and the only men who are at home in it, apart from the tyrannous bureaucrats — and even they regard us as their real enemies. It is impossible to live, to think, to create without bearing witness against the terror. Etc."

Mind, has been "stranded." He no longer, it seems, hopes to be an actor in history, a social engineer. But in fealty to the Light, he accepts the role of light bearer, even if all that he can do in a world of darkness is to show men "where the abyss drops."

The tidings of *Cyprian's Prayer* are more hopeful because this parable of our time is not set in the future, which is always dark, but in the past, in fifteenth-century France, and we know already what the future will disclose. Here again Wilson depicts the frightening political developments of recent history and his own withdrawal from active engagement with them. In a sense, the aging Merlin speaks for him when he says that "the dull old world [is] losing its interest for me. . . ." What he has lost interest in are the day-to-day shifts in alignment in the struggle for power between East and West. Power itself has become its own ideology, and he will not serve it. It is as if, after all the intervening years, he found himself in the world of the pony-cart, but at greater disadvantage than ever before, forced again to affirm "the instinct to give light and life against the lethal concentration on power. . . ." Yet the withdrawal enacted in this play is not a yielding — not the old fogeyism Wilson attributes to himself when he speaks in *A Piece of My Mind* of his unwillingness to be bothered with "the kind of contemporary conflicts that I used to go out to explore."

Cyprian Leclerc — Cyprian-the-intellectual — eventually frees himself from the power entanglements of East and West and chooses to remain alone in his castle, his "own domain — the kingdom of thought and art. . . ." He is the prototype of the Enlightenment man of the future. He makes his decision in 1465, and we are expected to take heart from the fact that his withdrawal to mind his own work made possible a better future. He has the great courage personally to hold the future in trust and, if need be, to withdraw in order to further the progress of mankind. And we are not permitted to see this withdrawal as a retreat to Axel's Castle, for he does not follow the example of the Moonlight Drunkard, that pure soul who finds refuge from political conflict in the world of imagination. Cyprian remains the rebel who tells the Moonlight Drunkard that it isn't enough to evade the brutal and strong but that one must oppose them, and it is clear that he intends to oppose them by doing his work.

The play, however, is creaky and farcical, and is interesting only because it rehearses many of the problems of Wilson's career. The young peasant who seeks diabolical power in order to redress social wrongs is the child of the century that Gauss had once believed Wilson to be. Aware of neither the ambiguity of motives nor the ways of power, he must learn, as Max Weber said in his essay on "Politics as a Vocation," that "he who lets himself in for politics, that is, for power and force as a means, contracts diabolical powers and for his action it is not true that good can follow only from good and evil only from evil, but that often the opposite is true." Experience teaches him this, and Mr. B (Beëlzebub, now a reformed devil) draws the moral for him. By way of exploding the myth of Heaven and Hell, he also depicts for his instruction the archetypal pattern of power, and he advises him to rely not on myth but on himself, on "the light of the mind." In a world where diabolical forces are competing with each other — those of the East are led by a genie with a mustache like Stalin's — this is what Cyprian does. Having turned from black magic to science, he no longer appeals to Satan but to the "Spirit of Man that speaks, that imagines, that plans, that contrives!" In his prayer he now invokes the beneficent powers that make it possible, as Mr. B says, for man to "remake the earth."

III

The themes of the works just surveyed were initiated during the long composition of *Patriotic Gore* (1962), Wilson's homecoming to American myth. "I shall try in the years still before me," he said in concluding *Red, Black, Blond and Olive*, "to deal in a more searching way than I have yet succeeded in doing with the life that I ought to know best." The reporting of foreign travels is now behind him; he has returned home — returned home in the special sense of all of his homecomings: turned back on himself. By the time he acknowledged this in *Red, Black, Blond and Olive* (1956), he was well along with his studies of the Civil War and had declared himself on much that informs *Patriotic Gore*. In *A Piece of My Mind* he spoke of Americanism, ex-

pansionism, and war, and by putting his thoughts in order tried
to tell us, as he says in *Red, Black, Blond and Olive,* "what we are
and what we are doing on earth." [8] Yet in explaining his homeward-turning, he does not make much of his work on the Civil
War. He speaks instead of trying to understand the history and
meaning of Talcottville and his relation to it.

This is deeply appropriate because the Civil War, and especially the years of the Gilded Age that followed it, are for him a
watershed era in his family's history, a history, we remember, that
reaches back to the Mathers but begins to live in his imagination
with the founding of Talcottville in the early years of the Republic. The old stone house there is his personal landmark of the old
America, the America of noble Romans, of which he now writes
so wistfully. Among the best pages of *Patriotic Gore* are those
eddies in the stream of prose in which he describes the spacious
countryside of the America of Jefferson and Audubon — in such
an interval, he has time to write a brilliant Whitmanesque catalog
of the animals Audubon had sketched. And living in the old stone
house, it is easy for him to respond to Lee's estate at Stratford: to
describe the huge brick house and its outbuildings, and to place
Lee, who had restored his family's status and had become for all
Americans a reminder of "the classical antique virtue, at once
aristocratic and republican," in that "headquarters of responsibility." In his own self-portraiture, Wilson asks us to see him in
much the same way — he has created, and is creating in *Patriotic
Gore*, a personally significant American history which enables him
to play his part to the end. The emotional key to this history is
perhaps to be found in what he says of Kate Stone's return to her
plantation at Brokenburn after the war. Kate writes that "Nothing
is left but to endure," that "Everything seems sadly *out of time*";
and Wilson, who italicized the phrase, comments: "Time is after
all a function of the life of a society, and as to pass from one to
another is to shift one's perception of time, so to have one's society destroyed is to find oneself 'out of time.'"

He has had a similar feeling of dislocation in his own life, which
in a way is projected in the Civil War, as well as in the history of
his family. The primary cause of this dislocation is the direction
that society took after the Civil War. The crucial period to which

[8] See also "Postscript of 1957," *The American Earthquake.*

he always turns is this period of commercial expansion and business ascendancy; and whenever he considers a writer of that time, he relates the difficulties of the professional class that by training in the antique virtues was unprepared to meet this new America.[9] (In *Patriotic Gore*, Sarah Morgan speaks directly for this class.) Wilson's explanation — repetition has made it a formula — was used as early as 1924, in an article on Stephen Crane; and strengthened by the Beards' theory of the Civil War as a second revolution, the theory which underlies the historical interpretation of *Patriotic Gore*, it is given its fullest statement in the account of his father in *A Piece of My Mind*.[10] Here we realize the intense filial necessity that has made it a refrain of his work and why, in order to answer the questions of who we are and what we are doing on earth, he turns to the Civil War.

In 1933, another time of crisis and homeward-turning, he gloomily confessed at the end of the essay on the old stone house that he was incapable of leaving the America of Talcottville. At that time, he read there Herndon's *Life of Lincoln* and could hardly bear the thought of that man of genius coming out of the wilderness, "rejoining by heroic self-discipline the creative intelligence of the race, to find himself the conscious focus of its terrible unconscious parturition. . . ." He is, of course, speaking of the role he himself felt called upon to play and for which *To the Finland Station* was to be the prompt book. But Herndon's *Lincoln* had for him a deeper, inescapable association: his father admired Lincoln and identified himself with him, an identification that puzzled the son until he found the clue in Herndon. Herndon's portrait revealed "a great lawyer who was deeply neurotic, who had to struggle through spells of depression, and who . . . had managed, in spite of this handicap, to bring through his own nightmares and the crisis of society — somewhat battered — the American Republic." His father, broken by a crisis in American history, had tried to follow the Great Commoner and, as one surmises from Wilson's exemplification in the portrait of General Sherman

---

[9] Though Wilson may be said to have successfully met his new America — that in fact is one way in which to interpret the significance to him of endurance — it cannot be said that he has achieved the social mastery he desired.

[10] His father died in 1923.

of the "sins" (traumas) of the fathers being visited on the sons, had left to him the legacy of the Republic.

Wilson seems to have been impelled to do what John Jay Chapman did in *William Lloyd Garrison* — to relive in the writing an episode of history that was not his but in which he nevertheless has a stake. *Patriotic Gore* is perhaps best read as such a personal encounter with history. As the critical response indicates, it is unsatisfactory if one turns to it for a systematic or balanced presentation of the history or literature of the period or, to borrow a phrase Wilson uses in connection with the work of Thomas Nelson Page, for the "soft poultices of words" to which we have become accustomed in a time of national celebration.

The book is large and ill-proportioned, made up for the most part of pieces previously published in *The New Yorker* and little revised, and these are often linked by the simple expedient of introductory paragraphs. Yet the book has a significant architecture: it moves from the Northern myth of the war to Northern soldiers and observers, and instead of repeating this development for the South, works back, in a somewhat inverse order, with accounts of Southern ladies, soldiers, and apologists, to Alexander Stephens, with whose *Constitutional View of the Late War Between the States* Wilson is sympathetic. (In a recent interview he said that the South should have been permitted to secede.) The complete development would include the section on the myth of the Old South in the following portmanteau chapter with which Wilson changes the course of the book. The first half of the book, beginning with the eruptive force of *Uncle Tom's Cabin* and ending with the postwar deliberations at Liberty Hall dramatized in the *Constitutional View*, is contained by the rival myths and by the sturdily principled personalities of Harriet Beecher Stowe and Stephens. This organization apparently gives the Northern myth a causal priority and softens whatever hostility one may have towards the South and its myth: the book would appear to be addressed to Northerners but only because, as a Northerner, Wilson has had to work through his prejudices, and because for him the myth of holy war, now a national susceptibility, is more reprehensible than the defeated South's "Great Alibi." This part of the book is devoted almost entirely to the coming of the war and to the conflict itself — here the literature is used to present the living moment — and it creates a sense of action that the remainder, with its treatment of literature and the literary consequences of the war, does not have. The chapters on the poetry and prose of the Civil War are sometimes superficial in their scholarship; the imbalance in treatment and the serious omissions are most noticeable here. But after this necessary but rather desultory excursion, for which the subtitle, "Studies in the Literature of the American Civil War," seems as fitting as *Patriotic Gore* does for the first part, one comes to Justice Holmes. His life, rich in military action as well as thought and, if one considers his forebears, spanning almost all of the history of the Republic, allows Wilson to recover the ground of the book. And Holmes, whom one feels yields more completely to identification than any of the some thirty figures whose lives enact the book, brings it to a successful emotional close. One feels that the great crisis, the war and its aftermath, has been lived through and that Wilson has found in Holmes one of those phenomenal men whose example is still sustaining.

The organizational groundwork may be partly explained by Wilson's dissatisfaction with Van Wyck Brooks's *The Times of Melville and Whitman*. Reviewing the book in 1947, when he had already begun to study the Civil War, he noted that the scheme of *Makers and Finders* diverted Brooks from "featuring the war as the crisis it was in the development of American society" and that one missed in his book "the stress of the period. . . ." Wilson himself recreates for us this "moment of bankruptcies and wounds, of miscarriages, distortions, frustrations," and to some extent, by considering De Forest, Bierce, and Lanier in relation to their war experience, overcomes the defect he found in Brooks's regional treatment. Perhaps Cable figures so largely for him because he felt that Brooks had not made enough of the "strain and waste" of his life — though scope of treatment, one suspects, depends also on the scholarly research that is available to him and, as the case of De Forest suggests, on his personal interest. Making the war the focal point of the book may account for the failure to treat in an adequate way the most important literary figures — Melville, Whitman, Howells, Twain, James, Adams, and Emily Dickinson. And his admiration for Brooks's work may have led

him, in the case of Frederick Tuckerman, to the delving into
corners that is justified by a *trouvaille*. Certainly, the excessive
quotation, necessary as it often is for his purposes, is an adapta-
tion of Brooks's still freer practice.

An even more interesting aspect of the organization of the book
is the clue it provides to Wilson's present assessment of his role
as man of letters. The two parts of the book are joined in a way
that has the deepest meaning for him, and the impression that
the movement of the book makes is related to this. The Civil War,
in its scale, technique, brutality, is "modern"; the Southerners
remind us of war's time-honored but foresaken rules. But in spite
of the parallels this permits Wilson to draw to more recent enor-
mities, and in spite of the verbal equivalents that call to mind his
favorite Callot's *The Miseries of War*, we are struck by his vicari-
ous excitement over its action and, especially in the portraits of
Grant, Sherman, and Mosby, by the extent to which he identifies
with the men of action who are making history. He remarks of
Henry James that he liked to read military memoirs and books
about Napoleon, envied the qualities of "'the brilliant man of
action,'" and planned his literary career as if it were a military
campaign; and we feel that he, too, would like to experience, as
he says of Sherman, "the real exaltation of leadership." Still unsatisfied with the role of sayer, he would be a doer — and it is not
fortuitous that one remembers in reading *Patriotic Gore* how he
had dramatized once before in *To the Finland Station* a glorious
imperative to action.

Although the biographical method and the spotlight technique
of *To the Finland Station* are employed again in *Patriotic Gore*,
the theory of history exemplified in the earlier book has been
abandoned in the later. Wilson puts aside the dialectical theory
that willy-nilly contributed to the dramatic narrative of *To the
Finland Station*. In *Patriotic Gore* the *view* of history is more complex and the narrative, accordingly, less single-minded. *To the
Finland Station* moves irresistibly toward the acting of history, but
in *Patriotic Gore*, except for the opening chapters where the Provi-
dential theory of the Northerners is assimilated to the Marxist
assurance of historical backing, such movement is absent. Instead
one finds a tapestry being woven before one's eyes. Various
threads appear and reappear in the fabric, and scenes already

visible fill out in other unexpected forms and colors. This is accomplished by the skillful use of perspectives: by seeing the war as it is seen by various characters, by the varied personal response of character to character (for example, Adams on Lincoln and Grant), by the careful threading of themes (Mrs. Chesnut on Mrs. Stowe's *Uncle Tom's Cabin* and, in a different vein, Alexander Stephens' recording in prison the "irrepressible conflict" of the bedbugs and their victim). The individuals of *Patriotic Gore* do not, as in *To the Finland Station*, subserve a theory: no one arrives at last at a Finland Station; the "key of a philosophy of history" does not "fit an historical lock"; no one achieves the almost superhuman grandeur of Lenin. The individuals have only their personal destinies. They make history — the way in which Wilson uses the literary record shows them, whatever the nature of their action, making it — but the history in which they are immersed is neither directed by them nor using them for its own certain purpose. In a way the book gives one the impression that the Civil War, as a historical moment or crisis, is fixed, while the destinies of individuals move through it and beyond. How brief the moment of action! How long the life that remains! What really matters when these individuals confront history is their destinies, the lives that they live out afterwards and that constitute for them the essential weight of history. In effect, Wilson is saying: "Confront the crisis, as you must. But remember that it will have consequences for you, and, through you, for generations to come. The moment of confrontation may be glorious, but it may also destroy the moral props of your life." History in *Patriotic Gore* moves all at once, like an agitated sea, and casts up debris from which the mind eagerly takes the hope of some significance. Or to return to the tapestry: although it is finally completed, one follows its threads beyond its borders, and since it is so vast, an incredibly richly detailed work with subjects of various proportions sometimes compelling attention, sometimes demanding it, one cannot grasp it in its entirety and find beyond complexity itself a design of history. The book gives one, as Robert Penn Warren says, a sense of "roles and dooms in a single drama." It does not stir us to glorious action but teaches us to work out our private destinies with stoic resignation.

This conception of history has not put to rest Wilson's own

desire to play an active, responsible part in the present crisis. In speaking of the chastening of American prose style after the Civil War, he relates its terseness, precision, and lucidity to the demands of wartime communication. The language of Lincoln and Grant, which he uses to assay their qualities of mind and character, is, he says, "the language of responsibility"; [11] and those who served in the war, like Bierce, De Forest, and Holmes, carried on its "accent of decisiveness," while nonparticipants, like James and Adams, developed a style prolix, ambiguous, and ironical. In *A Piece of My Mind*, he tells of his own devotion to the stylistic trinity of lucidity, force, and ease, and though he employs long prose rhythms, his style is readily associated with the chastened prose of responsibility, with the language of leadership. In the matter of style, he places himself with the men of action.

But some men who had known action were disillusioned. The experience of war robbed Holmes and Bierce and De Forest of a "compelling faith," the lack of which, as in Adams, too, is felt in a certain "aridity and bleakness." Yet disillusioned as Wilson himself has been by war and revolution — the ostensible purpose of the book is to clear away their enabling myths — he will not relinquish his faith or succumb to the aridity and bleakness of his own satanism. "A Lincoln or a Harriet Beecher Stowe," he writes in one of those abrupt comments that tells so much, "was impassioned by a vision, a purpose. The one sought to obtain for his nation that it should have, under God, a new birth of freedom and prove to the sneering old world that such a government as the Revolution had tried to establish could survive internal dissension; Mrs. Stowe, who had been read to in her childhood from Cotton Mather's history of New England, still believed that America was 'consecrated by some special dealing of God's providence.'" In its context, this passage conveys conviction, a conviction supported in the book by Wilson's adherence to the Lincolnian idea of the Republican experiment and elsewhere by his notion of the United States as a "society." "The United States," he says at the beginning of the chapter devoted to it in *A Piece of My Mind*, "is not a nation. . . . It is a society, a political system, which is still in a somewhat experimental state." This explains

[11] See also the analysis of Lenin's literary style in *To the Finland Station*, Anchor edition, pp. 382–383.

for him our various panics, of which the most consequential was the crisis of the Civil War, and, accordingly, the one to be used typologically to illuminate the present crisis. In fact, what he concludes from these crises — that "the Republic has thus had to be saved over and over again, and it continues to have to be saved" — declares his purpose in writing *Patriotic Gore*. With it, one might put for a motto the sentences that conclude the passage in which he redresses his strictures on James and Adams by acknowledging the outstanding achievements their nonparticipation made possible: "They also serve who only stand and watch. The men of action make history, but the spectators make most of the histories, and these histories may influence the action." Writing history in order to save the Republic, commanding the language of responsibility, he is perhaps as much a man of action as an intellectual, with little inclination for the actual work of politics, can be. It is to his credit that he at least sees this moment as one of action, of dispatch for the intellectual. He has always had the courage to make his private troubles public issues, and (reversing this brilliant formulation of C. Wright Mills) to make public issues his private woe. In doing so, he communicates, as before, from the most important battlefronts of our time.[12]

What has Wilson made of history and how does his history influence the action?

The most explicit use he makes of the literature of the Civil War is to introduce us to a supreme occasion in history and to strip away its melodramatic trappings. He had written in *Red, Black, Blond and Olive* of the need to discourage myths and had remarked that he hoped "to return to the subject in connection with the American Civil War — so much obscured, then and now, by the semi-religious myths in terms of which we have liked to conceive it." In *Patriotic Gore* he restages the competition to which he believes such myths inevitably lead. At the same time, he further discredits them by showing the ironies that the competi-

---

[12] Whatever one may think of Wilson's tax delinquency, he must grant the courage of his protest, *The Cold War and the Income Tax*. Its importance is representative, as an example of the kind of gesture open to intellectuals. Its content is hardly new, Wilson himself having summarized it earlier in the introduction to *Patriotic Gore* (pp. xxviii–xxix).

tion produced in the lives of the participants, some of whom served a standard without accepting the myth, others believing the myth and serving only to become disillusioned, and in the affairs of the nation, which lacked a statesman prescient enough to see the economic and social consequences. War, he explains in the introduction, is promoted by myths but motivated by animal appetite; it is a struggle for power — in the nineteenth century, a struggle for unification and centralization — in which sea-slugs devour each other.[13] America, too, has been driven by this hunger for expansion, and her history is indeed a chronicle of patriotic gore — he reviews our wars and the myths that glorified them, and lists the casualties.

This reductive, biological view of American history and its application to the competition between America and Russia has angered rather than sobered most readers. They fail to see the introduction as an expression of profound revulsion at the present state of history with its masquerade of power, and they assume that showing up the ways in which moral appeals have been used to dignify a cause is equivalent to saying that morality itself is cant, when the very metaphor of ingurgitation is not without its own moral appeal. In fact the harsh realism of the piece is a moral club for those who do not recognize the morality of truth-seeking, who do not see the advantage in the conduct of foreign affairs of tempering the competition, and who have nothing of the genuine concern for the experiment which on hearing the Declaration of Independence read stirred Mrs. Stowe to desire "to preserve the integrity of our unprecedented republic." Wilson, it seems, is addressing in the introduction those of his countrymen who have been dissociated by the very media that gives them the voice and image of America from the actual America, the on-going Republic in which they truly have a stake.

The sense of urgency that inspired this book breaks through in the introduction where Wilson, instead of letting his history speak for itself, speaks for it. "One cannot care so much about what has

[13] In *The Children of Light and the Children of Darkness*, a critique of the liberal ideology, Reinhold Niebuhr remarks that "a modern nation does not dare to go to war for reasons other than those of self-interest and cannot conduct the war without claiming to be motivated by higher motives than those of self-interest." (New York, Charles Scribner's Sons, 1944, p. 170n.)

happened in the past," he said of the writing of history in *To the Finland Station,* "and not care what is happening in one's own time." And he added, though at the time it was with the intent of following a course of direct action, that "one cannot care about what is happening in one's own time without wanting to do something about it." He has chosen to do something by probing myths still vital and cherished: the Northern myth of the "Treasury of Virtue" and the Southern myth of the "Great Alibi," [14] legacies of the Civil War, "fraudulent traditions," he says, that will not save us. If the affairs of nations, however, are truly as elemental as those of sea-slugs, nothing can save us. Still the import of the book — even that of the desperate image of the sea-slug — is that the Republic must be saved, and saved at home, saved in us; and that it can be saved by increased devotion to the cause for which many have given the full measure of devotion. Wilson's view of American expansion may be wrongheaded, but his intentions are noble and his history salutary. He follows Mrs. Stowe in wishing to fight for *his* country and to make some declaration on his own account. As far as possible, he will be responsible for the making of history. And his way is to write history, to revive in us an ardor for the tradition of our Republic, for the great revolutionary experiment whose unfinished work is the burden of our history.

Biological tropism hardly explains the history he has written nor the view of Michelet that it exemplifies — that history is primarily the matter of man, his proper study. The encounter between Mr. Beebe and the iguana, which Wilson says still represents his idea of man's relation to nature (instinct), is not won by the sluggish reptile. Long ago, Whitehead helped him overcome the despair of naturalism; and he is still too much a man of the Enlightenment to forswear the idea of human progress. At times, ever more so now that he speaks for what he believes to be eternal in human history, one feels his kinship with the type of someone like Alexander Stephens, who adhered to unalterable principles and aimed at the construction of a perfect society — indeed, one feels, at times, that he wished history would stand still. But the true kinship is not so much with any figure in the book as it is with Michelet, its presiding genius.

[14] The terms are Robert Penn Warren's, in his *The Legacy of the Civil War,* New York, Random House, Inc., 1961.

One feels this not only in the method of the book but in the situation of the author. In a number of ways Wilson had tried in *To the Finland Station* to identify with Lenin, when, in fact, he had more in common with Michelet whom he said was a "man of an unsettled and passionate generation . . . [who] forged his own personality, created his own trade and established his own place." [15] Time has secured this identification and deepened the inspiration Wilson has drawn from Michelet. And now one finds him in the position of Michelet, writing in a time of reaction, perhaps with the hope of setting in motion, as he shows Michelet doing, a vision of man's immemorial struggle against limitation, and certainly in order to rejoin through his history, as he says again of Michelet, "a part of the human world of which he believed in the importance and destiny."

The best gloss on what Wilson has now achieved in the writing of history is his own description of Michelet's. In Michelet, he says, "what we are aware of is not a surface, but the thing he is presenting, the living complex of the social being. Michelet's primary concern is to stick close to men and events; he succeeds in dominating history, like Odysseus wrestling with Proteus, by seizing it and holding on to it through all its variety of metamorphoses. . . ." By identifying with the people and the period, he relives, and reconstitutes, so that we experience "the peculiar shape and color of history as it must have seemed to the men who had lived it." Great men, for him, are "ambitious marionettes" set at work by the impulse of history the people supply (consider Wilson's Lincoln); these he shows "in their relation to the social group which has molded them and whose feelings they are finding expression for, whose needs they are attempting to satisfy"; and, at times, it is to his purpose to bring them "so close to us that we can note a change in their health or morale, their manner or their way of dressing . . . [and] follow their private relationships, enter into their love affairs." To recreate history in this way is not to suggest the warfare of sea-slugs but the sense of incredible complexity that is humanity creating itself. "There is no book,"

[15] Wilson makes this comment in order to distinguish Michelet from Renan and Taine, "members of learned castes." It is quite possible that even now, in so obviously following Michelet in the writing of history, Wilson unconsciously makes the same distinction in his own behalf by treating scholars and their work carelessly and with minimal acknowledgment

Wilson says of the *History of France*, "that makes us feel when we have finished it that we have lived through and known with such intimacy so many generations of men. And it makes us feel something more: that we ourselves are the last chapter of the story and that the next chapter is for us to create."

The method, if not the focal action, of *Patriotic Gore* makes it a history of America, a study of generations, not unlike Michelet's masterpiece. Much that on first sight seems irrelevant serves to extend its historical vistas or to fill them out. We are told, for example, of De Forest's books on Salem witchcraft and on the Indians of Connecticut, and introduced to the old Connecticut judge of *The Wetherel Affair*, of whom De Forest writes, "All of his ancestors, as far back as the days of the *Mayflower*, had been not only Puritans, but Puritans of good social position and of high breeding"; Mrs. Chesnut tells us of her father-in-law, "partly patriarch, partly *grand seigneur* . . . the last of the lordly planters who ruled this Southern world," and we see him old and blind, still attended by his Negro servant, surviving the war with dignity; Harriet and Calvin Stowe lead us through scenes of clerical life, Tourgée and Cable tell us of the era of Reconstruction, and Holmes, who comments on the Sacco-Vanzetti case, lives on into the New Deal. This excursion in time is made with sympathy but directed by a passionate humanitarianism and combativeness for freedom similar to Michelet's. Where Michelet used his history to make war on superstition, Wilson uses his to make war on Calvinism. "Everything past, present and future, takes its place in the legend of American idealism" — this statement, made in reference to our myths, announces the theme of the book and relates particularly to Calvinism, the obdurate enemy with which Wilson wrestles throughout book and finally, in Holmes, subdues to his own purpose.

Wilson reveals his mixed response to his own religious inheritance at the start, in the chapters on the Stowes. Harriet, daughter of Lyman Beecher, one of the dynasty of ministerial Beechers, fights out New England's long battle with the "hanging God" of Jonathan Edwards — the "monstrous conception of God," Wilson remarks, that "was carried along well to the end of the nineteenth century."[16] Calvin Stowe, her hypochondriacal husband, lives

[16] See *The Little Blue Light* in *Five Plays*, p. 505.

with the devils of a "Calvinist fantasy," is crippled by a terrible anxiety much as Wilson's father has been and he himself to a lesser extent had. Harriet turned to the milder Christianity of Episcopalianism; Calvin, like Wilson, was attracted to Judaism. But meanwhile the Calvinist vision of judgment served the fanatical ends of holy war and unrelenting Reconstruction. It enlisted the freethinker Lincoln, inspired *The Battle Hymn of the Republic*, and took the field with idealistic men like Oliver Wendell Holmes, Jr. and Thomas Wentworth Higginson, the latter a "Bible-drugged" supporter of the "lunatic" John Brown. (Calvinist-inspired fanaticism also drove the Southerner, Stonewall Jackson.) Fulfilled by victory, it contributed heavily to the nation's righteousness — to the "Treasury of Virtue."

It is hard, perhaps, to separate the religion from the sturdy character of its believers, but this is what Wilson would like to do. He extols the moral fortitude of New Englanders, and in the chapter on Holmes speaks approvingly of "the spirit of Puritan protest." But here, as when he had had Beppo say that this "tradition of protest is perhaps the one sound thing we've got," he is referring not to Calvinism, but to a general protestant spirit, to a secular and rationally critical idealism and moral individualism such as that which fired the liberals in his early manhood.

One sees the virtues of Puritanism that he is seeking in men like Cable and De Forest and Holmes. Cable's piety and conscientiousness, for example, distressed Lafcadio Hearn and Twain — Twain wrote Howells, "You will never, never know, never divine, guess, imagine, how loathsome a thing the Christian religion can be made until you come to know and study Cable daily and hourly." But Wilson, reviewing Cable's career, amends Twain's opinion: he says that Cable's Puritanism was not as inflexible as Twain made out, that under no circumstances could he be called a prig, and that, lacking as he was in the artistic temperament of Twain and Hearn, he had "a stronger intellect and more integration of character than either." And this strength, he adds, "was no doubt [the result of] the New England blood which was mingled in him with that of Virginia." The strengths and weaknesses of De Forest are also the result of his New England blood: on the one hand, "his sense of his own competence, his pride, which is, however, quite without ostentation, in his principles, his abilities and

stamina"; on the other, his tightly reined curiosity and inability
to respond emotionally to experience which give his writing a
"curious dull and chill touch. . . ." These deficiencies in the novel-
ist, however, he attributes to his "background of Calvinist theology." They are not so much a personal fault as liabilities of his
situation, general conditions that have constrained the imaginations of many Americans: "You could hardly get a Shakespeare
or a Balzac or a Tolstoy or a Dostoevsky," he asserts, "out of a
mind that had been molded by this doctrine [Calvinism]."

Holmes, wounded on the battlefield, denied God and lived, but
the Calvinism he had rejected still persisted in his desire to win
salvation by achieving the "superlative" in his calling. War taught
him the error of the Abolitionists' apocalyptic vision — "I detest,"
he wrote Harold Laski in a letter in which he compared the Abolitionists to the Communists, "a man who knows that he knows."
It also taught him that "everything is founded on the death of men,"
a conviction that enabled him to serve a law no longer sacred
but the precarious result of the experiment of human life. Holmes
was not a liberal, though there were times when he seemed to be,
and his personality, as Wilson makes it out for us, is bleak. He
determinedly followed his career, not even turning aside to read
the newspaper or, for the sake of the cases he was trying, to
acquaint himself with industrial, labor, or economic facts. He
did not believe that man had any cosmic significance, yet he had
a sense of his own importance and of the inferiority of others.
Nevertheless, Wilson finds much to admire in this man of "negative convictions," especially the devotion to career which, however
much it narrowed his range and checked his sympathies, helped
him to weather the postwar conditions that wrecked so many.

Holmes's conception of a career is not to be confused with
careerism, a phenomenon of the bureaucratic world that Wilson
depicted in the character of Ellis in *The Little Blue Light*. The
careerist is a self-seeker, an opportunist; he eschews public service. The "jobbist" — to use Holmes's term — is not ambitious in the
vulgar sense; he chooses a calling such as the law, which Holmes
considered a significant part of the human enterprise, and in this
calling he seeks to attain intellectual mastery, to excel, and (God
willing) to touch the "superlative." The conception of vocation
here, as Wilson explains, is simply that of the Brahmin scholarly

tradition, to which Holmes has added his own personal need to find in intellectual distinction the proof of his "justification." One might say that where the careerist is selfishly other-directed, Holmes-the-jobbist is selfishly inner-directed. The "dedication to an ideal of excellence which is not to save others but to justify oneself" — this is the last vestige of Calvinism that Wilson would remove, the perversion, which he disclaims, of the tradition to which he belongs.

But Holmes was in fact all of his life holding back the idealistic sympathies his experience of war had caused him to renounce. This was the high price he paid for coming through, and it is gratifying to see him, an old man, warming to the young men who were working for social justice. In any reckoning there is, of course, his solid legal and literary achievement. Equally praiseworthy, as Wilson insists in an essay on the Holmes-Laski correspondence, is the fact that "he figured in his field as something of a priest and prophet . . . [as] a lawgiver and moralist who held himself quite superior to worldly considerations." [17] And, finally, there is the grandeur of the man who, in spite of negative convictions, among them an uncertainty about democracy, left his fortune to the government of the United States. "The American Constitution was, as he came to declare, an 'experiment,' — what was to come of our democratic society it was impossible for a philosopher to tell — but he had taken responsibility for its workings, he had subsisted and achieved his fame through his tenure of the place it had given him; and he returned to the treasury of the Union the little he had

---

[17] "The Holmes-Laski Correspondence," *Eight Essays*, Anchor Books, Garden City, New York, Doubleday and Co., 1954, deals with a later stage of Holmes's career. It rounds out the chapter in *Patriotic Gore* and gives prominence to some aspects of Wilson's identification with Holmes not treated there. Of most importance in understanding the prophetic direction of his own work is Wilson's comment on the Judaic elements in New England culture that accounted for Holmes's friendships with Brandeis, Frankfurter, Morris Cohen, and Laski: they shared, he says, "the conviction that what we do in this world must have the sanction of non-worldly values and be acted in the sight of eternity." Just as important, because it provides a clue to Wilson's profound satisfaction in writing of Holmes, is the fact, brought to our attention by him, that Laski "needed a Jewish father" and found one in Holmes. But, happily, a priest and prophet himself, he is as much father as son: a patriarch, a thinker "whose position has something of the rabbinical," like "Marx or Trotsky or Freud, Arnold Schoenberg or Alfred Stieglitz."

to leave." With this explanation of Holmes's gesture, Wilson concludes the book.

Holmes, of course, is not, as Wilson purports, the last of the republican Romans. In giving us what is now recognized as an American Plutarch's *Lives*,[18] and in his own long career which is wonderfully fulfilled here, he has taken his place with them. And Holmes is not so remote as to be merely a figure of the past, only remote enough to strike us as old-fashioned — old-fashioned, however, in a reassuring way, and in a way that Wilson, too, is old-fashioned. Commenting on the enthusiastic response of audiences to a second-rate movie about Holmes, Wilson explained how inspiriting, in a time of national uncertainty, was the reminder of the "just man," the "man of the old America," the man who had "triumphed in remaining faithful to some kind of traditional ideal." The film, produced in 1951, carries the studies of the Civil War into our own time and exemplifies how history, by means of art, tells its story and renews itself. We may consider it to be Wilson's own commentary on the uses of his book, especially if we keep in mind that he wishes most by means of his book to renew our sense of the necessity of virtue — our sense of what Herbert Croly meant when he said at the end of *The Promise of American Life* that "the principle of democracy *is* virtue. . . . " The common citizen, Croly said, needed models that he could sincerely and enthusiastically imitate; and Wilson, who had himself once cited this statement, has tried to offer him "acceptable examples of heroism and saintliness."

Now Holmes is especially important here because he represents the tradition of republican patriotism that Wilson upholds. In *A Piece of My Mind*, he defines this tradition, the crucial distinctions being those of having a sense of America's role and a stake in her success; and his example again is Holmes who, he says, "felt a stake in the United States of a kind that his friend Henry James did not feel." What distinguishes the kind is something more than concern for or loyalty to America, both of which, in his way, James had. The difference, Wilson explains, "derives from the fact that Holmes had, as James had not, *identified* his own interests

[18]Alfred Kazin first made the comparison.

with those of the American Republic." Such identification of interests, he maintains, is not a measure of the human achievement of men like James whose stake was art; but one feels that he thinks otherwise — that he believes that as a man of letters he has given his whole life, like Holmes, to the service of his country.

And it is true that in *Patriotic Gore* he has once more and in a direct way given his skill, intelligence, awareness, and devotion to the treasury of his country. He has even put himself forward as a model. For here we find him an upstate New York republican patriot such as Harold Frederic portrayed in *The Copperhead*: a man of principle, who champions the right of the South to secede and refuses to contribute to the war effort, is attacked by his neighbors, yet after the war (this detail of the comparison he would spare us) earns their respect for his allegiance "to his own ideal of American republican freedom." [19]

[19] The parallels here and in *Patriotic Gore* are fairly loose, speaking most forcibly for principled obstinacy and, in the championship of the right to secede, for coexistence and the national determination Wilson has recently considered in "My Fifty Years with Dictionaries and Grammars," *The New Yorker* (April 20, 1963). One understands how appealing to Wilson now the example of Alexander Stephens or Abner Beech in *The Copperhead* might be, but one wonders if Wilson, had he lived at the time of the Civil War, would have yielded his principled devotion to the "experiment" that secession jeopardized.

Epilogue

The language of citations is seldom felicitous or exact, but in the case of the Presidential Medal of Freedom awarded to Wilson on December 6, 1963, it is at least correct: "Critic and historian, he has converted criticism itself into a creative act, while setting for the nation a stern and uncompromising standard of independent judgment." The first part of the tribute suggests, though perhaps perfunctorily, the lifetime work without which the achievement of the second part might have gone unnoticed and unproclaimed.[1] But the second part has point and refers unquestionably to *Patriotic Gore,* the book which brought Wilson, after years of indifferent attention, once again into the light of publicity.

Because of coincidence of publication and Wilson's absence from the ceremony, the second part of the citation seemed also to refer specifically to *The Cold War and the Income Tax: A Protest,* in which Wilson concluded that he had finally come to feel that "this country, whether or not I continue to live in it, is no longer any place for me."[2] And so the occasion, which for other

[1] I have taken the citation from the report in the *New York Times,* December 7, 1963. I have corrected an obvious misprint, and though I am suspicious about "creative act" — "creative art" seems more likely — will let it stand as recognition of Wilson's intention.

[2] The awards were announced July 4, 1963; the book was published in the autumn of 1963. In leading up to his conclusion, Wilson mentions Thoreau, though not the following sentences from "Civil Disobedience" which seem to express his feelings precisely: "How does it become a man to behave toward this American government today? I answer, that he cannot without disgrace be associated with it."

recipients may have properly honored a full career, only dramatized the fact that the first literary critic to be recognized by the
government was more estranged than he had ever been from the
country in whose service he had spent his life.

He has always been an outsider, the very continuity that sustains him having been with an America that antedates the society
in which he finds himself. And as he indicates in *A Piece of My
Mind* when he remarks that "my own generation in America has
not had so gay a journey as we expected when we first started
out," history itself has had something to do with the estrangement
— history and the progressive attitudes with which he had been
prepared to meet it. Wilson is a child of the Progressive Era and,
although he has criticized its intellectual and moral simplicity,
still responds to its sentiments. His hope for social change — the
fine expectancy he showed in the economic crisis of the thirties —
has its well-spring in the Progressive Era, as does the moral tenor
of his work; and his fundamental criticism of America in *The Cold
War and the Income Tax* is a progressive one — that the *bigness*
of government itself is "making it more and more difficult to
carry on the tradition of American individualism. . . ." He has
the progressive's sensitivity to the qualitative human possibilities
that comprise the promise of American life. He believes in the
"experiment with political and social ideals" that Croly said was
of more than national importance because it "stands for the highest hopes of an excellent worldly life that mankind has yet ven-
tured," and in its behalf he follows the progressives in wishing both
to liberate and discipline the people. In making this his work,
he has always, to use Max Weber's terms, upheld an "ethics of
responsibility" rather than an "ethics of ultimate ends." It is what
he now admires in the early Theodore Roosevelt, whose " 'practical politics' " of accommodation he prefers to the intransigence of
reformers like John Jay Chapman; and however intransigent his
own opposition to the cold war and its financing, it is more to the
issue of the present discordant encounter of our culture that he
remains an independent intellectual who with art contests the
ideology of the careerist.[3]

[3] Daniel Bell, in *The End of Ideology*, revised edition, New York, Collier
Books, 1961, p. 302, uses Wilson's remarks on Theodore Roosevelt to explain
Weber's distinctions. Harold Rosenberg in *The Tradition of the New*, New

His posture is defensive and appears conservative, though conserving better describes it. We recognize in Wilson the union of "conservative impulse" and "radical idea" that Richard Chase in *The Democratic Vista* considers to be a characteristic of our best minds, and we recognize also what Chase, taking Edith Wharton for his example, calls "piety toward civilization." Conservatism, here, is a way of speaking of one's profound sense of relationship with the past, the necessary kind of relationship that confirms one's feeling that "the style of integrity developed by his culture or civilization" is, as Erik Erikson says, "'the patrimony of his soul'. . . ." Wilson is not a conservative in any other sense; is not, for instance, a John Dos Passos, the Virginia squire of whom he writes: "On account of Soviet knavery, / He favors restoring slavery."

"Old-fashioned" is the word Wilson himself most often uses in describing the values he conserves, and one can use it to describe him if it is remembered that to be old-fashioned is merely to be out-of-fashion, not out-of-use. And to define it, one can turn to Wilson's review of Dreiser's *The Bulwark*, published in *The New Yorker* in 1946. Here Wilson notes that when Solon Barnes "finds, in his garden, a beautiful green insect devouring an equally beautiful rosebud, he does not . . . think of 'Nature, red in tooth and claw'; he rises, on the contrary, to the realization that 'there must be a Creative Divinity, and so a purpose, behind all of this variety and beauty and tragedy of life.'" This view of the universe of Dreiser's last hero — it is advanced by the narrator of *Memoirs of Hecate County* — admonishes the Manichaean-inspired Strykers of our society; and it is the view of the gardener in *The Little Blue Light*, one which may be said to be the result of a metaphysics such as Whitehead's having been certified by personal religious experience such as John Jay Chapman's. Indeed, the gardener, the doomed rabbi of Wilson's play who derives his gospel from conscience alone, may have been modeled on Solon, the Quaker, who asks one of his daughters, "'If thee do not turn to the Inner Light, where will thee go?'"

York, Horizon Press, 1959, p. 263, approves of Wilson's repudiation of *kitsch* — of his proper regard for the responsibilities of art. The organization man, the intellectual or professional who in purchasing "social place" redeems alienation by paying the higher price of self-alienation and for whom *kitsch* is an article of ideology, is Rosenberg's equivalent for Wilson's "careerist."

Solon's faith, Wilson insists, is an old-fashioned American faith, as much so as his own faith, which it underprops, in the reform, progress, and survival of mankind — a faith, Wilson said in a recent interview, that he holds to "entirely instinctively" as a part of his nineteenth-century birthright. And because of this faith his self-confidence, as he says of Solon's, cannot be shaken. He identifies with Solon Barnes, whom he finds "almost unique, in this new American world of fast motor cars and Main Line riches, in being able to withstand the current. Taught that the appetite for money conflicts with the service of God and that the voice of morality is not a convention but something that speaks within, he is proof against the lust for speculation and blind imitation of one's neighbors that dominated and debauched the eighteen-nineties and early nineteen-hundreds." The tides of society have not swept him away, and by identifying with men of spirit like Solon as well as by creating others who speak for himself, he has continued to affirm the humanism which has given him the moral strength to resist the authority of the pony-cart.

Bibliographical Note

For the convenience of the reader and by way of acknowledgment to publishers, this list of editions of the books of Edmund Wilson is included.

The Undertaker's Garland, in collaboration with John Peale Bishop, New York, Alfred A. Knopf, 1922.

Discordant Encounters: Plays and Dialogues, New York, Albert & Charles Boni, 1926. "The Poet's Return: Mr. Paul Rosenfeld and Mr. Matthew Josephson" and "The Delegate from Great Neck: Mr. Van Wyck Brooks and Mr. Scott Fitzgerald" are reprinted in *The Shores of Light*; "In the Galapagos: Mr. William Beebe and a Marine Iguana" is reprinted in *A Piece of My Mind*; "The Crime in the Whistler Room" is reprinted in *This Room and This Gin and These Sandwiches* and in *Five Plays*.

I Thought of Daisy, New York, Charles Scribner's Sons, 1929. Reprinted by Farrar, Straus and Young, 1953; Ballantine Books, paperback edition, 1953. Available in Penguin Books.

Poets, Farewell!, New York, Charles Scribner's Sons, 1929. Most of the poetry and prose in this volume is reprinted in *Night Thoughts*.

Axel's Castle: A Study in the Imaginative Literature of 1870 to 1930, New York and London, Charles Scribner's Sons, 1931. Available in paperback, Scribner's.

The American Jitters: A Year of the Slump, New York and London, Charles Scribner's Sons, 1932. Except for "The Independent Farmer" and "The Case of the Author," reprinted in *The American Earthquake*.

Travels in Two Democracies, New York, Harcourt, Brace and Co., 1936. The American portion, with some additions, is reprinted in *The American Earthquake*; the Russian portion, with the addition of suppressed materials, is reprinted in *Red, Black, Blond and Olive*. These reprintings omit the prologue, flashback, and epilogue.

This Room and This Gin and These Sandwiches: Three Plays, New York, The New Republic, 1937. Contains "The Crime in the Whistler Room," "Beppo and Beth," "A Winter in Beech Street" (later retitled, "This Room and This Gin and These Sandwiches"). All are reprinted in *Five Plays*.

The Triple Thinkers: Ten Essays on Literature, New York, Harcourt, Brace and Co., 1938. Revised and enlarged edition published by Oxford University Press, 1948; available in paperback, Galaxy Books, Oxford University Press.

To the Finland Station: A Study in the Writing and Acting of History, New York, Harcourt, Brace and Co., 1940. With omissions and substitutions in the appendices, available in paperback, Anchor Books, Doubleday and Co.

The Boys in the Back Room: Notes on California Novelists, San Francisco, The Colt Press, 1941. Reprinted in *Classics and Commercials*.

The Wound and the Bow: Seven Studies in Literature, Boston, Houghton Mifflin Co., 1941. Available in paperback, University Paperbacks, Methuen, London.

Note-books of Night, San Francisco, The Colt Press, 1942. Most of the poetry and prose of this volume is reprinted in *Night Thoughts*.

The Shock of Recognition: The Development of Literature in the United States Recorded by the Men Who Made It, Garden City, New York, Doubleday, Doran and Co., 1943. Available in paperback, University Library, Grosset and Dunlap.

Memoirs of Hecate County, Garden City, New York, Doubleday and Co., 1946. Reprinted by L. C. Page & Co., New York, 1959; available in paperback, Signet Books, New American Library of World Literature.

Europe Without Baedeker: Sketches Among the Ruins of Italy, Greece, and England, Garden City, New York, Doubleday and Co., 1947.

The Little Blue Light: A Play in Three Acts, New York, Farrar, Straus and Co., 1950. Reprinted in *Five Plays*.

Classics and Commercials: A Literary Chronicle of the Forties, New York, Farrar, Straus and Co., 1950. Available in paperback, Vintage Books, Random House. Contents partially reprinted in *A Literary Chronicle: 1920–1950*.

The Shores of Light: A Literary Chronicle of the Twenties and Thirties, New York, Farrar, Straus and Young, 1952. Available in paperback, Vintage Books, Random House. Contents partially reprinted in *A Literary Chronicle: 1920–1950*.

Eight Essays, Garden City, New York, Doubleday and Co., 1954. An Anchor Book paperback containing four new essays.

Five Plays, New York, Farrar, Straus and Young, 1954. Reprints all previously published plays and "Cyprian's Prayer."

The Scrolls from the Dead Sea, New York, Oxford University Press, 1955. Available in paperback, Meridian Books, The World Publishing Company.

Red, Black, Blond and Olive: Studies in Four Civilizations: Zuñi, Haiti, Soviet Russia, Israel, New York, Oxford University Press, 1956.

A Piece of My Mind: Reflections at Sixty, New York, Farrar, Straus and Cudahy, 1956. Reprinted in paperback, Anchor Books, Doubleday and Co.

A Literary Chronicle: 1920–1950, Garden City, New York, Doubleday and Co., 1956. An Anchor Book paperback selection from *Classics and Commercials* and *The Shores of Light*.

The American Earthquake: A Documentary of the Twenties and Thirties, Garden City, New York, Doubleday and Co., 1958. Available in paperback, Anchor Books, Doubleday and Co.

Apologies to the Iroquois, New York, Farrar, Straus and Cudahy, 1960. Contains "The Mohawks in High Steel" by Joseph Mitchell.

Night Thoughts, New York, Farrar, Straus and Cudahy, 1961. Incorporates most of the previously published poetry and sketches. Available in paperback, Noonday Press.

Patriotic Gore: Studies in the Literature of the American Civil War, New York, Oxford University Press, 1962.

The Cold War and the Income Tax: A Protest, New York, Farrar, Straus and Co., 1963. Available in paperback, Signet Books, New American Library of World Literature.

O Canada: An American's Notes on Canadian Culture, New York, Farrar, Straus and Giroux, 1965.

Index